Anthony Barnett is among Britain's foremost radical writers and journalists. He is the author of *Iron Britannia*, and *Aftermath: The Struggle of Cambodia and Vietnam* (with John Pilger). A regular contributor to the *New Statesman*, *The Guardian* and *Art Monthly*, he is currently working on a documentary about Henry Moore and England.

SOVIET
FREEDOM

Anthony Barnett

and
Nella Bielski

PICADOR original
published by Pan Books

First published in Picador 1988 by Pan Books Ltd,
Cavaye Place, London SW10 9PG
9 8 7 6 5 4 3 2 1
© Anthony Barnett 1988
ISBN 0 330 30268 X
Photoset by Parker Typesetting Service, Leicester
Printed in Great Britain by
Richard Clay Ltd, Bungay, Suffolk

FOR JOHN BERGER
who writes from life

Every five years there is an All-Union Rally of Young Pioneers on the shore of the Black Sea. In the summer of 1987, 2500 of the Soviet Union's keenest children, aged between ten and fourteen, gathered for the ceremonial parade. The official resolution had been written by adults. 'We do not ag-ree! We pro-test!' chanted the children, when it was read out to them. *Moscow News* reported that the lights were then turned down, which 'enraged the TV cameramen'. But the kids stormed the platform and seized the microphones. A girl shouted into it: 'Comrades! We must fight for freedom!'

CONTENTS

ACKNOWLEDGEMENTS

Really, these are unacknowledgements. Most of those with whom I spoke in Moscow said they did not want their names used. Even the old Bolshevik displayed her training. Many over here requested anonymity for reasons of visas or business. This widespread caution is a judgement on how far the Soviet reforms still have to go. It also means that the list of those whom I can thank by name for their conversations and advice is too brief to be fair to the others. So I thank them all: journalists, lecturers, Communists, bankers, my agent, and above all my hosts in Moscow and Leningrad.

A special mention, however, to Tamara Kate for her guarded curiosity; to Geoffrey Mulligan at Picador for making the book possible; to Patrick Cockburn of the *Financial Times* and Martin Walker of the *Guardian* for helping to open doors in Moscow; to Joan Burchardt for sending me cuttings; and to Guy Boanas for solving my software problems.

And a big thank you to the Soviet, as he likes to be called, whom I mention in 'Leaving', and those who along with him read the manuscript so speedily and gave me detailed and helpful comments on it: John Berger, Hugh Brody, Eleanor Herrin, Judith Herrin, Nick Lampert, Zhores Medvedev, Valerie Mendes, Francis Wheen, and Nella Bielski who is also part author.

I want to thank Hugh Brody especially (although he doesn't like adverbs) for his unwavering judgement. And Judith Herrin; *Soviet Freedom* was written under pressure, she made it a pleasure – for me at least – and if the reader finds it enjoyable, it is in large part thanks to her.

PREFACE

Something is changing in Moscow. New men (but almost no new women) are legislating policies they say will add up to 'a revolution without the shots'. They do not claim to have found a solution to the organization of the world, as their predecessors did after 1917. Nor do they assert that they have caught up with the rest of Europe, albeit by means of a forced march, as Stalin could argue by the late 1930s. Nor do they brag, like Khrushchev in 1960, that their society's economic growth means it will overtake America in twenty years. These are not men consumed with victory or success.

On the contrary, they are leaders plagued by the failures of their society, who have called for dialogue and truthful criticism, while admitting, in Mikhail Gorbachev's phrase, that 'No one has the right to final judgement'.

Their aim is perestroika, reconstruction. Their stated means, economic and political democracy and glasnost or openness. These are fine words. There is also action: laws, policies, disarmament, brilliant films, painfully true criticisms in the newspapers. Yes, such words are deeds as it remains brave to publish them. But one word tends to be left unsaid. Glasnost, democracy, initiative, reconstruction, involvement, legal and human rights, all these are also a way of *not* saying 'freedom'.

What is the momentum behind the new words? Are they an attempt to approach freedom from a direction different from that of 'capitalist slavery'? Or do they signal in advance a steel barrier that will limit change? Is the aim of the new leaders to go as far as they can, or to concede as little as possible? At the conclusion of his recent book, *Perestroika*, Gorbachev writes: 'We want freedom to reign supreme in the coming century everywhere in the world'. Which is all very well, but what are the prospects for freedom in his own country during the remaining years of this century?

I went to Moscow in the summer of 1987 with this general question in mind, to see what is changing, what the change feels like and why it has come about. In the first few sections of this book I describe the incomparable opportunity I was offered by Nella Bielski. Only a few hours after our plane touched down, not only was I in the Soviet Union for the first time, I was peeling potatoes in a Moscow kitchen, observing how well-dressed everyone was but that the tap dripped rather badly.

Our sense that developments in Moscow were at a historic turning point now seems borne out. At the beginning of 1987, the reformers committed the Communist Party to 'democracy'; as I left in June, the Plenum of the Central Committee approved the economic and legal reforms that are at the heart of perestroika. The 'revolution' had been set in train. The much harder task remains: that of putting the programme into effect.

Nella stayed a fortnight, having introduced me to the city and many of her friends. The pages that follow record some of their feelings and those of other Soviets at this critical time. The book is based on conversations, arguments and missile agreements; news reports, films, explosions in nuclear power stations, policy statements, resignations, strikes and the reaction of people to them. It is a book about hopes and fears, written to give a picture of the changes under way. Fiction claims a privileged access to lived experience, while 'ologies' and 'omics' supposedly interpret material reality. Well, this book is neither. It has no obvious model. It is more a travel book of ideas than places. Like life, for good or ill, observation, memory, stories and analysis, are here mixed together.

One thing is absent: statistics. This is not because I do not find them fascinating and helpful, it is just that statistics in the Soviet Union today – especially such basic ones as the number of people at work, or what they earn – do not seem to add up to Soviet realities.

On the other hand, there is a lot of history in these pages because people in the USSR breathe history as they speak, in a way that we do not in the West. One of the first sharp exchanges under glasnost was about the Stalin period. Four ranking professors, whom some would describe as Brezhnevite, protested at Yuri Afanasyev's account of the thirties. 'Perestroika', the four professors wrote, 'does not mean destruction, it means construction, an ascent to new heights in historical science'. Afanasyev's reply raged against the 'monumentality' of this formulation:

Perestroika certainly implies construction, but not on a vacant site. It means the restructuring of already occupied space, thick with well-established economic, political and ideological structures . . . I wonder if my opponents can tell me how the new methods of economic management can be established without destroying the old ones. How can democracy prevail without destroying bureaucracy?

. . . how can the new historic vision of Soviet society be attained without doing away with primitive clichés, deliberate silences and even distortions?[1]

It is a small example, but you can see how explosive is the fusion of past and future. To defend his profession, an academic archivist feels he must pose the question 'how can democracy prevail without destroying bureaucracy?' – a question of power no less, of who rules and by what methods.

One reason why history and the present walk together in the Soviet Union is that Soviet identity remains uncertain of itself. Abroad we tend to talk about Russians not Soviets. Although Slavs – that is Russians, Ukrainians, Byelorussians – make up about three-quarters of the Soviet population, only half of the overall total are Russians. There are fifteen Republics in the Union of Soviet Socialist Republics, and many more national minorities, among a total of more than 280 million. Because it is so much more than an economic programme, perestroika may be seen as an attempt to resolve this problem of identity: to establish what kind of people the Soviet people are and how they intend to relate to the rest of us.

For some, Moscow is the head, for others the heart of this great body. Either way, the limbs are elsewhere. There are at least as many Soviets who resent, despise or just ignore the capital, as there are those who regard it, like Chekhov's three provincial sisters, as the only real place to be.

I was just in Moscow, with a short trip to Leningrad. On the whole, I would say that the majority of those whom I met were still wondering whether they should dare to hope that change is really going to happen. I spoke with lots of people, of different ages, and then read avidly the English-language papers and translation services. I wanted very much to meet and talk with a die-hard opponent of glasnost, but failed, perhaps for the obvious reason. Nor did I have a heart-to-heart discussion in a working-class family.

But even within these limitations, I found my June enquiry taking me into deep waters, sometimes chilly but always very interesting. It became less a report on what is happening and more a discussion of what is at stake, and of the larger forces now in play. It turned into an exploration not just of their history but of our own, and hence our future also.

The reader is invited to join me on this intellectual journey that was also an investigation into the domestic and global reasons for Moscow's reforms. Like many expeditions it remains unfinished. More important, the situation in the Soviet Union itself – its new revolution – is dramatically unresolved. My hope is that the reader will share in some of the excitement, fear, enjoyment and tension this creates, aptly crystallized by the Young Pioneer's call to her Soviet comrades for freedom.

OPENNESS AHEAD

In March 1987 I had to make a brief trip to Paris. After I landed I rang Nella Bielski from Charles de Gaulle airport, just to say hello. She told me to come over for a drink. She is not a 'dissident' or an émigré. She came to France in 1961 because she fell in love with a French journalist – and married him in Moscow. As it was still in the Khruschev era, she had no great difficulty in obtaining permission to leave the USSR. This meant she could remain a Soviet citizen, hence hers was a migration that allowed her regularly to fly back. She says that in her soul she has never left the Soviet Union. Over the last few years, whenever we have met, we have talked about her country.

The conversation I recall most vividly was on a train journey from London to Bristol. As the English countryside whizzed past the large picture windows of the InterCity 125, I asked her why the Soviets did not just abolish special shops for the elite. Such privileges must be a source of inefficiency, I argued. We know this from England. If the Soviet bureaucrat in charge of the distribution of shoes has to put up with a barrage of complaints from his colleagues about the unavailability of shoes for their wives and families, next year he is likely to make sure shoes are in the shops. Whereas, if they themselves are well shod, why should they care about the shoes of the rest of the population?

I was going to continue in this vein. Special shops were established for party leaders during periods of scarcity. And I have heard it argued in Vietnam that such privileges are not unfair because Party functionaries are often poorer than those who work in cafés or factories. At least this argument is practical, although I remain unconvinced. But unlike Vietnam, the USSR no longer suffers from primitive scarcity of the basic necessities of life. So a regime of party privilege must compound inequality, create needless differentials, even help to create shortages, deplete motivation, distort priorities, generate inefficiency and cause waste. In short . . .

Nella would not allow me my speech. Long before I could get into my stride, I was squashed. She rolled her 'r's' saying, 'You do not understand RRRussia. You must go there and see for yourself'.

How could I disagree? I loathe bureaucracies and could not endure to go there. But why didn't it change?

Perhaps the fast new Paris train reminded me of this conversation. As it headed for Nella's suburb, I wondered what she was thinking now that Gorbachev demanded changes I did understand. *Pravda* had recently reported that among the thousands of letters of complaints and suggestions it had received prior to the Party's 27th Congress was one from a veteran Communist in Kazan. He wrote:

We can no longer close our eyes to the fact that party, soviet, trade union, management and even Komsomol officials sometimes deepen existing social inequalities through their use of special canteens, special shops and special hospitals . . . Let the bosses go and stand in line with everybody else at the ordinary shops. And then perhaps at last we'll see the end of those queues which depress us all so much.

Pravda was ticked off for allowing this issue to be aired. But it was nice to feel that there was at least one good old party member out there on the Volga sufficiently foolish to ask the same question as myself.

So as soon as the usual talk was over, about the children and life, I said,

'Nella, are you going to Russia?'

'Why don't we go together – we could write an article.'

Nella claims she saw my eyes gleam behind my spectacles. I recall that I knew immediately that I was heading for Moscow.

She remained incredibly suspicious of the news. I asked her when she first thought something was really happening. She described how a friend who works in the Russian theatre visited Paris, someone 'very sovietical'. I must have looked puzzled. Nella paused, 'She was in the Moscow Soviet'. Which seems sovietical enough.

'Nella', her friend had said, 'we are dizzy with freedom'. But when she returned to Moscow her bags were searched minutely at the airport.

I told Nella I first thought there was something original about the new leadership when I read some quotations from Gorbachev's speech to writers, published by *Time* magazine. He said that the US really feared the possibility of democracy in the USSR and not Moscow's nuclear strength. Therefore, he argued, Washington is relying on the bureaucracy to break his, Gorbachev's, neck just as it broke Khruschev's.[2] This was followed by his January 1987 speech when he called for the promotion of women and non-party members to key jobs. I began to think that the new leadership was seeking quality change, and not just the renewal of the old macho Kremlin machine.

But going to see if this is so? Hah! A few weeks later, after I tried to get tickets, I wrote in my notebook:

'Our idea is to go to Moscow as we would to any other major city. We do not want to go with a party on an official tour. I do not want to go officially as a journalist although I have a little yellow plastic card marked PRESS. I call it my licence to lie. But we are not going to wave that at them either. We just want to go as individuals. We have the idea of talking to people, starting with Nella's friends, with the aim of writing about the changes that are taking place. Just as if I was going to Washington, where I would use my contacts to make contacts so as to interview, on or off the record, people who might know what is going on, so Nella and I hope to go to Russia. I would not ask the US State Department for their permission or co-operation, nor will I approach the press attaché at the Soviet Embassy. For a start, we have no need for an official translator. We want to take glasnost at its word and go to Moscow - now supposedly the capital of "openness" – for ourselves.'

The travel agent round the corner couldn't book independent visits to Moscow. So I rang Progressive Tours. They can and such trips are arranged by a Mr Mohammed. He proved to be competent, and explained that there are two sorts of hotel available for visitors like us in Moscow. One has some rooms at £45 a day. Otherwise the cost is £80 a day. I asked if any of the less expensive would be available in June. A reasonable question. Could we ring up the hotel to find out?

Mr Mohammed looked at me and laughed.

The laugh was gentle, the look one I'll never forget. I might have been seven years old.

'You can't phone hotels in Russia', he laughed again. 'You have to telex Intourist, who arrange with the hotels, who confirm with Intourist, who inform us.'

'Oh dear', I said, 'It's a big price difference. Will you mark the request "urgent"?'

'All my telexes to Moscow are headed URGENT', he replied.

Everything is supposed to be fixed in advance. Only when the booking is accepted can I apply for the visa, which must state all my movements. I am not allowed to stay in one town for more than two weeks at a stretch. The Embassy checks that the application on the visa accords with the booking taken by Intourist. Only then will the visa be issued and openness lie ahead . . .

RUSSIA

One definition of being a European is to feel the heavy breathing of Russia to the East. Is it the bear waking up from hibernation? Is it the gasp of emphysema in its lungs? Is it the sigh of Tarkovsky's wind stroking the vast steppes, calling us to our roots? Is that long slow drawing of breath threatening, antiquated, or inspiring? Is its message from the past or the future?

Who could not be aware of the USSR? But its meaning is not the same all over the world, unlike the meaning of the USA, which is perceived in a similar fashion in South America, India, Tokyo and Moscow itself. The actual experience and impact of the United States varies in every case, of course. But each would recognize the America of others, and in a larger sense there is a common comprehension of its singular global influence. It isn't the same for the Soviet Union. The Americans think of it as a bunch of missiles pointing at them from the other side of the North Pole. For China it is a perplexing mixture of achievement and failure, strength and weakness, role model and demon. Latin America regards the Soviets as Americans-without-dollars, actually a contradiction in terms; India as convenient allies. Finally, while Europe wants to think of itself as the centre of the world – that world which it was the first to circum-navigate – Russia reminds it that it is a peninsula, an appendage.

Yet the Soviet Union is also the great Other to the North Atlantic alliance, and the mighty presence of the USSR helps define the world. When its breathing changes, therefore, we may change too. And suddenly it *has* changed. What is taking place in Russia concerns us, not just in terms of arms agreements and peace, although that is hardly insignificant, but also in terms of what we think our civilization stands for and who we think we are.

Should glasnost succeed – should the Soviet Union become an 'open' society – this will affect the closures over here. And what new kind of Other will it be if Siberia is stripped of its political Gulag, if Moscow bookshops sell *First Circle* and *Doctor Zhivago*, if the Russian encyclopaedia includes truthful accounts of Trotsky and Stalin, if Soviet factories elect their management by secret ballot, and if private enterprise flourishes for family firms and restaurants?

Most of these are now possible developments. Of course, they are not the same as having the right to strike (not that this is so highly esteemed these days in the West), and above all – literally as well as in every other way – they do not alter the Party's monopoly on power and the privileges that accompany it. Or perhaps what will really remain unaltered will be Mother Russia . . .

A window has opened slightly, a window previously painted over for you to admire or scorn, but not to see through. It has become in part a mirror, a window on ourselves.

For me it closed with a feeling of permanence when the Kremlin ordered the invasion of Czechoslovakia in 1968. At a stroke this ended all hope of any movement to socialism in Europe for my lifetime – or at least for my early, more active lifetime. By socialism I do not mean heavy-metal centralized planning, with its state control, bureaucratic inertia and labour-movement philistinism. For me, socialism is the contradiction of almost everything that the popular mind is supposed to associate *with* socialism. Not just freedom, equality, justice, and a sense of the common good, but also people having power over their own lives rather than having it removed from them, whether by the State or big money.

In 1968, the Prague Spring promised a combination of collective control of the economy with democracy. Instead, it is still capitalism that delivers more freedom. Whatever its injustices and swinishness, therefore, I much prefer to argue for its downfall from within. For if you are interested in politics or writing, or indeed any kind of creativity, including the creation of business, then democracy counts most of all. Even from a socialist point of view, the West is best. That was the lesson reinforced by the way the Kremlin snuffed out the Prague Spring.

I recall being woken by my flatmate at the time, who banged on my door and came in aghast saying, 'The Russians have invaded Czechoslovakia'. You often hear people talking about how they remember exactly the moment they heard that Kennedy was assassinated. I remember that too. But Kennedy, bah, he was a false hope really. The Prague Spring was larger than one man. And it was a different kind of example: not a 'great power' one, nor a celebration of a new leader for humankind. The Czech experiment said something simpler; that people should feel at home with themselves. It was a chance, if you will, to begin the end of boastfulness.

Which is why, when I hear Gorbachev being compared to Kennedy, I groan. The importance of what he is saying is that his country needs less direction not more, that it accepts the co-existence of different sorts of socialism, without a 'leading country'. Whether the Soviets will now behave differently is open to question. And this is our question, it concerns change of a political kind.

Someone more expert than I is needed to report on the economic changes the new Soviet leadership seeks to introduce. There have been many attempts to reform socialism, beginning with Lenin's New Economic Policy of the early 1920s. From then on, to Kosygin's relaxation in 1965, to Poland in the early '70s, these reforms have been reversed or just petered out. Only two attempts have lasted so far (the present Chinese one remains in its infancy). Yugoslavia's attempt has lasted forty years and, to judge by results, has brought the country to the edge of disaster. The Hungarian effort has given its people not only the best standard of living, but also the largest per-capita hard-currency debt of Eastern Europe, and is about to introduce steep price rises. The balance sheet of socialist reform is almost completely negative.

Reform means a marriage of bureaucracy and the market. Some say that this is like trying to unite fire and water: the relationship cannot be consummated. Others distinguish between the markets involved. There is the 'produce market' of consumer goods that we shop for. We can have a market here, which means no rationing and few subsidies. Then there is the 'labour market'. Is the distribution of labour - who is to be employed where in what numbers – to be decided by market forces or by administered criteria? Third, there is a 'capital market'. Is the distribution of investment itself to be decided only on the basis of profit? Some experts argue that there cannot be an effective market in products without a market in labour, and for that to work there must be a market in capital also, which means capitalism. Others suggest that you can have a market in one but not the other, or even that a dominant state sector is compatible with a small capital market.

All this is fairly abstract. One thing is clear: all the reforms attempted hitherto have sought to isolate economic change from political reform. They have been attempts to marry the market with a monolithic, one-party regime, open to no independent criticism and argument, let alone autonomous political organizations. Thus in China, student demonstrations at the end of 1986 were rapidly crushed, not in order to put an end to reform but to ensure that economic change was inoculated against political initiatives.

The only exception to this catalogue of restricted economic reform was the Prague Spring, and twenty years ago the USSR was not prepared to let its political dimension succeed. Twenty years is a very long time, however, and has produced a new adminstration in the Kremlin. Moscow now insists that democracy is crucial to economic reconstruction. It is this new spirit, at once political and cultural, that Nella and I in our different ways wished to test. Its outcome will be determined by what happens in people's pockets. We went to learn about what is going on in their heads. The journey would be a voyage to the superstructures.

WHO GOES THERE?

We are not the first to have made such a trip. There is a long history – not just of fellows travelling to Moscow but of fellow-travellers going there, drawn by their sympathy and preconceptions. They went to lend the Fatherland of Socialism support against fascism and imperialism or to describe and defend, and even celebrate, the Kremlin's system as a world model.

Among the first of those who made the pilgrimage was Bertrand Russell in 1920. His response is still in some ways an outstanding report on a visit to the USSR. He did not allow his hopes to blind him to realities. He saw more clearly than the Marxists who 'knew better' or the socialists who just wanted it to 'be better'. Among the latter was the American journalist and 'revolutionist' Lincoln Steffens, famous for his remark made in 1919 after his second trip, 'I have been over into the future, and it works'.[3]

Russell reported that it did not. 'The fundamental ideas of Communism are by no means impracticable, and would, if realized, add immeasurably to the well-being of mankind.' But, he concluded, 'Over the whole development of Russia and of Bolshevism since the October revolution there broods a tragic fatality'. In his introduction, the philosopher stated his new attitude 'as unambiguously as I can':

I believe that Communism is necessary to the world, and I believe that the heroism of Russia has fired men's hopes in a way which was essential to the realization of Communism in the future. Regarded as a splendid attempt, without which ultimate success would have been very improbable, Bolshevism deserves the gratitude and admiration of all the progressive part of mankind.

But the method by which Moscow aims at establishing Communism is a pioneer method, rough and dangerous, too heroic to count the cost of the opposition it arouses. I do not believe that by this method a stable or desirable form of Communism can be established. Three issues seem to me possible from the present situation. The first is the ultimate defeat of Bolshevism by the forces of capitalism. The second is the victory of the Bolshevists accompanied by a complete loss of their ideals and a regime of Napoleonic imperialism. The third is a prolonged world war, in which civilization will go under, and all its manifestations (including Communism) will be forgotten.[4]

It is easy to see why Russell's approach should have aroused universal irritation. Intransigently hostile to the greed and hypocrisy of capitalism, he antagonised the Right and most liberals. Aloof and undaunted in his expression of the need for toleration, he alienated the Fabians and social democrats. Implacable in his exposure of the failure of the Bolsheviks, he outraged the Left. In 1920 he insisted, 'The Russian failure should be admitted and analysed . . . I cannot enter into the conspiracy of concealment which many Western Socialists who have visited Russia consider necessary'. And in a private letter to a mistress he was more colourful:

No vestige of liberty remains, in thought, or speech, or action. I was stifled and oppressed by the weight of the machine as by a cope of lead. Yet I think it the right Government for Russia at this moment. If you ask yourself how Dostoevsky's characters should be governed, you will understand. Yet it is terrible. They are a nation of artists, down to the simplest peasant; the aim of the Bolsheviks is to make them industrial and as Yankee as possible.[5]

This attitude of Russell's, that the revolution was necessary though terrible for them but far too terrible for us; that it should be supported over there while being opposed over here or as a model for the rest of the world, was hard for others to share. Only outrageous philosophical self-assurance, and aristocratic breeding, could maintain such galactic distance. To argue sim-ultaneously positions that sat so ill with one another, and to be for communism and against the Communists, defied the realities of public advocacy.

Russell's was a unique kind of distance. In his neat 1973 essay on 'Tourists of the Revolution', Hans Magnus Enzensberger discerned another sort of distance between most visitors and existing socialist realities:

No matter what attitude or position one takes towards these countries – and they run the gamut from blind identification to vitriolic dislike – the verdicts are invariably reached *from the outside*. No one who returns from a sojourn in socialism is a genuine part of the process he tries to describe.[6]

The Soviets in particular have designed a special system to ensure that visitors remain well outside, even as they are given the impression of being intimate observers. The key instrument for the organization of such distance, Enzensberger argues, is the *delegatsiya*, the system of delegations invented to handle foreign 'guests'. Often invited with expenses paid, given specially trained interpreters, who are themselves observed by hotel and other state employees, the delegate is separated from the very society she or he is fortunate enough to visit.

Ordinary tourists everywhere, but especially in countries poorer than their own, enjoy an episode of leisure and perhaps unaccustomed luxury. Most are quite unaware, for example, when they go to Morocco, that its workers have been shot down in their hundreds. But few think that the hotel swimming pool or beach party represents the 'real life' of the inhabitants. The revolutionary tourist in a socialist country, on the other hand, visits a factory, maybe sees a special school, is sung to by children at their best, finds it hard to leave the arranged itinerary, and is expected to return with an interpretation of the whole society and its quality of life. As Russell showed, it is not impossible to make up your own mind. But the more carelessly you accept the status of delegate, the less you see.

Unlike Stalin, who almost never went abroad after he assumed power and who was pathologically distrustful of the foreign, Khruschev was curious by temperament. He began to open up Russia's relations with the West after 1954. Commercial sightseeing then began in the USSR itself. The Soviets still ban large areas to foreigners. As often as possible they ensure that tourists are guided on their trips, especially through the bribe of cheap tours. But this is not compulsory. One of the first accounts of Soviet tourism was Laurens van der Post's, who travelled around the USSR for the American magazine *Holiday* in 1963. His *Journey into Russia* became a bestseller. ~~book.~~

At one point he describes his reactions to the 'delegation country' of the Black Sea coast. Most of the delegations were from other socialist states: the Romanians enjoy themselves, the Czechs are pragmatic, the Bulgarians obstinate but disillusioned, there are no Poles. The East Germans offend him, but worst of all were the delegations of Communists from the West: 'There was no joy in them. They ate and drank sparingly and hardly ever spoke to one another.'[7]

During my last week in Moscow, after Nella had left, I met people from a couple of East European groups. They struck me as uneasy prisoners of their delegations – supposedly forbidden to talk to westerners, older members keeping an eye on the younger when they could. At this rate, the Communists will be the last people on earth to trust each other.

But the real problem for foreign visitors with any political sympathy and interest in socialism is less the controls of the *delegatsiya* than the insidious appeal it makes, the special status it bestows, that of becoming 'a friend'. Once, on my first visit to Hanoi in 1980, I had to correct an official who called me 'a friend' of his country. I told him that while I supported it against the grotesque invasion from China that had taken place the year before, I was no 'Friend of Vietnam'.

'I like a friend the better for having faults that one can talk about', Hazlitt wrote. The friendship badge offered by Communist states is not at all an invitation to such frankness or the discussion of faults. On the contrary, it invests the bearer with a kind of a isolated status. It invites you to become one of *their* diplomats. Now diplomacy, being by its nature a profession of representatives who can lie convincingly, the invitation

15

presupposes that you will at least dissemble and above all avoid awkward questions. At best, as a 'friend' you will function as an unofficial and uncritical ambassador to the world outside.

Nella was concerned not to become a laughing stock among her friends and relatives in Moscow. I was aware of the long history of suckers from the West. We were thus doubly paranoid about avoiding all official contact or approval.

A FREE PRESS

Paranoia may also seize those who write about Russia for other reasons. The Western press can be blindly dishonest. Just like apologists, those dedicated to hostility make honesty seem more difficult. While preparing for our visit an apt illustration of prejudice appeared in the *Independent* (the paper that has now taken over from *The Times* as the organ of Britain's official opinion). It was particularly striking because the *Independent*'s Moscow correspondent, Rupert Cornwell, is a shrewd and balanced observer who is well worth reading. In contrast, its East European editor, Edward Steen, does not always allow facts to get in the way of his judgements.

Gorbachev was about to visit Romania, a country that poses a dilemma for right-wing commentators on the Soviet bloc. It has been much the most independent of the Warsaw pact countries diplomatically. It recognized Israel, pioneered cordial relations with China when Peking and Moscow were hissing threats at one another, and welcomed Nixon who bestowed an exceptionally friendly visit on Bucharest. President Ceausescu even dined at Buckingham Palace on an official visit to London. But while much supported by the West, Romania is also the most Stalinist of the societies of Eastern Europe.

There are four vicious and frightful regimes that claim the epithet socialist: North Korea, Albania, Romania and the Pol

Pot outfit which sits in Cambodia's seat at the United Nations and is known as Democratic Kampuchea. Of these four the latter two are directly favoured by the Free World, while Moscow has an uneasy or hostile relationship with them all. This is what is known as 'an irony of history'.

I visited Bucharest briefly in 1973 and found it genuinely ominous. It was the kind of thing you read about in political thrillers: chilling empty streets, vicious heavies lurking, a constant sub-current of fear that hovered around the top of your spine. It was a general fear, different from that in other East European states, where dissidents, because they actually are subversive, might try to talk out of the range of police mikes. In Romania there was a smell of terror everywhere, at once arbitrary and ubiquitous. The fact that now, fifteen years later, there are open revolts, may signal the long deserved end to a detested regime – and perhaps Gorbachev's first East European crisis.

Romania's President Ceausescu has also distinguished himself, in the words of the *Economist*, by being 'the only European leader who has turned the cult of the personality into the cult of the family'.[8] His wife and a large network of their relatives head different Ministries, control state committees, and benefit from cushy jobs. Their effect on the economy has been disastrous: grandiose plans, ludicrous monumental edifices in the capital which have had a catastrophic effect on old Bucharest (last year they tore down a seventeenth-century church), a wretched standard of living . . . With its giganticism and dishonesty, Romania provided a piquant backdrop for a Gorbachev visit.

Steen's report in the *Independent* opened as follows:

Like squaddies subjected to a short-back-and-sides, the Soviet bloc countries have been Gorbachevised – all, that is, except Romania.

'Gorbachevised' gives the game away in the first sentence. Steen goes on to attack Romania's cult of the personality, having done what he can to contribute to Russia's. He is anyway wrong, if the term is supposed to mean 'liberalized'. East Germany has resisted the new Soviet example. The description hardly applies to Hungary either, which far from being subject to Moscow's dictate pioneered some of the reforms now being tried in the USSR.

Steen handles the problem with aplomb. Towards the end of the article he states the opposite of his beginning:

Judging by his (i.e. Gorbachev's) diplomacy in other Pact satrapies, he is none too keen to force change, and risk real instability – not yet, at least.

So it seems that the other countries of Eastern Europe are far from having to undergo compulsory 'Gorbachevisation', because the Russian leader is against any such change! Steen's final sentence, though, is the most cruel: 'Mr Ceausescu and his police can be relied on to hold down the lid for the time being.' Relied upon, that is, *by Gorbachev*. So he is blamed for making them follow his line . . . and is blamed if they don't.

This is 'independent' news all right, independent, that is, of a relationship to the news. Life itself is full of inconsistencies, so it is not surprising that newspaper stories should be too. But this is not why the assertions at the beginning and end of Steen's report contradict each other. A similar prejudgement unites them both: a prejudice revealed in his description of the countries of Eastern Europe as 'squaddies' and 'satrapies'. The first term means recruits under marching order; the second, provinces of an ancient empire. Perhaps this is supposed to be good writing, but once these countries are cast as mere extras in the Soviet system, with no political life of their own, nothing can happen within them that is not Kremlin-inspired.

These countries are not free. But as Gorbachev tries to blow some change into his own for whatever motive, relations with other socialist states have begun to shift. Once movement begins it may not be easy to control.

Gorbachev addressed the assembled Romanian elite and talked to them about glasnost and perestroika in his country. He described how, under the old Soviet system, 'our development began to slow down'. He declared: 'The human being is the goal, means and dramatis persona of our policy. People alone can accomplish it . . . There is only one way to do it, and that is more democracy.' Further on, he added:

> Another side to the issue is removing those who prove incompetent, who cannot keep pace with the time, and particularly those who lack principles and honesty, who *cultivate kinship* and personal gain . . .[9]

A Romanian could get shot for saying less. And not so long ago a Soviet citizen would hardly have dared to use such words in public. There were too many stories about Brezhnev's daughter and her collection of diamonds for such reflections to be safe.

So some space is opening up in Soviet life, tragically small perhaps, but fascinating and with great potential. The need to argue with the likes of Steen, even if he's on a bad day, spoils the mind. The closed minds of the fellow traveller and the resolutely hostile observer must both be avoided. An equilibrium of judgement is called for which takes into account the inevitable distance of the visitor.

INTOURIST STINKS

It is not hard to sense why people turned to the glamour of diamonds during the Brezhnev era. There has to be some outlet for the lust for revenge that builds up in your breast. My experience with Intourist was hardly a blip on Moscow's scale of frustration. But it left me gnashing my teeth.

It took a long time to get a reference number, which at least allowed us to apply for visas. We were put on a waiting list for rooms at £45 a night each (without bathrooms *en suite*). Otherwise it would be £80 a night. *They* (whoever 'they' are) would decide, and they would do so too late for any change of plan.

It colours your attitude. We've decided to take glasnost at its word. But at what price? I despise being treated with an indifference that feels like contempt. It also makes me angry to be made angry about something I've no desire to be angry about.

The visas and places were finally confirmed just two days before we were due to leave. This is normal, I was told. In fact, it is more than normal. Margaret Gardiner, for example, decided to accompany Desmond Bernal to the USSR when he was invited to lecture as an honoured guest. They chose to go by boat. But he wasn't there as arranged. Instead he arrived as they were pulling up the gangway.

There he was below, wild-haired and shouting against the wind. "I haven't got my visa", he yelled, "They haven't given me my visa. I'll have to wait. I'll fly out as soon as I can".[10]

With that the ship pulled away. It was 1933.

Thirty years later in 1963, Laurens van der Post wrote, 'The visa itself was another story . . . just thirty-six hours before I was due to leave . . .'[11]

The standard explanations seem inadequate. It isn't due to 'chaos', 'sloth', or 'bureaucracy'. After more than fifty years, three generations of Intourist officials know the score. It must be more than a policy to keep people waiting, treat them with contempt, and once in the Soviet Union bully them when they wish to alter arrangements that they could have made better by themselves. Intourist exemplifies an abiding structure of behaviour. Not that it is planned. On the contrary, it is a way of resisting planning. The USSR, I discovered, should have a large warning notice:

ABANDON PLANNING ALL YE WHO SEEK TO ENTER HERE.

Western societies and western life, I was to discover, are far more organized and far better planned than the Soviet Union.

RUST

Six days before we hoped to set off, Matthias Rust got there first, in his club Cessna 172 aircraft. The TV news showed the tourist video of his plane over Red Square and taxiing to stop in front of St Basil's. As I complained about the visa wait, friends joked about Rust. Perhaps he was another frustrated Intourist customer . . . maybe I should just hire a plane myself; it seemed such a quick way to get to Moscow. The same spirit of enjoyment – but more intensely appreciated – reigned in Moscow itself. The delight was still palpable three weeks later in one of my last conversations. Earlier, in a cabaret at a Moscow Artists Club, a stand-up comic had his audience roaring with his lines about small aircraft bringing down great ministries.

The bloated apparatus had been punctured. It was not just that the pompous self-importance of 'developed socialism' had been made to look ridiculous. It *is* ridiculous. Rust simply showed it up, through the simple device of flying there on his own, as a nineteen-year-old having fun. His success somehow linked Moscow to the outside world. It was an unplanned opening that exposed the façade of official controls, as well as the generation gap that lay behind it. The head of the Soviet armed forces who was summarily retired as a consequence was 3.8 times as old as the West German, who could have been his great-grandson. So I was very grateful to my Common Market compatriot: he helped to normalize my journey and relaxed the atmosphere. Moscow seemed an easier place to go to in the wake of his Cessna.

He was also earnestly discussed in the first week of our stay. Few of Nella's friends really believed that he had done it on his own. Some had their own reverse versions of the right-wing conspiracy theory (which suggested Rust was the agent of a scheme to damage detente with the West by having him shot up in a type of mini Korean jet disaster). They thought that, on the contrary, Gorbachev's allies had let the plane through deliberately, to give him a stronger hand against the military. I was particularly impressed by a shrewd critic who dismissed my feeling that Rust could have acted on his own. Yet later in the evening she told us about reports in a Soviet paper of a young country boy said to be able to ignite things at a distance with his gaze. She listed the extraordinary fires that had occurred and the tests supposed to have taken place which apparently confirmed his exceptional powers. When I expressed a degree of disbelief, she warned me not to be so incredulous – amazing things happen.

Perhaps because it was one of my first conversations, or because the critic was so distinctive, I often reflected on her two judgements. It is possible that Rust's flight was planned by someone else, but it is not inconceivable that he acted for himself. Whereas, even though it is possible to feel someone's glare on the back of your neck, it is more than a rare day on which ignition follows. According to her, however, we should reject the idea that the young man who flew a borrowed plane to Red Square could do so of his own volition, but believe that provincial Russia can produce a superboy with laser-vision capacity.

I suspect that like many Soviet citizens Nella's friend has an intense desire to believe in the force of the individual, as something alive and still burning in her country. But she also shares a massive disbelief that such freedom can really exist in today's world. Hence the displacement of conviction about the individual into supernatural forms. This, I thought, might account for her refusal to dismiss the ludicrous reports of a superboy while being all too 'knowing' about Rust.

I was discomforted by such thoughts. They made me feel superior. I loathe priggy westerners who patronize life in the USSR. I was determined in advance to have none of the same attitudes myself. But time and again I found a political culture that suffered from evident insularity.

Mrs Thatcher had also preceded us to Moscow, and they loved her – especially for her interview with three leading Soviet journalists. She did to these senior representatives of Moscow's current affairs establishment what Rust did to its air-defence command. She interrupted their ponderous questions, made them squirm with counter-questions, revealed them as complacent and out of touch and deflated their pretentiousness. It was marvellous television and healthy politics.

In Britain, however, Thatcher's technique has quite the opposite effect. She manipulates her questioners, grants knighthoods to interviewers who are properly slavish or serve her cause, interrupts and bullies others and prevents fair debate. Muscovites were not interested to hear this, however. I gibed them, and said that it was well known that Russians adored 'strong leaders'. They bridled rather than laughed. It was possible for me to appreciate Thatcher's positive impact in their country; but they did not seem able even to try to see why I should dislike her role in mine. They suffered from a lack of irony, an inability to appreciate different perspectives.

Americans often suffer from the same failing. They think everyone else should be like them. Russians think nobody else should be like them. Both regard their own situation as defining. To suggest that any aspect of official Soviet analysis of Margaret Thatcher might be right, like arguing in favour of a free health service for all in America, is the social equivalent of bad acne – an unfortunate if superficial blemish that is best ignored.

Soviet insularity is not the same as provincialism. Discussion in Moscow of European theatre, or music, or cinema, ranges from Paris and Milan to Berlin and London with an informed ease that puts the ignorance of Anglo-Saxons to shame. I was taken to a fashion show put on by Giorgio Armani of his latest designs, at Moscow's All Union Centre for fashion. Around the sweeping modern auditorium hung the slogan in large letters: LONG LIVE MARXISM-LENINISM THE ETER-NALLY LIVING INTERNATIONAL THEORY. Below, pastel shaded clothes were displayed by models who walked along the cat-walk to the sound of soft rock. The collection was unoriginal, too clever for ordinary clothes and insufficiently stylish for expensive ones. The audience was professional in its reactions, distinctly cool and highly selective in its applause. Moscow knew better than to embrace the second rate.

At the same time, politically its society is second rate. Its international theory, far from living eternally, has been mum-mified. A western journalist told me that it is so simple for him to get books on Soviet society and history in London, that it took him some time to realize that even well-placed, young Party officials could not obtain equivalently thorough studies

27

about their own country in their own language, in Moscow. In the USSR there is nothing like the same availability of different material – whether specialist, balanced, crazy, or essential reading – as in the West. Ironically, it seems that this applies above all to the now lively Marxist or leftist theory written in German and English, if no longer French. An implacable poverty of perspective follows from the insistence on slogans such as that which adorned the fashion hall.

What is the result? I was seriously assured by a professional woman who had visited Western Europe a number of times that unemployment in the United Kingdom was a myth. She was so overwhelmed by the availability of consumer goods, that I just couldn't open my mouth to oppose her. My family includes someone better trained than she who has been stripped of waged employment by the policies of Mrs Thatcher, and I know very well the intense demoralization and insecurity that the reality of mass unemployment, which runs into the millions, creates in its victims. In the USA the problem is vaster; nearly 30 million live below the poverty line. To be poor in America is to be crushed and despised. Yet it is impossible to discuss this reality in Moscow. Conditions there are so much worse in general, society so choked with dissatisfaction, that many are incapable of considering how bad things might be for a section of the people elsewhere, particularly in western societies.

Occasionally I teased my hosts by saying that Moscow reminded me of Hanoi. Such a remark is in distinct bad taste and produced long faces. But it was not untrue. Apart from the unique fragrance of Soviet petrol, both societies have a battered feel, with peeling historic buildings in their European style city centres. The big difference, of course, is that Moscow is rich and powerful. But I was struck by the way in which Soviet influence parallels American, in that it creates an amplified version of its own worst features in its allied states. The Muscovites didn't want to know. (I suspect that they even hold their victory over America against the Vietnamese.) They couldn't go to Hanoi and they were not glad to learn that I could and did travel there as a journalist to try and see what it was like.

A major source of Soviet insularity is their imprisonment through travel restrictions. I was in Moscow, free to come and go. Intourist made things difficult; my own society did not. Yet my hosts could never go at will to see London or Rome or Paris; even if they were invited all expenses paid it might make no difference. On a short trip I met two people who had been asked to speak in the West or to visit colleagues, on scientific trips whose costs would have been completely covered. They were refused permission to leave. Things are said to be improving, especially for those who wish to visit their families. But travel papers will still be routed through work collectives and institutions. The permission of others remains necessary in order for Soviets to travel.

While this fundamental restriction remains, all visitors from the West have an advantage over their hosts in the USSR. We breathe a different air. Like Matthias Rust who flew legally from West Germany, first to Iceland and then to Sweden before he headed illegally across the Soviet border, we are citizens of the world and they are not.

still largely true — hassle # ×

29

FIRST APPROACH

'You must look out for the difference between the way people are in public and in private. On the streets their faces are hard and off-putting. While in their homes they are kinder and more warm than Europeans.'

Nella didn't want me to be put off by my first impression. She feared the stony immigration officer, an unrelenting five-hour wait and baggage search. In fact it was easy at the airport. Nella was amazed. It was the first time they had not gone through her papers on arrival. But the contrast she alerted me to, between appearance and reality, hovered over Moscow; everything seemed capable of dissolving into something different.

On the plane I asked her when she first learnt of Stalin's terror.

She was a student at the time of Khrushchev's speech to the Communist Party's 20th Congress in 1956. Although this was secret and, incidentally, has still never been published in the USSR, it was read out to millions of Party and Komsomol members in local meetings throughout the country. An older graduate friend who attended one of them told Nella what Khrushchev had said. She was shocked and appalled.

But how can someone grow up in a society where millions have died in purges and where five per cent of the population is incarcerated in camps (as they were by the early fifties in the USSR) and not know? Didn't Nella's parents know? Did no one whisper in the ear of an intelligent student the secret Khrushchev 'revealed'?

'Afterwards, my father recalled how, just before the war, his Army commander was denounced as an enemy of the people, and how no one really believed it. And I had a girl friend at school. Like me, she was very good at her lessons. We spent a lot of time together. Her father, she said, was an engineer. But he was never at home, he was always away in the country. "Why is he away so long?", I once asked her. Perhaps we were twelve. It upset her a lot. She didn't want to talk about it I could see. And I never asked again. People just didn't know. It was unspeakable. But afterwards, I thought back and realized that he was in a camp.'

Our plane turned to descend, and as it banked fields and trees came into view,

'You will see that the organization of the fields is chaotic. Ah, my country.'

NELLA'S VERSION

One evening I dined with Anthony, a friend from England, in the Parisian suburb where I live. The conversation centred on what was happening in the USSR. We recalled the film *Reds* and talked about John Reed and his *Ten Days That Shook The World*. My friend said that Reed was naïve.

Being a novelist, I then had the idea of taking this friend to my country, especially as for him it would be his first visit. Behind my friend's glasses I saw his eyes gleam. We distributed the roles: he would be the real explorer, I the guide.

After my departure from Russia at the end of 1961, things began to go badly there. It was visible. From one year to the next it got worse and worse. I went to see my family and friends. Each time I went with more concern. Each time I came back with an even more heavy heart.

When I was first a student at the Philosophy faculty in Moscow, I was labelled an 'abstract humanist' – which was not a compliment. With time it seemed that I gradually became a 'concrete pessimist'. Even so, I have to say that for the entire month before my departure, I almost regretted my impulsive decision to leave. But one must keep one's promises and I kept mine.

So here we were in a plane for Moscow, my friend and I. During the flight I tried to prepare him for the phenomenon of the customs and police formalities. This spectacle is extremely familiar to me, I've gone through it so many times. I told him, for example, that in 1983, on my return from Moscow, they confiscated a handful of grass from my father's tomb. It was dry grass from the previous year which the snow had covered and preserved for me. I was told I did not have permission to export agricultural produce. I warned him about other absurdities and humiliations. In short, I didn't want to give him any comfort about what to expect at the entrance to this country.

There's no need to draw optimistic conclusions from the procedure which we experienced at the passport control in Moscow airport on 3 June 1987; it was simply correct. Quite a surprise for me, for Anthony it probably seemed normal.

We arrived at the Hotel Berlin which had been booked for us by Intourist. Instead of two rooms reserved in our names, there was only one. It was already early evening and knowing the system I began to run through in my mind the friends who might put me up for the night. And then the second surprise of the day: the lady at reception resolves the problem in a quarter of an hour by telephone.

In the corner of the hall of this old hotel which used to be called the Savoy, there's a stuffed bear. I was struck by how much cleaner he looked. They must have restored him. Opposite the bear there's a counter with newspapers. I immediately bought some. The lady added up the cost on her abacus with the usual rapidity. In contrast, it is much less fast at the shop where they sell for hard currency the 'deficit', a term which designates rare goods (all alcohol, Russian or foreign, Marlboro cigarettes or fizzy drinks like Schweppes). This shop has a computerized till and three cashiers, no less, and there is an interminable filling in of papers by hand – buying things here takes much longer than with the aid of the abacus.

After reading through the newspapers late into the night after we had supper with some friends – from *Pravda* to *Izvestiya* to reviews such as *Communist* and *Agitator* – I had to admit that foreign correspondents posted to Moscow can't get much rest.

Unless they carry on like the journalists who helped to write the issue of *l'Express* devoted to the USSR (12 May 1987). In the article titled "The Gorbachev Illusion" I read, 'The last echo coming from this mysterious planet never fails to intrigue the fascinated Earthlings that we are: a man with a head, two arms and two legs, a bit more than 50 years, a smiling wife and a few legal friends, has been elected General Secretary of the Party which *rules everything*, over there, where there are some 280 million subjects'. One would have thought they were describing a film like *Close Encounters of the Third Kind*.

Given the manner in which information about the Soviet Union has been presented in the western press these last two years, it's necessary to define a word that is repeated endlessly: *glasnost*, in French *transparence*, or transparency rather than openness.

Soviet reality, perhaps more than any other, has its own particular laws and its own history, whose course was turned in a radical fashion, away from the general march of the western world in 1917. It was an experience that created, even on its own, a civilization, not just another form of power or economic control, seen as mere social organization.

The most widespread error made by nearly all observers without exception, whether they are favourable to this historic development or not, has been a mechanical application to this civilization of categories formed by a tradition of thought and action in the West.

In this respect the translation of the word glasnost by 'transparency' is fairly symptomatic, although the English 'openness' is perhaps better. In my dictionary of 1955 the word glasnost is a judicial term which means publicity, in the sense of making a judicial procedure public. The opposite would be clandestine, in secret.

What is publicity? Malraux once said that, 'the most efficient publicity is American, which plays on conditioned reflexes, and attempts to preserve the Museum of the Imagination for commodities'.

If we refer to the famous Makharoff dictionary of 1902, when publicity didn't have the sense we give it today, the definition of glasnost is: to make something known to the people, to proclaim publicly, before all the people, before all the world.

And if we look at the history of Russia we can find a primitive form of Russian social organization, the *obtchina*, also called 'community', rural or urban, whose affairs are decided in public, on the public square. People are summoned to come together by voice, '*glas*'. Whenever there is a threat of danger, fire or war, for example, they used to cry out and ring the bells.

We can see therefore that the choice of the word glasnost by the new government of the USSR marks a rupture with words previously in vogue in Soviet social life: propaganda, agitation. These last go right back to the revolutionary tradition of Lenin's party.

If one imagines a world that is closed, opaque, inaccessible, a sort of gigantic self-enclosed thing peopled by heartless fanatics without souls, incapable of thought, then the western perception might have some justification. Transparency would then become a ray of light in a kingdom of shadows.

There have been shadows, nameless horrors, even aspects of

a huge farce. Blood has flowed, women have been beaten, men treated like animals, orphans created by the shovel-full, words ripped out of the true Russian language to become slogans. All this happened and there's nothing to add. Except the fact that on this patch of the earth there are 280 million humans who live, breathe, beget children, eat bread, drink pure water or fortified water, build houses, think, create, write books and poetry of great beauty, and who resist as they resisted during the Second World War, as they survived collectivization, the camps, the Brezhnev swamp, as they now lift their heads and raise their voices.

What has changed in Moscow since my last journey there in 1983? I had one immediate impression which affected everything. The fences have been dismantled. For me, the symbol of Moscow has always been the contrast between the immensity of the city, its streets of huge modern buildings, and the intimacy of the interior courtyards, with their grass and trees and the small kitchen windows looking onto them. Before, the little historic courtyards were fenced off, as if they refused the change of regime. Today, these barriers are down and it is as if old Moscow lives once more, and has opened itself to the outside world. Perhaps more than anything in a dictionary, this for me is now the first meaning of glasnost.

MOSCOW

I had expected the capital of seriousness. Heavy architecture, grey streets, black cars. Maybe it was because it was June. They say that the long Russian winter drains colour and saps the soul. But when we arrived at the height of summer there was abundant greenery and it was warm. At midnight, I joined the Soviet tourists who lolled around Red Square in their shirt-sleeves or dresses. During the day the pavements were packed thick with crowds. In various places there were even stalls with little tables and tulip-shaped parasols over them where you could get soft drinks and sometimes snacks. I was told that these were a recent innovation.

Not that Moscow is adapted to the stroller or the shopper. There is almost nowhere to pee, for example. But I was so prepared for there being nowhere to drink at all, nothing in the shops, long lines of people everywhere, brutal rudeness from shop assistants when you did get to a counter, that instead of being struck by how bad things are compared to the West I was more impressed by the crudity of my preconceptions. Moscow is not dullsville plus Lenin's tomb. Shopping there is not the end of the world; there are even some bargains, including clothes and hats.

Also the centre of Moscow is beautiful. Much of the old city exists and if it is peeling that is because the quality of the paint is poor and not because it hasn't been renovated since 1945. South of the river especially, but also at many places within the inner ring-road, there are fine structures, small churches, and the older buildings with courtyards that would be very attractive if they were not in a state of sometimes sordid neglect.

Moscow has been likened to a spider's web. It has a web-shaped pattern on maps and the image is also suitably sinister. It's inappropriate. There is nothing gossamer or gentle about Moscow, it does not blow in the wind or look to chance, nor is it uniform. Although it is also a clumsy comparison, I came to think of it as an onion. There is the tight centre of the Kremlin, in fact a complex of major buildings within its towering brick walls. On my second day I took a walk around the Kremlin and there on the river bank below its walls were some men fishing, in the centre of Moscow: its river was neither grey, grimy nor badly polluted.

Around this heart of the onion are the squares, and bridges over the River Moskva. Then the remains of the old City. As you move outward, new periods dominate in successive rings. Stalin's with heavy and then heavy and ornate structures. Khruschev's prefabricated and now decayed apartment blocks. The sweeping high-rise estates of the sixties and seventies. When you get to the outer ring-road, which is 60km in diameter, Moscow stops. The transition from big city to poorly developed countryside is almost instantaneous. Later I learnt to pick out the little dachas or weekend houses in the woods.

But it is misleading to describe Moscow as a series of packed rings as if they circle one another intact. What keeps the city together are the wide arterial roads that blast out from the centre. They give Moscow a tremendous sense of energy.

Watching the traffic at a big intersection quite close to the city centre, I tried to imagine the feelings of a British or French diplomat observing its construction, or the first waves of modern traffic, in the early sixties, as their own empires entered terminal decline. 'Damn the Soviets. This thing is unmovable!', they must have said, green with jealousy. Moscow draws into itself something of the enormous extent of the Steppes, the Baltic, the Caucasus. It is a city of power.

We went to look at Moscow from the Lenin Hills, a steep escarpment on a bend of the river: the Lenin stadium and the Novodevichy Convent below, just across the water, the vast city beyond them disappearing rapidly into the haze. On the hill behind stands the New University, one of the six sprawling 'wedding cake' constructions Stalin had built after the war. Nella went to student dances there every week. She told me a story that she heard then. The university was built by convict labour. One day, as the tower neared completion, one of the builders smuggled up some pieces of wood and cloth he'd carefully prepared. With the wind behind him, he put them on, leapt from the top and glided away on the up-draught from the escarpment, over the construction site to freedom.

One evening, after the theatre, one of Nella's friends took us to see the same view of Moscow by night, and we walked and slipped down the hill-side to the river-bank. Across, on the far side, a terrible mechanical noise slowly and repeatedly rent the air. Perhaps it came from a machine crunching waste or a moving belt shifting scrap metal; it moaned and rasped and roared. 'Moscow's digestion', we agreed: a sometimes beautiful and extraordinary city still in atrocious pain.

Towards the middle of the month there was a massive downpour accompanied by thunder and lightning. Sheets of rain blew sideways between the buildings, bounced off roofs and scattered pedestrians. The road below our hotel turned into a sea that lapped over the pavement; drains lower down the hill became fountains that added to the flood. I understood why Russia has such great rivers. It also gave me a glimpse of the way the Soviet system works – a lasting image of its preposterous stubbornness. Every night water lorries would circulate to wash away the dust from the centres of tourism around the Kremlin. The storm had diminished to gusts and drizzle, yet that evening there it was under the street lights in the rain, adding its gallons to the tons of water that had already washed down the Great Square of the October Revolution: the water lorry continued on its round, the City plan was being fulfilled.

THE RUSSIAN
ECONOMIC MIRACLE

*They remind me very much of their predecessors, except that the
housing shortage has soured them.*

Mikhail Bulgakov[12]

Compared to an equivalent city in the West, Moscow is poor. In the centre, its people look and dress as they might have in a mid-western American town fifteen years ago. I found the almost complete absence of blacks (and punks) unnerving in a great metropolis. Quite often young people stand out, when they are exceptionally well dressed. The number of people with bad teeth is very noticeable; to judge by results, Soviet dentistry must be abominable.

It was not the people, or their teeth, but the rottenness of the system I found surprising. I had expected a centralized society like East Germany but with fewer goods available. In other words, a set-up that was deliberate rather than careless, cold rather than stupid. I suppose this was due to the constant pressure of Western propaganda, including notions of spiders' webs, and totalitarian efficacy. But Moscow's daily life is not like this at all.

There is quite a lot in the shops, for example, but its

whereabouts and quality is unpredictable and erratic and the queues are ridiculous. 'You don't buy things in Russia', one housewife told me angrily when I brought the conversation round to shopping, 'you *get* them'.

Getting things means seizing opportunities, playing the system, using contacts, bribery and barter, in cash, kind or in favours. Because of the clamp down on vodka, which is sold during very restricted hours to huge and unpleasant lines of drinkers, a favoured gift from a westerner is now a bottle that we can buy at any time from foreign currency shops. I often took one along. It was rarely opened, not just because it wasn't chilled, but because if you want your plumbing seen to, for example, a bottle of hard stuff is a far more acceptable means of exchange than roubles.

If you don't have the means but only a little money, getting things means wasting time; an enervating and exhausting amount of time is spent to obtain your share. The result, year in year out, is a peculiar social exhaustion. In his *Moscow Diary*, written in the Christmas of 1926, before Stalin brought the New Economic Policy to an end, Walter Benjamin wrote:

> I don't think there's another city with as many watchmakers as Moscow. This is all the more peculiar since people here do not get particularly worried about time.

Then he notes that a club has a poster on its wall stating:

LENIN SAID, 'TIME IS MONEY'.

And Benjamin adds, 'Just to express this banality, the highest authority has to be invoked'.[13] Sixty years later an article by Anatoly Rubinov in *Literaturnaya Gazeta* describes how much speedier and efficient the London postal system is than Moscow's:

Capitalists look after their money better than we do, and so in Britain they know that the saying 'time is money' should be taken literally.[14]

But whether it has taken time, money or contacts, it also adds pleasure to the dinner table if you have beaten the system and got something rare – such as tomatoes, which were completely unavailable for the first two weeks of June.

Shopping in such circumstances becomes completely irrational. It is exacerbated by the hundreds of thousands of people who pour into Moscow from even worse-served provincial towns to get whatever they can. Walking down Gorki Street, I noticed a line of people out in the open waiting to buy green bananas, from a woman with a white coat and a large pair of scales. At the head of the queue was a small elderly man in a battered suit. The assistant put a large bunch on the scales, then another and another. There was restlessness in the line as another large bunch went on. By now, the bananas towered above the old man's head. Yet another bunch went onto the pile. Even if he had been starved of his greatest passion, he could never have consumed so many bananas before they went bad. He was buying for the future, for exchange with neighbours, and because he might never have another chance to get to the head of the line of people trying to buy bananas. Everyone buys today as if there will be nothing tomorrow, because all too often there isn't any coffee/tea/lemons/toothpaste or bananas tomorrow or the day after that. It struck me as a miracle that the old man could even carry that many bananas.

If you comment with surprise on the delicious food in people's homes, that's what they say too: 'It is the Russian economic miracle'. Namely, the way so much gets on to the tables when so little is in the shops. A Sociological Institute survey found that:

> Moscow's average young man was wearing clothes with a street value of 500 roubles and the average girl wore clothes worth 700 roubles.

But their average household income was supposedly around 100 roubles a month![15] Socialism has extended The Miracle of the Loaves and the Fishes to the latest fashions. In part, it is thanks to administered allocation that is hidden to strangers shopping in the street; each workplace, factory or institute will have special access to supplies for its employees. With an ironic grin a British journalist commented on his surprise when he first observed, 'The contrast between private affluence and public squalor'. The phrase is from Kenneth Galbraith's critique of American capitalism . . .

It's no joke. Rather it is an indictment of the inefficiency, and worse, that has accumulated in the Soviet Union. The retail system is riddled with crime and fiddles. Walking near the Bolshoi I saw a line forming, with nobody selling anything at the front. But there was a lorry in the square which was about to be unloaded. I nosed up to have a look. Inside were wooden trays of tomatoes from Romania, which were being stacked beside a couple of weighing machines. Given the value of tomatoes at the time (they were the first I'd seen in Moscow), and the low wages which people are paid, it is inconceivable that the salespeople wouldn't take the opportunity to borrow a tray-load for themselves if only to deal in kind. As for payments made and taken to have the opportunity to run a temporary stall of that sort . . . Muscovites would have to belong to another species for such a system not to be corrupt. Pushing the sale of fruit and vegetables into the streets is a way of cutting across the abysmal distribution system to get foodstuffs into the *avoska* – the bags Muscovites carry around 'just in case' there is something to buy. But even if it was conceived as an attempt to improve things, only the tomatoes smelt fresh.

Buying petrol provided another vivid example. Twice I was in a car that needed fuel. On each occasion the Moscow station had a mere two pumps but only one worked. The result was a long line and a fifteen and a twenty minute wait respectively. Each time the driver assured me that the second pump was deliberately kept out of order. The men in the grotty little huts who took the money had less work to do watching one pump and no incentive to look after two. On the contrary, because the lines are always so long there is a black market in petrol. So attendants pump out their own special supply when the stations are closed, or so everyone believes, which they sell at a profit. In other words, the shortage is created deliberately because it generates revenues outside the official system, while everyone is paid poorly within it. And thus in the capital city of the world's largest oil-producing country, everyone has to wait in long lines to buy fuel.

Arbitrary mis-allocation is most noticeable and most painful for those involved when it comes to housing. There is a tremendous demand for apartments and living space in the Soviet Union. You could say that the Soviet Union has achieved a lot. From being a predominantly peasant country even under Khrushchev it is now 70 per cent urbanized. But a similar demographic shift has taken place in western countries without the same degree of over-crowding and lack of apartments found in the USSR.

Thousands of villages with relatively good buildings and

potential are depopulated because of needlessly harsh conditions in the countryside. Village roads are so bad, or non-existent, that children can't get to school. According to the new Minister of Health, Yevgeniy Chasov:

> In only 35 per cent of the rural district hospitals of the country is there a supply of hot water and in 27 per cent there is no sewerage system and in 17 per cent no running water. [16]

People flee to the towns to escape such unbelievable conditions. Thus, the shortage of even small urban apartments becomes more acute, as ghost villages multiply.

One of the country's most influential, reform-minded economists, Abel Aganbegyan, is impatient:

> In many areas I don't know what we are waiting for. Approximately a million people want to buy apartments with their own money, but we don't give them the opportunity to do this. [17]

The Soviet Union is the planet's largest country, they say that it covers one-sixth of the world's land surface. This is misleading, since the taiga supports only sparse habitation. Nonetheless, the living areas are still vast for the relatively small Soviet population. Even the most casual traveller is impressed by the immensity of the spaces that surround Moscow. Furthermore, they are full of forests and woods, that stretch for hundreds of miles. The three crucial resources needed for housing are: first, space; second, timber; and third, bricks. Bricks need only fuel to be made from clay, and Siberian natural gas supplies are plentiful. All the basic ingredients are at hand to transform the housing situation in the USSR. There is also capital, labour and even machinery. It is impossible not to conclude that the system functions more to prevent the building of housing than to encourage it. Indeed, only an immensely powerful and entrenched structure of power could have managed to stop more living space from being built in a country so over-endowed with all the necessary materials.

An English language *Pravda* carried a long article by one Valeri Parfenov called 'Putting the rouble back to work'. Its long columns certainly forced one's eyes to work, yet a certain tension in the prose encouraged me to persevere. For example:

There must be a good reason for the proverb that if you are holding an elephant by the back legs and it bolts, the most reasonable thing to do is to let go.

Well, yes. And Mr Parfenov continues:

To be more precise, one should not hold onto unnecessary things, but should sell what one does not need oneself as soon as possible.

Is Valeri Parfenov attempting to sell us a bolting elephant? As his assessment moved to its conclusion, the reason for his desperate proverbs became clear. He cast aside his Aesopian language and gave an example of the problem the Soviet economy has created for itself. It concerns refrigerated railway stock, in which it seems tens of millions of roubles have been invested:

It turns out, that many of the carriages go back and forth empty, transporting air. But the way indices are evaluated it is still worth the while of the railway depots to do this. Their efforts are measured according to kilometres covered by the carriages. Just link up the empty cars to the locomotive and let it race backwards and forwards from one end of the country to another. The more kilometres the carriages mark up, the bigger the bonus . . . the Kak-hovka refrigerator depot overfulfilled its plan for ten months of 1986: with a distance set of 224,000 km to be covered by refrigerated carriages, it managed to clock up 233,000 km, mainly with empties. These transported six times less freight than normal goods wagons.

The mind can do nothing other than boggle. Across the largest and coldest country in the world, empty refrigerated carriages 'race backwards and forwards from one end to another', covering a distance that is equivalent to many times around the world. Was the air inside kept at the stipulated low temperature?

The fascination of this example is that it demonstrates how the Soviet economy has involved wastage on a huge scale that crosses numerous time zones. Wastage that is itself criminal and naturally creates crime, as stupendous resources are poured away for no purpose. The right-wing American Soviet expert, Marshall Goldman, concluded a recent study with the observation that the Soviet economy 'has to rely more on its natural riches than on its creative potential'.[18] Both the extent of these riches and the loss of their potential is breathtaking. As I watched the tomatoes being unloaded into the square it seemed that the Soviets had turned their society into the biggest back of a lorry in the world.

SOVIET CONTRASTS

Before I went to Russia, I thought that people there lived relatively badly. Instead I found that many were much better off than I expected. Yet everyday life was even more intolerable than I had imagined, and not just because of the cramped housing. A mother of two, after telling me how coffee had just that week disappeared, said, 'The real difference with the West is that you do not have the economics of life on your mind the whole time'.

Crucially, I'd not realized how rich and impressive the Soviet Union really is. The major surprise for me, therefore, was this contrast between this wealth and the poverty of Soviet existence, especially what people have to do to get what they have. The scale of this contrast strikes you immediately yet is difficult to put into words. The system is wanton. It runs on waste, both of resources and people, and can do so because the country is so big and rich. I was astonished by this concurrence of extravagance with the material impoverishment of people's lives.

Capitalism, the early Russian Marxists argued, created uneven development. Indeed, in Manhattan today you can leave a glass palace heated to almost insufferable temperatures throughout a hundred floors, and walk out into bitter winter snow to see dozens of freezing bag-ladies lining up for a hand-out from church soup kitchens. In Russia the Brezhnev years created their own sort of unevenness, one more stifling and less economically dynamic than capitalism. Senior Communists, for example, were granted their own private forests for hunting, while ordinary citizens hunted desperately for living space.[19]

On our first weekend we went to a dacha north of Moscow up by the river and the next morning went for a long walk along the bank, picking huge bunches of wild lilac. A splendid passenger ship passed us. The Moskva is navigable to very large vessels; I'd not realized that one can virtually sail across Russia. On the bank opposite there was a marina of small boats. An Ilyushin jet passed overhead at the same time, to complete the perfect picture of successful modern development. Then we approached a broken jetty with a cracked wooden diving board. It extended into a quiet bend of the river. Overhead there was the skeleton of a look-out tower. It belonged to a magnificent holiday camp, apparently built in the late 1950s, now disused and overgrown. Gingerly, I walked out along the jetty, undressed and plunged into the water to feel mother Russia on my skin. When I asked our guide why such a wonderful site should had gone to ruin when there were thousands of children who would have loved it, he said:

> Who knows? Perhaps it belonged to a factory and they could not afford it any more and they had no way to exchange it, perhaps the influential occupiers of the nearby dachas objected to vacationers nearby.

The following weekend was spent in a dacha more than twenty kilometres south of Moscow, where again we went for a long walk, this time to see a village. We approached it across the huge collective fields. The houses were all bunched close together. We went down a narrow path between the fruit and vegetable gardens of the wooden houses into the centre of the village, which was built around a large pond. At first sight it was as if we had walked straight into the eighteenth century. The antique look – the appearance that reminded me of paintings of olden times – stemmed from two facts that were obvious as soon as I recovered from the surprise. First, there was no pavement or metalled surface. The road in the village that went around the pond was mud, very uneven yet at that time hardened mud. The heavy rain that fell later that week would have made it thick, sticky and virtually impassable. The second thing that was missing – or at least seemed to be – was a little store. In most equivalent settlements close to the outskirts of a great modern city would there would be some kind of public shop with basic supplies.

The contemporary element, which reassured me that I had not walked into a time-warp, were the cars in most of the gardens and driveways of the wooden houses. The residents are not badly off; some work at a nearby dairy complex, others sell their own vegetables, and they rent out holiday rooms in summer to Muscovites at a good price. Some of the cars belonged to the villagers, some to their summer tenants. We walked out along the wide mud track towards the highway, our guide cursing the leaders who

> swear every year by the blood of their heart that they will
> build roads that will stop the harvest being wasted and lost
> even when it's grown, every year, and *never* is it done!

Walking back along the mud road, I thought about a conversation I had had in London just before setting out for Moscow.

I'd been introduced to an executive of a big multinational who manages his group's Soviet bloc sales, and thus knew Russian business quite well. He gave me an alarming picture. Everything is centralized, yet no one person can give you a decision. To sell a product that contained oils might need permission from ministries involved with both transport and chemicals. Furthermore, each wing of an organization stores away as much information as it can, while circulating it to as few other places as possible. 'How does it work, then?', I asked.

It does not work. Nothing gets transmitted into action until production stops because of a lack. Then there is a panic. Pressure to work regularly does not exist.

This, I came to realize, is why there is a new team at the top. Gorbachev and his colleagues have emerged from the bowels of a 'systems-failure' of continental dimensions. I only sensed the problems in Moscow. But that sense was enough!

A solution must involve further disruption in the short run. How the population will react is a question discussed incessantly in Moscow. Will the workers accept austerity measures? One observer there told a colleague of mine, 'the key thing is *kolbasa* (sausage)'. He is wrong. This is an example of the old thinking; the old military approach which concentrates on one main front, as if a victory in the battle of sausage, and a decisive blow at the transport salient, will allow a pincer attack on housing, and you will be in Berlin. It just isn't like that anymore in the USSR, if it ever was. What is wrong is that everything is out of synch. The system is clogged with dislocations. To have sausage, to take that example, demands pig feed. Which means agricultural machinery:

The USSR produces four and a half times more tractors than the USA. What for? The volume of plant-growing output in our country is about one-third of that of the US. Besides, we produce only half the amount of trailers and mounted implements required for normal agricultural work.[20]

Then there are the roads along which the feed-stuffs must travel to get to the pigs. Even after sausages are made, the distribution system might provide them in Moscow but none in Gorki or only one kind in Kiev. So even if you think that it is all a matter of the battle of the sausage, to win that battle definitively rather than this year or next involves a battle over 'everything', until there are regular supplies throughout the society. In other words, an end to military style thinking.

When you plan a society on military lines, the people are treated like soldiers. Their role is to obey. Their task, to carry out the strategic plan. But when the objective itself is to respond to the wills, the aims and desires of the 'troops', then they are no longer soldiers – to be fed sausages so that they will not mutiny - they are the masters, even if they are not the generals. Except for some Third World countries, the economic struggle does not have a foreign enemy. When peace replaces war, planning becomes a different kind of activity. It starts by projecting a reckoning of people's needs and their effective demands. The capitalist world comprehended this far earlier than the Communist one, and as a result is far better planned.

It may be that the problem of putting an end to military style assumptions is rooted in Soviet identity itself, as it emerged from the Second World War. At any rate, the key task for the

Still behaving run wrong —

e.g. budget deficits

Soviet leaders today is to try to set in motion a dynamic which does not lurch from trying to solve this or that shortage, but which instead enables the riches and the potential of the Soviet Union to spread their wings.

THE BIRTH OF GLASNOST

That sounds wonderful. In fact, a Herculean task of cleansing Soviet society is needed – an effort bound to be unpleasant and arduous. How on earth has anyone come to the conclusion that they themselves must shoulder this Labour of Hercules?

At a press conference in London, Abel Aganbagyan, the Armenian economics professor who is now one of Gorbachev's major advisers, was asked when he first met the present General Secretary. He replied that it was when Gorbachev was brought to Moscow in 1979, from his home base of Stavropol, to take up a position in the Politburo and oversee agriculture. Perhaps they had to turn to a young bright outsider, as no one else would take responsibility for the USSR's greatest disaster. But with his sudden elevation he was twenty years younger than most of his colleagues in the leadership.

Gorbachev used to call in economists and specialists of all persuasions to discuss policy. In particular, Aganbagyan said, he talked with Tatyana Zaslavskaya who specialized in agriculture, 'but when general questions arose I was included'. After Andropov become General Secretary in 1983, Gorbachev began to work more on the economy as a whole and continued to gather specialists and economists for discussions; 'these meetings were very informal, everyone said what they thought, then Gorbachev integrated the ideas'. Sometimes these meetings were day-long discussions; one lasted for two days.

A key purpose was to try to work out how to speed up technical development and improve management. Aganbagyan said that earlier attempts at economic reform had been analysed carefully, and they also looked at the experience of other socialist countries. They came to the conclusion that previous efforts had failed because they were partial and 'the social organism as a whole was unchanged'. He gave the example of the Soviet reforms of 1965 which broadened the responsibility of enterprise management but nonetheless retained central administrative controls.

In a draft translation of the first chapter of Aganbagyan's forthcoming book, *The Challenge*, he describes as the core problem the command nature of the economy,

> The essence of perestroika lies in the transition from administrative to economic methods of management. For this, the basic link in production is the transfer of enterprises to full economic accounting, self-financing and self-management. The main development is economic democracy, the workers being widely involved in management, and now able to elect their own economic managers.

Mikhail Gorbachev's own book, *Perestroika*, bears out this commitment to democracy, politically, culturally and in international affairs. However, I have yet to meet anyone who believes that a majority of the Central Committee were persuaded to vote for democratization as a favour to the notoriously unreliable and ungrateful intelligentsia of Moscow, who have been among the first to benefit.

Of course, Gorbachev insists on the political aspect of the changes:

One cannot fail to see that a paradoxical situation developed: an educated and talented people committed to socialism could not make full use of the potentialities inherent in socialism, of their right to take a real part in the administration of state affairs.

And he had already admitted that:

the ideas of perestroika have been prompted not just by pragmatic interests and considerations but also by our troubled conscience, by our indomitable commitment to ideals which we inherited from the Revolution . . .

As a materialist he should not regard it as a slight to his sincerity if we note that the decisive factor was pragmatic. 'It was important to preclude the repetition of the past mistakes which in the 1950s, 1960s and 1970s doomed to failure our attempts to change the system of economic management', the General Secretary explains.

Repeated attempts to reform the upper management levels without support from below were unsuccessful . . . What is the main shortcoming of the old economic machinery? It is above all the lack of inner stimuli for self-development.

Inner stimulus is supposed to come from the self-determination of the enterprise, through a combination of the economic realities of the market place and the motivation of the work-force. In combination, it is hoped, these will shatter the 'braking mechanism' of the massive, ministerial, Moscow based, over-centralized system, Gorbachev emphasizes, and it is a point to come back to, that:

It is a distinctive feature and strength of perestroika, that it is simultaneously a revolution 'from above' and 'from below'.[21]

Yet from his own description he seems to have hesitated before committing himself to the awesome consequences of linking the Party to a revolution 'from below'. For the first year and a half in office this must have been one of the questions debated heatedly in the discussions Aganbagyan described. Meanwhile, according to Gorbachev, people in the Party thought perestroika 'just another campaign', while 'sceptics would chuckle in the office corridors'. Finally, in January 1987, the Plenum of the Central Committee was persuaded that only intensified democracy could 'eliminate the braking mechanism'.[22] This was, so to speak, the historic turning point for a programme that was given its economic outline by the next Plenum in June 1987.

One of the most interesting American experts in Soviet studies, Jerry Hough, says:

Mr Gorbachev is a dictator consolidating his power. We share common interests . . . But we should not have wishful thoughts about his commitment to democracy.[23]

I think the evidence is otherwise. Mikhail Sergeyevich Gorbachev has concluded that democracy, and hence glasnost, are essential for perestroika. Whether he can tolerate the consequences, or more important, persuade the Party and the KGB to live with them, and whether even the Soviet people will indeed embrace the opportunity, are still unresolved questions. But a powerful and intelligent team of economists and political theorists in the Soviet Union are convinced that monolithic uniformity must be abandoned because, in the words of Alexander Yakovlev, 'history has never achieved progress through simplification'. Instead, every successive form of society, he argues, is 'internally more complex than the previous one'.[24] They have therefore set the USSR on course for diversity.

PETTY MONARCHS
WITHIN OURSELVES

Alexander Yakovlev became a full member of the Politburo in June 1987. He was interviewed on 30 July 1987 by Andras Sugar for the Hungarian television programme *Face to Face*. Among other questions, Sugar asked, 'What changes are necessary in the system of political institutions?' This was Yakovlev's reply:

Democratization is needed first and foremost, second and third too. I do not think that there can be any more effective method for us to carry the economy forward, improve people's mood . . . or to be more precise to create the necessary mood in society. Nothing can be more effective than democracy.

One person wants to develop democracy, and the other does not because this does not coincide with his personal interest. A third person is on the side of democracy, but only for the time being provided it does not affect him in person. He wants democracy for his own sake, but only so that they should deal democratically with him. While he, of course, does not want to act accordingly, and perhaps he cannot do so either, because he has not got used to it, does not know how to do it. For, you know, when we look at it as outsiders, we like the fact that people criticize one another. But when they criticize us, then the situation changes immediately and radically.

We have not got used to really arguing, and what is more, arguing honourably, listening to one another's opinions. Yet this is essential, since collective wisdom is always stronger than the view of one person. For this reason, the issue does not consist of the perfection of the system of political institutions alone; what is at issue is that we should shape human thinking itself, that we should get people used to a democratic outlook, to a kind of democratic way of thinking.

I mentioned a few days ago here that we have overthrown the tsars, but we have not yet overthrown the petty monarchs hidden within ourselves. Within all of us there sits some kind of khan, tsar, I might say God almighty, in other words a sort of power-hungry being. When this starts to take hold of one, there straight away appears this inner-being, who starts to give out orders, to administrate. It starts to walk not upon our sinful soil but hovers somewhere above it. Such a person already thinks he is more clever, more learned; he starts to make pronouncements and everyone is obliged to attend in awe to his wise thoughts.

Therefore, we have got to get used to spiritual, human equality; we have to understand that a person, in the last resort, is only one among millions. If he attains greater or smaller office, then this only means that people trust him and have honoured him with their trust. To a certain extent, perhaps, it shows that they recognize one of his abilities or talents, but it in no way authorizes him to detach himself from the millions of human beings, to put himself above them.

I do not think it is a simple matter to recognize this; it is a matter of outlook. It needs a lot of time, and not just years or decades. Nor is it just a matter of teaching people, for it is also a matter of economic and social conditions.

CHERNOBYL

It was shortly after Mikhail Sergeyevich's first announcement of the policy of glasnost. Perhaps he hoped that his declaration would be greeted with enthusiasm. Surely he wished for a more positive response than the disbelieving, 'Oh yeah, we've heard that before' with which it was initially received. But scepticism towards Gorbachev showed that people wanted proof, and not another 'campaign'. The new General Secretary insisted that people drank less, especially at work, and he savagely reduced the availability of vodka. So if the first reactions to glasnost were distinctly sober, who was he to complain?

Reality, however, blew its top, like a mad over-fermented intoxicant, far more lethal than alcohol: the No 4 reactor at Chernobyl exploded. Emergency control systems had been switched off, if they worked at all. Cooling water hyper-boiled and separated into its component parts, releasing hydrogen. The hydrogen ignited, and blasted away the roof of the reactor building. In the intense heat the graphite – the carbon blocks designed to slow the fission – caught fire. Local firemen, without safety clothes, saved the contiguous reactor. As they fought, they began to die without knowing it. As they looked into the furnace which had been No 4 they were victims of a quite unintended 'openness'.

Unintended but in a way inevitable. Each society may have its own special style of nuclear disasters; only a social system that is without reactors or is incapable of decadence and deceit will never have a covered-up Windscale, a Three Mile Island or a Chernobyl. In this sense, Chernobyl was the incarnation of Brezhnevism. The formula of his regime was bound to have some such consequence. What particular value or site would be put on the right-hand side of the equals sign was perhaps a matter of chance. But greed, multiplied by economic growth, multiplied by mendacity, multiplied by bossism, equals x to the power of n, otherwise known as an almighty foul-up. It was a grim justice, really, that it went nuclear.

For this gave it world consequences. The fire plume raced to the stratosphere before the political committees could condemn it for being anti-Soviet. The machinery of 'developed socialism' creaked with buck-passing. Desperate yet inadequate secret messages went to Moscow. Ill-prepared, ill-informed and hence irresponsible meetings took place which could only presume that the world's most catastrophic and poisonous accident had not yet happened. While all this was going on, routine safety checks in a Swedish nuclear plant registered danger levels; neighbouring countries, including the USSR, were alerted! Chernobyl, however, was the ultimate form of dissent. The Geiger counter told you it was there, and even deadly, but no normal person could smell, see or touch its force. It was intangible but undeniable. Unlike Solzhenitsyn, responsibility for Chernobyl could not be exported to the West.

Logically speaking, therefore, I expected some kind of relationship between glasnost today and Chernobyl. It had been the policy's first serious test, it confirmed the need for a completely new administrative culture in the USSR and it showed that

Soviet development could never again be considered a purely 'internal affair'. So I often asked, over the kitchen tables in Moscow, if there was any connection. The idea aroused interest and discussion, but always the same answer: 'no'. No, they were separate things. Chernobyl was a massive tragedy, a Russian fate (though it took place in the Ukraine) rather than a Party policy like glasnost, with which it could hardly be compared or linked.

So I can report no evidence that allows me to persist in my belief. But most of my new Moscow friends know as little as I do about what goes on in the Politburo. And my suspicion remains that Chernobyl shifted the ground in favour of the reformers. At the same time it must have showed them how dangerous is the ship they steer and how close they are to a catastrophe, one that could sweep not only the 'old guard' but also themselves into oblivion.

Chernobyl favoured the reformers for three reasons. There is a Russian absolutist tradition of Potomkin villages, where the appearance of well-being is simply a façade behind which people groan. Such pretence is harmful in so far as it helps perpetuate the wretchedness it hides. Potomkin villages are one thing, Potomkin power stations quite another. For where pretence can be lethal, pretence itself really must be undone. The pretention of Brezhnev's Russia was harmful. The stupefying narcissism of its 'good news' not only perpetuated, it helped intensify the negative conditions that it publicly denied. By demonstrating the reality behind the façade on such an undeniable scale, Chernobyl assisted the wider dismantling of that official cheerfulness known to most of us as lying.

Secondly, Chernobyl demonstrated that if the Soviet economy is ever to work effectively – with the care and attention needed for high productivity with costly investments – then responsibility is essential at the work station. Russian officials have for too long been careless with their own lives not to speak of those below them. As for machinery! A society that does not look after its people is unlikely to service its inanimate instruments. Attention to detail starts at the top, yet it matters at the bottom. People need the morale and self-respect to take pride in the quality of what is in front of them, to solve problems on the spot, preferably being given credit for their actions. All this is one of the insistent themes of the new line. It can hardly have received a better confirmation than at Chernobyl. The court's judgement, prior to sentence, on those found responsible notes:

> One witness said that there had been quite a few violations, and that the administration was aware of them. In just one instance, when he was checking how work personnel were fulfilling work discipline, he discovered that twelve people were 'fulfilling' other things in their work time – playing dominoes and cards, writing letters, etc.

The court went on to report that between 1980 and 1986 out of 71 technical breakdowns, 'no research [into the causes] was done at all in 27 cases'. While, 'many cases of equipment failure have not even been registered in the operation logs'.[25] There is no reason to think such slovenliness was unusual in Soviet industry.

Thirdly, the new leadership claims to be keener on realities, rather than verbiage and medals. If Gorbachev's foreign policy may be summed up by the phrase that Soviets now use in talking about their nuclear deterrent – reasonable sufficiency – then it implies a desire to take a normal rather than an exceptional place on the planet. Psychologically, this presupposes dismantling the pathological aggressive defensive feelings that dog Soviet attitudes towards the outside world. A response especially noticeable among those military, economic and regional leaders, who have never been to the West, or even set foot in another country, outside, that is, those high ranking official delegations organized to cocoon their members from the most dangerous of viruses: other people living differently.

The Soviet system *is* different from the West's. It wishes to retain its originality. Ironically, this demands a genuine interest in how the West lives. The USSR cannot hope to compete with the successes of capitalism unless it is honest about them, and that means being honest about itself also – the two processes are linked. Gorbachev seems to have grasped this. One motive behind his desire for agreement with Washington is that it might relax tensions within the Soviet Union and so encourage a more creative, less commandist atmosphere. Chernobyl helped all this because it blew up the idea that the USSR can exist as an island unto itself.

As the long shadow from Chernobyl passed over north-west England, it rained, and the rain brought down the isotopes that entered the soil, where they were drawn into the grass, on which the ewes grazed, and were concentrated into their milk. In the summer of 1987, for the second year running, British farmers in Cumbria have been forbidden to slaughter their lambs for market because they are too radioactive for human consumption.

The Soviets are very sensitive to their image abroad. The people of the USSR have a tremendous sense of wounded pride. They have suffered many wounds, and their pride can be ludicrous. 'It is a proof of the advance of socialism that we have had the world's *greatest* accident', went one joke; not so far from the bone, for there was a perverse glory (or shame) in its scale. But it may have done the Soviet Union some good that its international influence can now be measured among other things with a Geiger counter. It raises one of the most interesting issues, that of the relationship between them and us. Are they part of the 'East' or the 'West'? Should they be true to their own special spirit and damn commercialism (or in the case of Solzhenitsyn, commercialism and socialism)? Can they, in the phrase of Stalin's that combined leftist defiance and national-aggrandizement, 'build socialism in one country'? There have been periods when the Kremlin felt it could tell the rest of the world to stop interfering if it took a close interest in the answer. But now we have a right to be involved. At the very least we have the right to know that their system – whatever it is – operates on an everyday basis at the highest standards. What we can eat depends on it.

Chernobyl emphasized the twist that has been taken in human affairs. Nuclear power held out the promise of clean energy and national autonomy, but delivered instead deadly pollution and interdependence. There can be no national borders against radioactivity.

There is thus a fourth way that the Chernobyl disaster has aided the reorientation associated with the new leadership. The old one sought proof of Soviet superiority through grand schemes. Expensive rockets blast off; new railway lines plunge through near arctic conditions in Siberia (when much needed city lines rust and the train takes eight hours from Moscow to Leningrad when it should take three); supersonic passenger aircraft (that crash); planning to divert giant rivers to make deserts bloom (when a quarter of the harvest is lost on the side of poor and non-existent roads). All these things were part of the Brezhnev era's flight into the future. A flight from the realities of the present. Lenin said that socialism was 'Soviets plus electrification', which could be taken to mean the combination of democratic power and high productivity. Brezhnev interpreted it as 'Me and my big schemes'. The crude, phallic vainglory of enormous triumphs hid the flaccid and sterile reality. Then Chernobyl occurred – a premature ejaculation so obvious that potency could no longer be proclaimed. The idea of continuous, triumphant progress collapsed with it. To take the Potomkin analogy further, it was not just that the façade of success was ripped away by the catastrophe at Chernobyl. The pictures drawn on the façades – the ideal picture itself of what progress should be like – will have to be recomposed.

To live better does not mean more of the same, it means to live differently. This lesson of Chernobyl could hardly have been more timely for Mikhail Sergeyevich and his colleagues.

But it was also too much for him to handle at the time. It took him nearly three weeks before he felt able to go on television and address the Soviet people about what had happened. The apparently detailed and frank report on the disaster made by the USSR to the International Atomic Energy Authority has not been published at home. Most disappointing was the trial.

In *Sarcophagus*, his play about Chernobyl, Vladimir Gubaryev, the science editor of *Pravda* and the first journalist to get to the burning reactor, has the official investigator say: 'In my opinion, there must be a trial. And an open trial, what's more'.[26]

Earlier, in a Soviet television documentary on the disaster, Gubaryev had urged that the most 'painstaking analysis' of the truth be made public. The play sees his *fictional* Director of Chernobyl argue:

You're wasting your time trying to pin the blame on me
. . . Go and see other nuclear power stations – take a good
look. Were we worse than them? No . . . we were better.
We've won the ministry's efficiency award three times . . .
So don't come looking *here* for the culprits. We're not the
ones to blame. But can you explain to me why the quality
of nuclear power-station equipment has got steadily worse
over the last ten years? Why we are given obsolete instruments and spare parts? . . . I could give you dozens more
'whys' of that sort – and I'm not the only one. Ask the
hydro-electric boys . . . It just so happened that the boil
burst at *our* nuclear station. It had to come, but it was still
just an accident.

This speech was made from a Moscow stage. But did the
actual director, Bryukhanov, make such a justification in
court? Although the opening and closing sessions were public,
the trial was indeed closed. In their sentence the judges criticized Bryukhanov for signing the acceptance of the reactor
before it was completed. He got ten years not just for this but
also for hiding the facts about radiation levels 'on purpose' after
the accident: 'the lack of broad-scale truthful information on
the nature of the breakdown led to the contamination of station
personnel . . .'[27]
Everyone knows that Bryukhanov must have been under
pressure from above. A month *before* the explosion at No 4
reactor an article appeared in the local *Literaturnaya Ukraina* by
Lyubov Kovalevska, a young journalist who was only saved
from punishment by the accident. She criticized the appalling
way the reactor complex was being expanded, and dared to
write:

The construction is not fit for assembly and never will be
. . . Equipment, machines and mechanisms started to wear
out and shortages of basic mechanical devices and instruments took place. Problems have multiplied and become
overgrown with a massive quantity of unknowns.[28]

Thus officials in the Ukraine knew beforehand of the terrible
danger. Yet Kovalevska's warning went unheeded. By whom?
But once you start to go up the ladder of responsibility, where
do you stop? The Ukrainian party apparatus under Shcher-
bitsky – a Brezhnev appointee – is still in place and he retains
his position in the Politburo. Nor is the nuclear lobby without
influence in Moscow. Bryukhanov, the actual as against the
fictional Director, was made a scapegoat.

The significance of Chernobyl for the USSR was played
down. It was one of the greatest crimes of the Brezhnev order.
Yet it was turned into a single, tragic exception, rather than a
powerful symbol and indictment of the way the country has
been run. By holding the Chernobyl trial in camera, did the
new men demonstrate a fear of their connection with – or
should we say their lasting contamination by – the system of
their predecessors?

'IMPOSSIBLE' 'NEVER'

THIRTY-YEAR-OLD: Perestroika is a lot too conservative for me. But most people are not really angry with the system. I'd say that they are more depressed. They get most of what they need, and a job even if they do not really have to work. Glasnost does not threaten any power, except for the most backward Party and government officials, who can be pensioned off. There will not be multi-parties, nor the right to travel abroad as you have. In my view, so far the changes are quite limited and safe. There will not be real changes ever, there will never be freedom in this country.

TEACHER: We have no tradition of public expression. I'd like to think that glasnost is for real. But people know that it is from the top. They say, it comes from them – he gestures upwards with his head – and they feel that it is not for people like *us* to criticize.

SIXTY-YEAR-OLD: The changes are coming from the top. This is very important. In our country all changes come from the top. The only exception was the October revolution, but even then the Tsar had gone and there was no authority. Serfdom was abolished from the top just like Krushchev toppled belief in Stalin.

HIS WIFE: Impossible! Russia can never change.

SCIENTIST: Russia is a black force, Reagan is right, all they understand is toughness. If it hadn't been for Star Wars forcing them to realize how backward the system is, there would never have been Gorbachev.

WRITER: I am in complete solidarity with what the government is trying to do. Six months ago I'd *never* have said anything like that . . . The Russians? You understand nothing. Just a hundred years ago their great-grandfathers were slaves. Then there was revolution and a bloody war, then a huge revolution, more war, red terror, collectivization, Stalin, another even more catastrophic war and still Stalin. What is surprising is not that Brezhnev ended up an idiot but that the whole country was not reduced to complete idiots after such a history.

MOTHER: This country will never change. Not for a very long time.

HER DAUGHTER: I have to have some hope, and in my profession of the arts it has become completely different over the last year.

EIGHTEEN-YEAR-OLD: I would like a car, a dacha, a good apartment, clothes . . . and perhaps a plane. Just a little plane, like Rust's, so that I could fly away.

BREZHNEV

I knew the Soviets had a problem with their past. I thought it was Stalin and coming to terms with what happened under Stalin. But the main difficulty may be Brezhnev – the not unkind buffoon, with his two eyebrows rather than a moustache. He had worshipped Stalin when he was a young political officer at the victory parade in Red Square in 1945. Thirty years later he made himself a Marshal and pretended that the Soviet people adored him in the same way.

The difference between them was that Stalin was a hater. If you had known him personally, then you were likely to hear the swish of the Grim Reaper. Most of the senior old Bolsheviks who served with Stalin and were not fortunate to die of natural causes, he eliminated. Perhaps the major exception was Molotov – but Stalin kept Molotov's wife in the Gulag as insurance. It was as lethal to have supported Stalin as to have coughed in his presence. Of the two thousand delegates to the 1934 Seventeenth Party Congress, more than half were killed. Of the Central Committee they elected, 70 per cent were executed. To appeal to him personally for your life, was to lose it.

Brezhnev enjoyed his power in quite a different way: with a slap on the back rather than a bullet. If, when you were young, fate had crossed your path with his, your reward was not death but a job. The better you knew him, the greater the chance of promotion. Ignaty Novikov was from Brezhnev's home town. He became chairman of the organizing committee for the 1980 Moscow Olympics. A lot better than going to Magadan.

Brezhnev created a cult around himself that took on more and more fantastical proportions. But he was not a Stalin. He was not so efficient or machiavellian. Suslov, the chief 'ideologist' and kingmaker, is said to have been the prime organizer behind the ouster of Kruschev in 1964, that made Brezhnev General Secretary. Stalin would have bumped both of them off. But Khruschev was retired and Suslov remained the official No 2 in Brezhnev's Politburo until his death in 1982. Furthermore, he retained considerable power independent of Brezhnev. Gromyko, in foreign affairs, grew in stature and influence during the Brezhnev period. Above all, Andropov was made head of the KGB and secured his own power base. None of these three seemed to have been touched by the grosser corruption of Brezhnev's own entourage, the so-called Dnepropetrovsk Mafia.

A peculiar form of relaxation took place in Brezhnev's USSR. You could take it easy if you were second rate, played the game, accepted bribes and didn't care about people other than your family and friends. If you tried to insist on principles, stood out for your views, or were awkward, then things could be . . . well, tough. Indeed, you had to have connections, and therefore protection to survive. Even the best were obliged to play the game.

There *was* space to play in. The social asphyxiation was not as all embracing as Stalin's terror. The system was hardly pluralist if that means a Western style unified system that provides for moderately different ideological parties, competing companies and one or two outspoken individuals. But there was a sort of pluralism in Brezhnev's USSR taken as a whole, in all its vast spaces. It was the pluralism of different Mafias, of quite a large number of city bosses, some worse than others. It was a regime of tough guys, with all their camaraderie and limelighting. It was the pluralism of mentally mediocre, but organizationally ruthless, benevolently oppressive Godfathers.

'Stalin was bad', I was told, as we drove south-west out of Moscow down the Lenin Prospect. On both sides rose the immense, new city-scape of long and high-rise apartment buildings. We were about to approach the Ring Road, 'but Brezhnev . . .' and my companion stopped in mid-sentence. 'What's this? I've never seen so much traffic!'

'It's Friday evening', I pointed out, used to the extra commuter rush at weekends.

'Of *course*, I forgot', said my companion, without thinking that he was witnessing one of the fruits of the Brezhnev era.

'But Brezhnev', he continued, 'in some ways he was *worse* than Stalin. Stalin killed people. But Brezhnev killed their souls. Under Brezhnev people forgot how to live. Just as they forgot how to work. In Stalin's time at least people lived for the future, even many of the camp inmates. Under Brezhnev it didn't bother them whether they lived for the past or the future. The spark went out of them. They just wanted to eat a little, to drink and to steal.'

The Brezhnev period lasted two decades. It started with considerable self-confidence within the leadership. Brezhnev himself had been in charge of part of the Soviet rocket programme; he was one of the main organizers of mankind's initial conquest of space. (When they first discussed strategic arms in the Kremlin in 1971, President Nixon noticed that Brezhnev 'used a red pencil to sketch missiles on the notepad in front of him'.[29]) Through the early space programme Brezhnev consolidated his contacts with the military. In the aftermath of the Cuban crisis of 1962, they pressed for a gigantic missile construction programme, to gain parity with the USA. Khruschev resisted, aware that it might have adverse consequences for the economy as a whole. Brezhnev built the missiles.

Along with the military, there was Suslov, who had worked side by side with Stalin on ideological issues, including international questions, since the late 1940s, after he had overseen the postwar purge of Lithuania. Suslov was among the Soviet Union's main ideologists for thirty years, for seventeen of them its chief guardian of Marxist–Leninist orthodoxy whose principles are taught as a compulsory subject throughout the Soviet education system. The historian Roy Medvedev has explained:

> Ideology in the USSR is a vital instrument of power. As the Politbureau member responsible for ideology, Suslov stood at the top of a great pyramid with a mass of institutions beneath him. In the Party Central Committee he directed such departments as ideology, agitation and propaganda, science, secondary and tertiary education and two foreign sections. He controlled political education in the Soviet Army, Central Committee information, the foreign travel commission and the organizations for youth and social affairs. The Ministry of Culture, the State Committee for Publishing Houses, the State Committee for the Cinema and the media organization, all operated under his authority. The whole of the press, censorship, TASS, CPSU contacts with other communist parties,

even the USSR's foreign policy – all came under his juris-
diction. Naturally he worked closely with the KGB and
the Office of the State Prosecutor, with particular reference to that rather vague concept, 'ideological deviation'.[30]

What kind of a man was Suslov? Although 'the entire ideological life of our country and party in the 1970s' was under his
control, and although when he died in 1982 his obituaries
described him as a major party theoretician, Medvedev points
out that Suslov's 'actual contribution to party theory was nil;
he never said an original word on the entire subject . . . He
made not a single new contribution to party ideology. His
creative potential proved to be inconsequential to a remarkable
degree'.

Could this be unfair? To sustain an unchanging point of view
through the heady decades of the fifties, sixties and seventies,
to resist all novelty and allow no deviation while the world was
transformed, is the sign of a most singular character.

Suslov was spare with himself, it is said, austere and uncorrupt in his lifestyle. Although he was trained in the barbarities
of Stalinism and promoted by the dictator, Suslov supported
Krushchev's attack on Stalin. In 1959 when the Chinese sought
to outflank Moscow on the left, charging it with 'revisionism',
Suslov went to Peking. How can you demand that we reverse
our criticisms of Stalin, he asked the Chinese Communists,
when under Stalin no one knew if they or their loved ones
would come home in the evening?

To understand the paradox of Suslov the anti-Stalinist is to
comprehend what happened to official life in the USSR after
the mid-sixties. Monolithic, punitive and philistine in outlook;

hence intellectually sterile, yet also opposed to terror and inquisitorial domination. What holds this singular combination together? Suslov moved against Khruschev in 1964 not because he desired to reverse de-Stalinization but because Khruschev had become capricious and unpredictable. It was this that offended him: not despotism but its erratic and subjective character. He believed completely in rule from above, but also a safe, steady life. The wilful arbitrariness of Stalin's terror; not knowing from one week to the next if Khruschev would decide that half the virgin lands should be planted with tomatoes; and the unforetellable consequences of new ideas; all were equally unacceptable to Suslov. He desired the trajectory of socialist truth to be as predictable as the orbit of one of Brezhnev's rockets on a good day.

Even a Marxist ought to have realized that this is like asking for the moon.

The combination of rigid yet complacent ideology and grandiose military and economic schemes gave birth to Brezhnevism. There was an early attempt to liberalize the economy, with Kosygin's economic policies of 1965. But such reforms would have had political consequences (in terms of the organization of society) and ideological ones (in terms of the need for free exchange of information) that implicitly challenged the world view of Suslov and Brezhnev. Perhaps this became absolutely clear only with the Prague Spring in 1968.

The attempt to introduce market reforms in Czechoslovakia and abolish censorship was intolerable. And not only to the Kremlin leaders. Apparently Ulbricht of East Germany, Zhivkov of Bulgaria and Gomulka of Poland demanded intervention.[31] They feared that their own local domination would be threatened by the Czech experiment. An alliance of Warsaw

Pact tanks crushed a fraternal Communist Party, one that had gained the overwhelming support of its people. This meant more than the end of liberalization in one country: when the tanks rolled into Czechoslovakia, they also creaked across the USSR.

In their wake, the Party neanderthals sought to rehabilitate Stalin and chose his eightieth birthday, on 21 December 1969. They nearly succeeded. While the creative intelligentsia of the Soviet Union mobilized to frustrate the attempt, a long celebratory article was composed and set in type to be published in *Pravda*. But once more East European opinion made itself felt. Kadar and Gomulka flew privately to Moscow from Hungary and Poland to warn the Kremlin that their own parties would publicly dissociate themselves from anything so grotesque. So too, of course, would the Communist Parties of Western Europe.

Two or three days before the anniversary the question of Stalin was once again discussed by the Politburo and, according to one well-informed source, it was decided by a small majority of votes to cancel a large part of the arrangements for celebrating Stalin's "jubilee".[32]

Only in Ulan-Bator did the message to cancel publication of the anniversary article fail to arrive. So it appeared in Mongolian, with an acknowledgement to the *Pravda* of 21 December, which had in fact remained silent.

What a fantastic story! Brezhnev and his colleagues wished to rehabilitate a leader already excoriated in multiple detail throughout the world – a man charged with numerous murders both individual and collective. A mass of evidence – archive after archive of the stuff – was a mere instruction away

('Bring me . . .'). Just fifteen years before, Stalin had incarcerated five per cent of their own population in the Gulag for no reason sustainable by justice. And not only did they want to praise his contribution to theory and practice, they couldn't bring themselves to do it because of some interfering foreigners! Such was the burden of empire.

One does not know whether to laugh or cry more at the fact that they desired to vindicate Stalin or the reasons why they did not. The result was a stifling stalemate. Joseph Vissarionovich Djugashvili, also known as *Soselo* or 'Little Joe', entered a long afterlife of suspended rehabilitation. Brezhnev's politburo took Soviet political culture by the throat and neither crushed its wind-pipe nor released it.

JEALOUSY

Margarita was talking to me about her institute. Internationally well known, but not a Party member, she has never been allowed to travel despite her reputation. At the end of 1986 she was invited to a big conference in Paris. Again, no passport. She went to see the head of her institute and demanded to know why she was not allowed to go, especially as her expenses would be paid without cost to Soviet foreign exchange.

The Director said, 'My dear Margarita, may I tell you something in complete confidence. It is the KGB.'

'Impossible', said Margarita.

She went home and broke Bulgakov's rule, that you should never ask anyone for anything – especially those more powerful than yourself. She wrote a letter to Comrade Chebrikov, the head of the KGB. She told him that the name of the KGB had been used to explain why she could not go abroad, that she was not anti-Soviet, had never been a dissident, and was quite sure that the KGB had no reason to act in this way. Would he, she asked, confirm this was so and give her a paper stating the KGB did not disapprove of her going abroad.

A short while later Margarita heard from the KGB. She was summonsed to an appointment. Not with Chebrikov but with the officer who oversees the institutes in her branch of knowledge.

He was very polite and he agreed that, so far as the KGB was concerned, it was fine for her to attend an international conference.

'Then why,' asked Margarita, 'doesn't the Institute allow me to travel?'

'Jealousy,' said the KGB officer, opening his hands in a gesture of helplessness.

THEY SAW IT COMING

I was sitting outside a residence for visiting officials in Leningrad, on Khalturina Street just down the road from The Hermitage, when an exceptionally well-dressed woman of a certain age left the same complex and got into a car, where she waited. Then an older-looking man, balding and with a stoop went to join her. He looked round, and I realized with a thrill that it was Sakharov. Sakharov, at liberty in Leningrad.

The car conducted a strange manoeuvre. Sakharov then got out, went back towards the building and talked to someone on an upper floor. I would not have understood what they were saying, even if I had been able to hear. But I couldn't take my eyes off him. Some young people passed, and there were others on the far pavement. Sakharov noticed me staring and bowed slightly. I waved and shouted in English: 'Keep it up!' The passers by, I realized, although likely to know his name, had never seen his picture in magazines or on the television. Even though he is deservedly one of the most famous of living Russians, only the Westerner recognized him.

After I returned to Moscow from Leningrad I went to see Roy Medvedev, the Soviet Union's foremost Marxist historian, whose marvellous study of the Stalin period *Let History Judge* remains unpublished in his own country. He has a twin brother, Zhores, who works in London. Zhores is a geneticist who was persecuted before being driven into exile. They are identical twins; the only obvious difference between them is that Roy learnt German while Zhores speaks English. Zhores had asked me to take Roy some large, strong manilla envelopes which are unobtainable in Moscow. Although his own work remains beyond the pail, Roy was more optimistic about the new developments than his brother. Zhores explained it in completely objective fashion. 'You see, he is a historian and I am a scientist. So I understand much better than he does how far behind the Soviet Union is, and how difficult it will be.'

Today, Sakharov thinks that a convergence is underway between the systems of East and West. He can argue this publicly in Moscow, as he did at the International Forum in 1987. Roy Medvedev has been allowed to work from his flat in Moscow for many years, although when Chernenko was in power police were stationed at the entrance to his apartment block, and he was harassed. He would not concur with Sakharov's perspectives.

But at the beginning of the seventies Medvedev and Sakharov together with Valery Turchin, signed an extraordinary letter to the Soviet leadership. I found this document by chance in a volume of *samizdat* material. Fifteen years before it was born, they argued the case for the combination of policies similar to those now known as glasnost and perestroika. In early 1970, their letter recorded a systematic and far-sighted indictment of the Brezhnev regime.[33]

When I came across it after I returned from Moscow, I felt as if I had opened up a message in an old bottle that had tossed its way across the seas. Spreading out the yellowed paper before me, I read a sharp analysis of today's news. Here it is:

To:

L. I. Brezhnev, Central Committee of the CPSU

A. N. Kosygin, USSR Council of Ministers

N. V. Podgorny, Presidium of the Supreme Soviet, USSR:

Dear Comrades,

We are appealing to you on a question of great importance. Our country has made great strides in the development of production, in the fields of education and culture, in the basic improvement of the living conditions of the working class, and in the development of new socialist human relationships. However, serious difficulties and shortcomings are also evident.

This letter will discuss and develop a point of view which can be formulated briefly by the following theses:

1. At the present time there is an urgent need to carry out a series of measures directed toward the further democratization of our country's public life. This need stems, in particular, from the very close connection between the problem of technological and economic progress and scientific methods of management, on the one hand, and the problems of freedom of information, the open airing of views, and the free clash of ideas, on the other . . .

2. Democratization must promote the maintenance and consolidation of the Soviet socialist system . . .

3. Democratization, carried out under the leadership of the CPSU in collaboration with all strata of society, should maintain and strengthen the leading role of the party in the economic, political and cultural life of society.

4. Democratization should be gradual in order to avoid possible complication and disruptions. At the same time it should be thoroughgoing, carried out consistently in accordance with a carefully worked-out program. Without fundamental

democratization, our society will not be able to solve the problems now facing it, and will not be able to develop in a normal manner . . .

Over the past decade menacing signs of disorder and stagnation have begun to show themselves in the economy, the roots of which go back to an earlier period and are very deeply embedded. There is an uninterrupted decline in the rate of growth of the national income. The gap between what is necessary for normal development and the new productive forces actually being introduced is growing wider. In addition to many mistakes in industry and agriculture, there is intolerable procrastination about finding solutions to urgent problems. Defects in the system of planning, accounting and incentives often cause contradictions between the local and departmental interests and those of the state and nation. As a result, new means of developing production potential are not being discovered or properly put to use and technical progress has slowed down abruptly. For these very reasons, the natural wealth of the country is often destroyed with impunity and without any supervision or controls: forests are levelled, reservoirs polluted, valuable agricultural land inundated, soil eroded or salinized, etc. The chronically difficult situation in agriculture, particularly in regard to livestock, is well known. The population's real income in recent years has hardly grown at all; food supply and medical and consumer services are improving very slowly, and with unevenness between regions. The number of goods in short supply continues to grow. There are clear signs of inflation.

Of particular concern regarding our country's future is the lag in the development of education: our total expenditures for education in all forms are three times below what they are in the United States, and are rising at a slower rate. Alcoholism is growing in a tragic way and drug addiction is beginning to surface. In many regions of the country the crime rate is climbing systematically. Signs of corruption are becoming more and more noticeable in a number of places. In the work of scientific and scientific-technical organizations, bureaucratism, departmentalism, a formal attitude toward one's tasks, and lack of initiative are becoming more and more pronounced.

As is well known, the productivity of labour is the decisive factor in the comparison of economic systems. It is here that the situation is worst of all. Productivity of labour in our country remains, as before, many times lower than that of the capitalist countries, and the growth of productivity has fallen off abruptly. This situation causes particular anxiety if one compares it with the situation in the leading capitalist countries, in particular with the United States. By introducing elements of state regulation and planning into the economy, these countries have saved themselves from the destructive crises which plagued the capitalist economy in an earlier era. The broad introduction of computer technology and automation assures a rapid rise in the productivity of labour, which in turn facilitates a partial overcoming of certain social problems and contradictions (e.g. by means of unemployment benefits, shortening of the work day, etc.). In comparing our economy with that of the United States, we see that ours lags behind not only in quantitative but also – most regrettable of all – in qualitative terms. The newer and more revolutionary a particular aspect of the economy may be, the wider the gap between the USSR and the USA. We outstrip America in coal production, but we lag behind in the output of oil, gas and electric power; we lag behind by ten times in the field of chemistry, and we are infinitely outstripped in computer technology. The latter is especially crucial, because the introduction of electronic computers into the economy is a phenomenon of decisive importance that radically changes the outlines of the production system and of the entire culture. This phenomenon has justly been called the second industrial revolution. Nevertheless, our stock of computers is *1 per cent* of that of the United States. And with respect to the application of the electronic computer, the gap is so great that it is impossible even to measure it. We simply live in another age . . .

What is wrong? Why have we not only failed to be the pioneers of the second industrial revolution, but have in fact found ourselves incapable of keeping pace with the developed capitalist countries? Is it possible that socialism provides fewer opportunities for the development of productive forces than capitalism? Or that in the economic competition between capitalism and socialism, capitalism is winning?

Of course not! The source of our difficulties does not lie in the socialist system, but on the contrary, it lies in those peculiarities and conditions of our life which run contrary to socialism and are hostile to it. The source lies in the antidemocratic traditions and norms of public life established in the Stalin era, which have not been decisively eliminated to this day.

Non-economic coercion, limitations on the exchange of information, restrictions on intellectual freedom, and other examples of the antidemocratic distortion of socialism which took place under Stalin were accepted in our country as an overhead expense of the industrialization process. It was believed that they did not seriously influence the economy of the country, although they had very serious consequences in the political and military arenas, in the destinies of vast layers of the population, and for whole nationalities. We will leave aside the question of the extent to which this point of view is justified for the early stages of the development of a socialist national economy; the decline in the rate of industrial development in the prewar years rather suggests the opposite. But there is no doubt that since the beginning of the second industrial revolution these phenomena have become a decisive economic factor; they have become the main brake on the development of the productive forces in this country. As a consequence of the increased size and complexity of economic systems, the problems of management and organization have moved to the forefront. These problems cannot be resolved by one or several persons holding power and 'knowing everything'. These problems demand the creative participation of millions of people on all levels of the economic system. In this lies the difference between modern economics and economics, let us say, in the ancient Orient.

However, we encounter certain insurmountable obstacles on the road towards the free exchange of ideas and information. Truthful information about our shortcomings and negative manifestations is hushed up on the grounds that it 'may be used by enemy propaganda'. Exchange of information with foreign countries is restricted for fear of 'penetration by an enemy ideology'. Theoretical generalizations and practical proposals, if they seem too bold to some individuals, are nipped in the bud without any discussion because of the fear that they might 'undermine our foundations'. An obvious lack of confidence in creatively thinking, critical and energetic individuals is to be seen here. Under such circumstances the conditions are created for the advancement up the rungs of the official ladder not of those who distinguish themselves by their professional qualities and commitment to principles but of those who proclaim their devotion to the party but in practice are only worried about their own narrow personal interests or are passive time-servers.

Limitations on freedom of information mean that not only is it more difficult to control the leaders, not only is the initiative of the people undermined, but that even the intermediate level of leadership is deprived of rights and information, and these people are transformed into passive time-servers and bureaucrats. The leaders in the highest government bodies receive information that is incomplete, with the rough spots glossed over; hence they are also deprived of the opportunity to utilize effectively the authority they have.

The economic reform of 1965 was an extremely beneficial and important start towards resolving key problems of our economic life. However, we are convinced that purely economic measures alone are not enough to fulfill all its tasks. Furthermore, these economic measures cannot be fully implemented without reforms in the sphere of management, information and open public discussion.

There is much talk these days about the need for a scientific approach to the problems of organization and management. This is true . . . But a scientific approach demands full information, impartial thinking and creative freedom. Until these conditions are established (not for certain individuals but for the masses) talk about scientific management will remain hollow . . . and under the conditions of the second industrial revolution, it is precisely creative labour that becomes increasingly important for the national economy.

In this connection the problem of relations between the state and the intelligentsia cannot be left unmentioned. Freedom of information and creative work are necessary for the intelligentsia due to the nature of its activity and its social function. The intelligentsia's attempts to increase these freedoms are legitimate and natural. The state, however, suppresses these attempts by employing all kinds of restrictions – administrative pressures, dismissals from employment and even courtroom trials. This all gives rise to a social gulf, an atmosphere of mutual distrust, and a profound lack of mutual understanding, making fruitful collaboration difficult between the party and the state apparatus, on the one hand, and the most active layers of the intelligentsia, i.e. the layers that are most valuable for society, on the other. Under the conditions of modern industrial society, in which the role of the intelligentsia is constantly increasing, such a gulf can only be described as suicidal.

An overwhelming part of the intelligentsia and the youth recognize the need for democratization, and the need for it to be cautious and gradual, but they cannot understand and justify measures of a patently antidemocratic nature. And, indeed, how can one justify the confinement in prisons, camps and insane asylums of people who hold oppositionist views but whose opposition stands on legal ground, in the area of ideas and convictions? In many instances, there was no opposition involved, but only a striving for information, or simply a courageous and unprejudiced discussion of important social questions. The imprisonment of writers for what they have written is inadmissable . . .

It is indispensable to speak once again about ideological problems. Democratization, with its fullness of information and clash of ideas, must restore to our ideological life its dynamism and creativity – in the social sciences, art and propaganda – and

91

liquidate the bureaucratic, ritualistic, dogmatic, openly hypo-critical and mediocre style that reigns in these areas today . . .

Carrying out democratization is not an easy process. Its normal development would be threatened from one direction by individualist and anti-socialist forces, and from the other by the supporters of a 'strong state' and demagogues on the fascist model, who might try to exploit for their own ends the eco-nomic problems of our country . . . But we must realize that there is no other solution for our country . . . Democratization, conducted on the initiative and under the control of the highest official bodies, will allow the process to be realized in a sys-tematic fashion, taking care that all levels of the party and government apparatus succeed in adopting a new style of work, differing from past work by its greater openness and fuller public airing of views, and its broader discussion of all problems . . .

We propose the following draft program of measures which could be realized over a four- to five-year period:

1. A statement from the highest party and government bodies on the necessity for further democratization and on the rate and means of achieving it. The publication in the press of a number of articles containing a discussion of the problems of democratization.

2. Limited distribution (through party organs, enterprises and institutions) of information on the situation in the country and theoretical works on social problems which at the present time would not be made the object of broad discussion. Grad-ual increase of access to these materials until all limitations on their distribution have been lifted.

3. Extensive, planned organization of complex industrial associations with a high degree of autonomy in matters of

industrial planning, technological processes, raw material supply, sale of products, finances and personnel. The expansion of these rights for smaller productive units as well. Scientific determination after careful research of the form and degree of state regulation.

4. Cessation of interference with foreign radio broadcasts. Free sale of foreign books and periodicals. Adherence by our country to the international copyright convention. Gradual expansion and encouragement of international tourism in both directions (over a three- to four-year period), expansion of international postal communications, and other measures for broadening international communications, with special emphasis in this regard on member nations of Comecon.

5. Establishment of an institute for public opinion research . . .

6. Amnesty for political prisoners. An order requiring publication of the complete record of all trials of a political character. Public supervision of all prisons, camps and psychiatric institutions.

7. Introduction of measures to improve the functioning of the courts and the procuracy and to enhance their independence from executive powers, local influences, prejudices and personal ties.

8. Abolition of the indication of nationality on passports and questionnaires. Uniform passport system for the inhabitants of cities and villages. Gradual elimination of the system of passport registration . . .

9. Reforms in education: increased appropriations for elementary and secondary schools; improving the living standard of teachers and increasing their autonomy and leeway to experiment.

10. Passage of a law on information and the press. Guaranteeing the right of social organizations and citizens' groups to establish new publications. Complete elimination of prior censorship in every form.

11. Improvement in the training of leadership cadres in the art of management. Introduction of special managerial training programs on the job. Improvement in the information available to leading cadres at all levels, increasing their autonomy, their rights to experiment, to defend their opinions and to test them in practice.

12. Gradual introduction of the practice of having several candidates in elections to party and Soviet bodies on every level, even for indirect elections.

13. Expansion of the rights of Soviets; expansions of the rights and the responsibilities of the Supreme Soviet of the USSR.

14. Expansion of the rights of those nationalities deported under Stalin. The re-establishment of the national autonomy of deported peoples with the opportunity for them to resettle in their homeland . . .

15. Measures directed toward increasing public discussion in the work of governing bodies, commensurate with the interests of the state. Establishment of consultative scientific committees to work with the government bodies at every level, such committees to include highly qualified specialists in the different disciplines.

It is also necessary to dwell for a moment on the international consequences of our taking a course towards democratization. Nothing could be more favorable to the enhancement of our authority and progressive Communist forces in the world . . . the possibility for peaceful co-existence and international co-operation would grow, the forces of peace and social progress would be strengthened, the attractiveness of Communist ideology would increase, our international position would become more secure. It is particularly important that the moral and material position of the USSR in relation to China would be strengthened . . .

What is in store for our nation if it does not take the course towards democratization? Its fate will be to lag behind the capitalist countries and gradually become a second-rate provincial power (history has seen cases of this); the growth of economic difficulties . . . exacerbation of national problems, particularly ominous if one also takes into account the danger of Chinese totalitarian nationalism (something we regard as a temporary phenomenon from the historical point of view but as an extremely serious one for the next few years) . . . Economic stagnation, lag in our rate of growth, coupled with an unrealistic foreign policy on all continents, can lead to catastrophic consequences for our country.

Dear Comrades!

There is no other way out of the difficulties now facing our country except the course towards democratization . . .

Roy Medvedev, Andrei Sakharov, Valery Turchin

19 March 1970

NIXON'S RUSSIA

The leaders of the USSR wilfully repudiated reality. What Sakharov, Medvedev and Turchin diagnosed as wrong in 1970 was borne out. So too were the consequences they predicted. But their solution – democratization – was spurned for more than wilful reasons. Clearly, it did not appeal to the psychology of Brezhnev, Suslov and their followers. But they had to come up with their own solution – one sufficiently effective for them to be able to suppress for so long the evident need for democratization.

They had the West to thank. Without detente and oil revenues, the Brezhnev group would not have been able to pretend that their stagnation was a triumph.

The events of 1968 in Vietnam, America, France, China and Czechoslovakia had a peculiar outcome. By the end of the year the Kremlin had a firm grip on Prague, a winning hand in Vietnam and Nixon in the White House. But for the American President the Soviet occupation of Prague was not inconvenient. It helped to justify his desire to retain an American dominated South Vietnam. In addition, the Czech invasion had also brought Sino–Soviet hostility to a new pitch. This allowed him and Kissinger to play at the triangular diplomacy, which brought Nixon himself to the Kremlin in 1971.

Equally alarmed at the prospect of an uncontrolled war in

Asia and at the prospect (as they saw it) of being reduced to a mere regional power, detente was both a relief and a vindication for the Soviet leaders, one that helped to justify their huge expenditure on strategic weapons.

Brezhnev was energetic and physically vigorous during the negotiations to limit the growth of the US-Soviet nuclear arsenals in 1971. He was a true machine politician. Nixon described him as being

> like a big Irish labour boss, or perhaps an analogy to Mayor Daley (of Chicago) would be more in order . . . As we were riding in the car out to the dacha, he put his hand on my knee and said he hoped we had developed a good personal relationship.[34]

Nixon was more powerful, his country much the stronger, even if he came to envy the Soviet leader his controlled press. The fact that they treated together, and traded, and that their talks not only reached a SALT agreement but also endorsed strategic parity between Moscow and Washington, helped make Brezhnev's position invulnerable at home. Nixon was one of the architects of Soviet stagnation.

Brezhnev's other gain, the oil price rise of 1972, gave the USSR a windfall of tens of billions of dollars. Butter, wheat, grain for livestock, factories, all this and luxury consumer items for the elite, could be imported, thanks to hard currency, without having to resolve the internal problems that prevented the Soviet Union from meeting its own basic civilian targets. Indeed, rather than making its own adjustments in good time Moscow helped to bankroll capitalism through its crisis; as Soviet supplies and sales assisted the West to undertake the painful reconstruction of the second industrial revolution.

Brezhnev's strategic parity was a deception. It fed his self-glorification and the official 'good news, happy days' character of so-called *Pravda* and its companion papers, while it reinforced an economic structure and organization doomed to fall further and further behind the West and Japan. Without Nixon and dollars it would hardly have been sustainable.

Two domestic developments also aided the Kremlin to consolidate its power. The KGB became an efficient and effective security force, tabbing dissidents, moving rapidly to silence protest or even discussion. At the same time, the airbrush took the place of argument. The suspended rehabilitation of Stalin had set the tone. People were no longer liquidated, problems were – they simply disappeared from the public agenda. Life expectancy declined, infant mortality rose (from 22.9 per 1,000 in 1970 to an estimated 30 per 1,000 in 1980). What did the Kremlin do? It stopped publishing health statistics.

A choice example of this concerned the fate of Nixon himself. The American President who did so much to make Brezhnev triumphant, and who was like him in many ways, resigned from his most high office in disgrace, about to be impeached for abuse of power, bugging telephones, illegally undermining his opponents and covering-up his mis-demeanours. Brezhnev must have felt for him, and invited him to Moscow to help avert his demise. Afterwards, however, it seems that Brezhnev may have feared that history would judge him by the company he kept. We do not know whether the authors of his official biography considered Brezhnev guilty by association. But when the Institute for Marxism-Leninism of the Central Committee of the Communist Party of the Soviet Union issued its official account of the Soviet President in 1977, a 45 page chapter entitled "Towards Detente", which lists innumerable foreign trips, receptions and agreements, makes no mention whatsoever of Richard Milhous Nixon.

Instead, it appends the Brezhnev constitution as the book's conclusion. The preamble to the 1977 Constitution of the USSR states: 'In the USSR a developed socialist society has been built . . . It is a society of mature socialist social relations . . . It is a society of true democracy'.

In place of democratization Brezhnev and his colleagues announced that true democracy had already been achieved.

It is easy to mock such nonsense from outside. It can be awful to live under it, when the consequences of any public protest may be drastic. It was particularly humiliating that Brezhnev's Constitution was promulgated after his vitality had met its natural limit. In 1975 Brezhnev suffered a major heart attack from which he took a long time to recover. Subsequently, his reactions were noticeably slower and his capacity to work diminished. His response was to gather more power and claim further honours. He pushed out Podgorny to become President of the USSR as well as the Party's General Secretary, and basked in gross eulogies to his potency. Today the 1977 Constitution can perhaps provide a useful basis for legal progress. But the preamble with its declarations of 'mature socialism' was a result of dotage and over-ripeness, and a system in which Brezhnev's incapacity – for all his power over nuclear war – could not be publicly discussed.

From the mid-seventies the rot really set in. An ironic moment, when the Vietnamese finally won the war in the South of their country, the Portuguese revolution opened the way to Soviet-supported independence movements in Angola and Mozambique, and Moscow seemed like a powerful player on the world stage. Within the Soviet Union a squalid underside was more evident than the triumphs. The response was a gathering, massive, uncoordinated but society-wide, private protest. One so sustained that it became for most Soviet citizens their natural way of life.

A huge 'go-slow' developed that had perhaps started back on the land, after collectivization, but extended under Brezhnev into the cities, to industry, including the most prestigious, even, as we have seen, to celebrated vanguard installations such as nuclear power stations.

Among the weapons of resistance developed by the proletariat under capitalism, is the 'work to rule'. It circumvents the adversities of strike action by the simple means of carrying out tasks exactly as specified and no faster than possible. The people of the Soviet Union began to work to rule. That is, when possible, they hardly worked at all. They did – or didn't do – whatever they could get away with. They complained about their own little boss and kept their heads down. They suffered their own housing disasters as best they could, delighting only when they could play the system to advantage.

Brezhnev set the example in terms of style and attitudes; a particular joy of his meetings with Nixon was the receipt of yet another large car. Not exactly malfeasance, simply the enjoyment of office . . . Brezhnev's appointment of Viktor Grishin as Moscow Party leader in 1967 is of special interest because Grishin would become Gorbachev's main opponent for the supreme prize of General Secretary eighteen years later. After he lost the last round in 1986, nearly 800 people in the capital's commercial life had been arrested for corruption, including the head of the trade network for the entire Moscow region.[35] Few doubt that Grishin himself was implicated.

The populace delivered a withering response to the growing

venality and hypocrisy of the Party and its system. Too fearful and disorganized to rebel, it turned against itself instead. An already chronic and brutalizing rate of alcohol consumption increased steeply, childlessness became widespread.

When Phil Donahue hosted some of his US TV shows in the USSR, they were also transmitted by Soviet television. There was a strong audience reaction. A Russian viewer wrote: 'All was well until the moment when a woman said that she had been waiting ten years to be given a new flat, a situation which made her decide not to have children.'

The low birth rate among the Russians in the USSR seems to have been a virtual biological strike of protest against the wearisome conditions of life, the arduous nature of shopping, the difficulties of child-minding, the drunkenness of men. Cheap rents, imported food, western goods for the privileged – there was economic growth, much of it as artificial as the declaration of the arrival of democracy. But the demoralization created by the – there is no other word for it – stupid conditions, ensured a profound social withdrawal and resentment.

This became clearer to me as I was having tea with an elderly lady at the tenth floor of a massive apartment building. I asked if the elevator ever broke down. She said it was not a problem. Even if it did, it was repaired swiftly. 'But,' she added, 'it is too small. You can't get a coffin in it. The stairs are too narrow to take a coffin properly either. We have protested. Soviet people die, after all. Yet they can't leave here with dignity.'

Almost everyone I met in Moscow told me jokes and, in their effort to explain the nature of the Soviet system, almost all repeated one particular one. At first I smiled and smiled. After the tenth time I strained to appear amused. It is not a long joke, really a one-liner, but it was given great significance. And it sums up the organization of the Soviet economy prior to Gorbachev:

THEY PRETEND TO PAY US AND WE PRETEND TO WORK

But if you think about it, it isn't such a bad deal. For a start you do not have to work. In return you get an apartment almost rent free, with heating and light, and food and enough clothes and a television.

But not very much more. Nor the truth. Or dignity.

GOOD AND EVIL

'Isn't it,' I asked, as we all sat in the apartment living room, 'that there are three sorts of change needed. First, it must touch the roots, and go back to what happened with Stalin. Second, it has to introduce enough of the market into the economy so that it can breathe and grow. Third, there has to be democracy in the sphere of politics.'

'No', she shook her head firmly in disagreement, 'such talk is without meaning. Most intellectuals and creative people just say, "We will do everything to use this moment of freedom while we can." We don't talk in larger terms. Democracy is too far off to think about. The economy needs to be improved, but actually, people have more than they admit. As for Stalin, that's important, but also history. What really matters is spiritual. It is the society's soul that has been lost. Only art and belief can regain it.'

She picked up a glass of water, put her hand firmly over the top of it and turned it upside down. 'Evil lies at the bottom of all societies while art is their highest expression. The revolution mixed them all up.'

She shook the glass, turned it back and put it on the table.

'Eventually, the good will rise once more to the top.'

We all clapped and laughed, and agreed that the way she said it was wonderful.

We were like an audience who had been to a good play but didn't believe a word.

POZHIVEM, UVIDIM

'For the first time in my life,' I scribbled in my Moscow notebook, 'I am in a country where all creative intellectuals think that their government is headed by someone who is honest, intelligent and progressive.'

Indeed, everyone, without exception, regarded Gorbachev as 'sincere', many even thought he was 'serious'.

But there were two aspects to this general approval. It was very recent. Some said that only a few months previously they had regarded him as yet another Komsomol loudmouth. The feeling of respect was growing, even if sometimes grudgingly so. This also meant that it was tenuous.

Second, although no one, including those frankly hostile to the Party and its rule, thought ill of the General Secretary, neither did anyone at all express confidence in the success of perestroika. Some said they would fight for it, others that they would do their best, yet more that they hoped for the best but feared the worst. One of these pessimists was actually taking a more considerable personal risk, in his attempt to push through grass-roots change, than those who spoke boldly. But still, I came across no complete or even quiet yet confident optimists in Moscow in the summer of 1987.

It would have felt happier, I thought, or at least more normal, if people had said that Gorbachev could not be completely

trusted, any more than anyone else, but that nonetheless reconstruction was bound to proceed. Too much was being placed
on the General Secretary personally, even while he was (and is)
trying to tell the population that it is up to them, not him, to
deliver. In effect, the personal endorsement of Gorbachev by
those whom I met underwrote their passivity towards his
policies, because it implied that perestroika and glasnost were
just the – sincerely held and progressive – ideas of the boss.

So I found myself trying to assess the source and nature of
this pessimism and passivity.

There is a Russian phrase *pozhivem, uvidim*: we shall live, we
shall see.

It is an attitude easy to comprehend amongst older intellectuals. Their scepticism draws on years of experience. The
big-dipper that raises hopes high, only to rush over into an
agonizing fall, goes back to 1945. Then, with victory, it
seemed that the purges and bloodshed could be left behind, and
everyone would build the country anew. Instead, the Gulag
groaned with millions of new prisoners.

After Khruschev's speech in 1956, the thaw that followed
Stalin's death began to turn to flood. But the *apparat* stymied
liberalization, and Khruschev himself became increasingly
arbitrary and dogmatic. When he was ousted in 1964, economic reforms began under the banner of collective leadership.
But the crisis of 1968 reversed even this palsied loosening of
restraints. The helplessness of dissidents after 1968 and the lack
of response in the population at large were not relieved by the
authentic conservatism of a well-fed cultural establishment.
You have to imagine what it was like in a society where the
calm, constructive, prescient and patriotic arguments of Medvedev, Sakharov and Turchin were suppressed, although all

the while what they'd said was becoming more and more true.

At last, the long period of Brezhnev's regime came to an end and Andropov started to clean up the regime and make some changes. Without him, today's new men would never have had their chance. But Andropov died within fifteen months and, unbelievably, the leadership in its collective wisdom seemed to have understood nothing and selected Brezhnev's sidekick Chernenko to take over. Nobody protested openly while everyone groaned inwardly. There is still little confidence that the same might not happen again.

But should concern focus on the leadership or on the response, hence also the character, of the people?

It is difficult to generalize about an entire people. Even if this itself is a generalization as weak as any other, we all know that there are national characteristics. We have observed them in foreigners, in ourselves, in our friends and even more in our enemies. As soon as you try to describe them, however, it is hard not to rely on stereotypes, and one of the characteristics of national characteristics is that their form is unpredictable in individuals. Historically, they are also surprisingly changeable. This is why it can indeed be dangerous to depend on such generalizations.

Especially about the Soviet Union. How does 'the good rise to the top' in a country that encompasses a number of Inuit, or Eskimo peoples, a large Islamic population, supposedly thinks of itself as European, yet has a major port on the Pacific Ocean? The first thing to say about such a place is that it is big. This hardly tells you much. What matters is the quality of the scale. The image of the Soviet Union as a country is one that is wide and grand, yet the project of political domination over it has often been narrow and petty. The two aspects go together and change each other.

In other words, the multinational yet singular character of the

Soviet people is less a matter of scale than of the combination of size and histories. In Soviet Central Asia there are mosques which date back to before the conversion of Kiev to Christianity a thousand years ago – there is thus a continuous Islamic tradition that pre-dates that of the Orthodox Russians. The three Baltic Republics were only incorporated into the USSR in 1940, and collectivized after the War. It was possible for many of their best farmers to return from Siberia after Stalin died and the bond between the people and the land has not been shattered as injuriously as in the Ukraine. Such histories could hardly be more different, yet they are joined to the Kremlin in an All-Union entity and share a common destiny.

The crucial question of these combinations of histories concerns modern politics. 'It is not socialism that is the problem, but 600 years of Russian history', a Czech friend told me, one who wants Gorbachev to succeed. Is socialism trapped in despotic form by Russian tradition? To put it more specifically, are the Russian people really incapable of democracy? Is it their past that crushes the possibility of a socialist liberty?

I felt a definite if uneasy contempt among the Moscow intelligentsia, including Party members, for the Soviet, and more particularly the Russian, 'masses'. But I could not work out for myself to what extent it was justified. It seemed to me that there was an element of bad faith.

Part of the reason for this may be that underdogs rarely feel that there is room for more than one kind of underdog. Those who are oppressed or crushed by a system claim to be the ones who know it from below. Those who, so to speak, are crucified by a society inevitably feel themselves the bearers of its real truth.

The independent minded have indeed suffered very badly

under the domination of the Kremlin since Stalin. They see the mass of people waiting in line obediently, or making connections to jump from their place, or stealing sausages and spare parts, 'pretending to work' in return for toy money, and they denounce these 'masses' (it is an old Communist term and not one that I like) as false witnesses. They are not the real underdogs! On the contrary, their passivity allows the system to continue.

There is a danger, they say, that perestroika and glasnost will prove to be no more than the campaign of a noisy minority, while the majority whispers to itself, *'Pozhivem, uvidim'*.

Yet there are different ways of living and seeing. Middle rank people in the bureaucracy who have not done so badly look both ways. They say, 'I hope Gorbachev succeeds, but I'm not going to stick my own neck out'. Having done quite well so far, they do not want things to get worse for them if perestroika is reversed. It does not follow that they are necessarily time-serving mediocrities. They may be perfectly capable, hard-working and ambitious. It is just that they are what in England would be called 'sensible chaps'.

The Soviet worker, on the other hand, especially if female, has paid for these people to have a life that is not so bad. There is anger and even desperation with conditions – and desperation should not be despised, even if it takes the form of passivity. The waiting of workers has been learnt in a harsher school. Their caution has good reason. Silent, perhaps, but not necessarily mindless.

Most of the Soviet population is within one or two generations of the land. The price of this transition – the word seems so gliding and easy – was terrible. Nor has the land benefited from its clearance. According to one calculation, Gorbachev's initial agricultural reform of October 1985, was 'the tenth radical reorganization of the agricultural administration since the war'.[36] The tenth – in the lifetime of a single tree! From above, demand followed demand to do something. The succession of new policies also had a common purpose: to preserve the *way* authority stemmed from higher up. This was the real mindlessness.

The distinction of the new reforms spearheaded by Gorbachev is that glasnost and perestroika imply a decisive change in the relationship between rulers and ruled, the leaders and the people. The tension this generates leaps off the pages of Gorbachev's own book, especially in the section 'A "Revolution from Above"? The Party and Perestroika' where he writes:

> The concept 'revolution from above' doesn't quite apply to our perestroika, at least it requires some qualifications. Yes, the Party leadership started it . . . True, perestroika is not a spontaneous, but a governed process. But that's only one side of the matter.
>
> Perestroika would not have been a truly revolutionary undertaking . . . if the people had not supported it so vehemently and effectively . . . In any case, everyone must work honestly and conscientiously . . . Maybe we have not yet fully realized ourselves and shown the people the full complexity of the situation . . . and what is to be done. But we have said the most essential thing and received support and approval in response.

Perhaps Gorbachev's problem is this: he must break the parasitic role of the centrally interconnected complex of Party and Ministries. Otherwise the energy and creativity of the people, especially the skilled ones, will never be released. Thus he needs their destructive potential to overthrow the restrictions under which they toil and wait. Yet this has to be a governed process. Not least because if he attempts to turn the people against the Party, not only will the Party win – for it has the guns – but it will also get rid of him, Gorbachev, in the process. The people are worried as to whether the leadership will pull it off. The leaders are worried that the people will not rise to the occasion.

The destiny of democracy in the USSR rests with the people not the Party, even though this makes the Party old guard nervous. Personally, I found the talk about people's passivity, lack of initiative, and love for strong leaders who will order them around, too crude to believe. The effort and skill put into getting things, when shopping is so hard, the size of the black economy, even the instinctive anarchism of many of those whom I met, gave me a positive impression of the Soviet people. At the same time there is the burden of history that they know all too well. Who pays for the errors of the leadership? The phrase *pozhivem, uvidim* does not just sum up a waiting attitude, it also expresses a desire to live. If you place the emphasis on the first word, it is about survival.

'The only mistake we need to fear,' Gorbachev told the Soviet public, 'is the fear of making mistakes'.

For a Westerner it is obvious to the point of banality. The economy demands creative initiative. This can only develop with trial and error. Mistakes are inevitable, perhaps even essential. Nothing can be learnt without them. An atmosphere of openness will allow results to be discussed and errors put right. Why should people fear this?

FEAR, WIDESPREAD
COWARDICE AND SHAME

The corners of the grey kerchief knotted under her chin were fluttering in the breeze. Her tall form stood out over the scaffolding, and behind her there was nothing but airy space, plains and Russian earth, the tortured earth of the Revolution, its black waters, its clouded waters, its clear waters, its frozen waters, its deadly waters, its invigorating waters, its enchanted forests, its mud, its impoverished villages, its countless living prisoners, its countless executed ones in graves, its construction sites, its masses, its solitudes and all the seeds germinating in its womb. Rodion saw it all, ineffably. All – even the germinating seeds, since they too are real. The woman, drinking brandy from the bottle, at that instant was truly, totally, a human being. He was entranced to see it so clearly.

'Listen,' he said softly, 'do you know what we are? Have you ever thought about it?'

She considered him with astonishment. And her direct, iron- blue gaze was tinged with fear.

Victor Serge, Midnight in the Century

Some are scornful: 'Bullshit. People here are not afraid any more, even if they say they are. We knew terror once but we are not afraid now, we are *tired* of being afraid.'

She partially agreed: 'It is different. Yet many people rather enjoy the whispering and the fear. It gives things a sense of importance while it excuses you from doing anything.'

An émigré I talked with in England after I got back cautioned me against believing all such talk.

'No, no, no. I remember the beginning of the Brezhnev era. Then we were not afraid to talk and to argue. That came later. Year by year, I watched it, people became afraid to talk. And they hated it. What were they afraid of? That they would not get promoted; or that they would not get an apartment; or that they would not be able to travel abroad; or, if they were intellectuals, that they would not be able to publish, or that even a technical paper would take much longer to appear; and also that life might be made harder for their children. Materially life got better, but in such a way that you had to behave, if you were going to have what was your due. The fear of not being promoted is not like being afraid for your life, but still you live under a punitive, controlling authority.'

Moscow may not believe in tears, but nor does it believe in celebrations. People argue that glasnost will be reversed. They say that it will only succeed if the economy is turned around, but that this is highly improbable and another clamp-down in the Soviet bloc will follow.

How, I asked, could the Party possibly reverse glasnost and instruct the media to insist on the superiority of socialism if the economy fails to improve?

'You don't understand', I was told repeatedly, almost always with the same, sad and knowledgeable shake of the head.

'They can just say that all the criticisms were anti-Soviet provocations,' one wise bird assured me, 'we are quite power-less'. Many seemed convinced that a Soviet mafia will assassinate Gorbachev, even if the CIA does not. Thereafter, the whole process of glasnost, if not perestroika, will disintegrate. The cynical joke: What will follow perestroika? Answer: perestrelka (shooting, or exchange of fire).

When Nella left, I asked a teacher whose English was very fluent if he would translate for me at one interview especially. He said yes, he'd like to, but then phoned to say that his wife had ruled it out. She argued that everything might be reversed and he could lose his job. And for what? To help a foreigner talk to dissidents?

The foreigner can only respect such reasoning. I felt like saying, 'You have got to be brave. You must claim your rights to speak to whom you please.' But one must never call on people to be more heroic than oneself, and I had a passport.

I thought of this incident when I got back and was reading a memoir by Krupskaya, Lenin's lifelong companion. It says little about his childhood. But one passage stands out:

When we had become closely acquainted, Vladimir Ilyich once told me about the attitude of the Liberals towards the arrest of his elder brother. All acquaintances shunned the Ulyanov family. Even an aged teacher, who had formerly come every evening to play chess, left off calling. There was no railway at Simbirsk at that time, and Vladimir Ilyich's mother had to go on horseback to Syzran in order to go to St Petersburg, where her eldest son was imprisoned. Vladimir Ilyich was sent to seek a companion for her journey. But no one wanted to travel with the mother of an arrested man.

Vladimir Ilyich told me that this widespread cowardice made a very profound impression on him at that time.

Widespread cowardice? Lenin's brother was no ordinary prisoner; he was charged with attempted regicide. Unknown to his family he helped in a plot that was supposed to assassinate his namesake, Alexander III. 'He perished at the hands of the Tsar's hangman before he had even come of age.'[37]

There is another burden. Alongside the widespread cowardice, doubt, pessimism, cynicism and fear, I felt there was something the Soviets I spoke with tried not to reveal.

Shame.

In all sorts of ways the Soviets are ashamed. It is not the kind of shame that exists in Third World countries, that comes from obvious poverty and outright backwardness.

The Soviet Union may be 'behind' in many ways, but it is not a Third World country and hasn't been since the revolution in 1917. It suffers from an acute mixture of being *both* ahead and behind. The unbalanced and incoherent character of its economy and culture is more than disabling. It is one thing to be very poor, for example, and thus have terrible housing. It is another to have terrible housing when you are in the middle of a vast amount of good building land, with a copious supply of timber, bricks, machinery, capital, and slogans proclaiming your incomparable achievements. That is really shameful. The scale and power of the Soviet Union feeds its pride and high temper. Because they have good reasons to be proud, the shame becomes unspeakable. That which is unspoken gets worse.

They are ashamed of the way they live. They are ashamed of the way the regime treats its people. They feel shamed because, while 'the Soviet people' send a rocket into orbit on an average of once every four days, actual Soviet people cannot make love with the same frequency without clumsiness or worry, due to the lack of contraception. They are ashamed of what they have done to each other, of the loss of meaning in their public language, and of their past.

The very same past, that is, which saved Europe from fascism, and in which they take such pride. They are therefore furious that there should be such shame among them. Part of the compelling tone of Soviet literature has its source in the inflection through very different individuals of this bitter, shameful mixture of their power and their past, and leads some to lose control: The roar of Alexander Solzhenitsyn, the scatological despair of Edward Limonov, the blind drunkenness of Benedict Erofeev, the sense of crucifixion about Boris Pasternak. It may even be embedded in the title of Nadezhda Mandelstam's final volume, *Hope Abandoned*. Nor is it just a matter of dissidents, this complex of pride and shame is craftily acknowledged by Julian Semyonov: 'I'm talking about the principle of cutting things because you are afraid of them'.[38]

Fear, shame *and* pride. We're talking about Stalin.

THE OLD BOLSHEVIK

Like all good Bolsheviks who survived the revolution itself, she had spent time in the Gulag. Usually it was with fatal results. In her case she survived seventeen years. I took the fact that we had a sudden chance to talk as a good omen for this book. She spoke broken English, very clearly for her age, which was apparently 86.

I had first learnt of her existence a few days before, in a conversation about the Gulag. Talk had turned to a friend of many of those present, a friend of Nella's now in Paris. A photograph of him was produced. It was one of the great surprises of my stay.

A little black and white Brownie snap from the Gulag was the least likely thing I could have imagined. This was not an official photograph taken by the police. There, in the background, were the wooden posts with their familiar Y structure. Between the uprights, which were less than ten foot, there was wire, and between the V tops of the Ys a roll of barbed wire. In the foreground two prisoners, one with an arm slung around the other, posed in strong Russian boots.

I stuttered that I never thought there would be photographs from inside a camp. 'Oh yes,' said the picture's owner, 'after Stalin's death in 1953 it was more relaxed.' I still found it fantastic. It was like a holiday shot. You wouldn't go away on a family holiday these days and return without some snaps. The snapshot is the record of the enjoyment of having been elsewhere. We expect people to say, I went to the seaside, let me show you some pictures. But not, 'I did five years, here's a snap, the window with bars is mine.' For this is a record of an even worse confinement than one's everyday life. Prison is a kind of nowhere. So as I looked at the little photograph of the two inmates posing in the camp, I understood that in the Soviet Union the Gulag had been a way of life.

I didn't ask the old Bolshevik if I could see her photographs. When I realized we had a little time I asked her if we could have some tea and talk about what happened to her.

'It was our fascism', she whispered, with conspiratorial emphasis, as if the walls might be listening and didn't yet know. 'Stalin – it was our fascism, it wasn't German fascism, or Italian,' she lowered her voice even more and hissed his name, 'Stalin, our own fascism.'

We went and sat down in the kitchen.

'Yes, I've had a hard life. My husband was in the opposition. Beria invited him to the Caucasus. Later he was killed. He did not know his wife was arrested. Two men came, at about two o'clock in the morning. One of them had the papers. The other searched the flat. I had my little boys. Luckily my mother was also there, I left the children with her. It was 1936.

'They said I was a counter-revolutionary, a Trotskyist. Yes, I saw Trotsky, he was a great orator, very great, and a good war leader. But he did not understand ordinary Russians.'

With this, she pointed with her thin, ancient arm, to the kitchen window, and by implication to the whole country outside. 'Trotsky was too hard. I talked with people who were with him in Siberia. They said he was too self-opinionated and not a good colleague. So yes, I'd thought about these things.' She leant forward and lowered her voice: 'I knew what Lenin said in his Testament, you see.'

'Was I for Bukharin? Ah, we were young, he was the theorist of socialism for us, we learnt from his books most of all. I knew many of them.'

This struck me as evasive, so I pressed the question. Her voiced dropped, for the walls were still listening. 'Who was I *for*? I was for Kirov as our General Secretary.'

She was arrested in October 1936. Interrogated for nine months, she was then sent to Siberia where she remained for nearly ten years. In 1946 she was released on condition that she lived at least 100 kilometres away from Moscow. In 1948 she was re-arrested without reason and returned to Magadan. She was freed in 1955.

'With Krushchev I was given a piece of paper saying that I had done nothing. I asked immediately to be re-admitted to the Party. It is not easy here now. But the system is the one with the best human principles. I am still an idealist.

'Ours was even harder than the French revolution. It is one thing to make a revolution. It is another problem to construct socialism. Our good people, all of them, they all made mistakes and had bad points. In science experiments are made in laboratories. But not socialism. Its laboratory is the world. The whole planet is the laboratory for revolution.'

As she used this phrase I knew that she was genuine. I felt the breath of a thousand arguments. No one who has grown up since Hiroshima would use such an analogy. The notion that the planet is a laboratory for revolution echoes back, right back to the time when it was spoken with supreme confidence in progress, in 1917. Afterwards it was uttered with a more sombre seriousness of purpose; next, with the resolve of self-persuasion; then, with lowered tones of concern, as the experiment refused to right itself; and finally, in whispered efforts to justify the tragedy.

'Glasnost? It is very good. But it will take another fifty years to recover from Stalin.'

PETROVA'S STORY

I met Petrova once. We talked for five hours. Her husband, who is now dead, was nearly twenty years older than her. After the Revolution, he had been caught up in the East of the country, where he had gone to continue his studies and keep out of trouble. Instead, Kolchak's White Army swept through the area and he was pressed into bearing arms until Kolchak was driven back to Vladivostock. He returned to Moscow, gained his qualifications and went to work. In 1926 his brief connection with the Whites was reported by a colleague. The police demanded to know why he had not told them about it, and he was advised to admit it and serve the minimum three years, rather than anything longer. He accepted the advice, and was given a three-year sentence. After Kirov was assassinated and the intense purges began in 1934, he was charged with having dealings with the Shah, because he had come back from holiday with a suit made in Iran that he'd bought on the black market. He was given eight years, served four and was released. Then he was re-arrested and in 1939 sentenced to death without trial. This was when Yezhov was Stalin's chief executioner. But then it was Yezhov's turn to be executed, and Beria replaced him. Our victim demanded some notepaper and told his prison guards he was going to write to Beria. He was released. In 1941 he was exiled from Moscow until after 1953.

In total he did nineteen years of prison and banishment.

Under Khruschev he didn't even want to ask for rehabilitation. But in 1956 he was summoned by a KGB Colonel. He spent a sleepless night of fear. The next day he returned. Petrova rushed to the door and found him ashen white.

'What's the matter?', she asked him.

'I've been rehabilitated.'

'But that's good.'

'The Colonel asked me about the charges and looked at my file. He said there was nothing in it at all. He had never seen one so empty. I did all those years for absolutely no reason.'

He never fully recovered.

When he was removed from her, Petrova did not talk to her neighbours about her husband. She was afraid to. I asked her if this didn't allow others to continue to believe in Stalin. She nodded assent, 'But not me. I was teaching when he was lying ill. A student came in at the back with the news. A big lad, weeping. I found it hard not to smile. I thought, "I'll have my husband back".'

'I suppose many did not realize what Stalin was like', Petrova continued, as we sipped tea in her small apartment. 'At the time I lived in the centre, in old Moscow. Stalin was laid in State for some days in the grand Hall. One day there was a strange radio broadcast saying that there was no need for people to go and mourn for him there that day. I recall thinking to myself that I had no desire to go at all. A little while later my nephew turned up at the door; he was twelve. He couldn't speak. We thought he was drunk, we couldn't understand it. He just asked us to ring his mother and say that he was OK. We laid him down and it took him some time to recover.

'He told us that he went with a school party to see Stalin.

The roads go downhill towards the Hall and it seems that they blocked them to try to control the crowds. My nephew said he felt a sudden pain in his chest and passed out. He woke up to find himself in a lorry in the central hospital surrounded by bodies. People were taking them out saying, "Dead", "Alive", "Dead", "Alive".

'He was not bleeding. He was told to go home, and tried to walk out, but had almost no idea where he was, except that he knew our place was close by. He used to come every week, but when he asked a policeman where the street was, he was told he was in it. He suffered from headaches for years. One of his school friends died, hundreds died.

'We could hardly believe it. Later I went there to see for myself. There was no sign that anything had happened except that the drainpipes were crushed flat just up to the height of a human being.'

She finished her tea.

'So I suppose that there must have been many people who believed in Stalin.'

Going back to the hotel I imagined Petrova thirty years ago, as in a silent film. She is in a wide street in central Moscow. There are only a few passers-by. While trying not to appear to be doing so, she is looking. Her eyes notice the drainpipes. They are flattened yet retain the discernable indentation of shoulders and heads.

'The clouds wore trousers,' wrote Mayakovsky, and 'the stars were beheaded, the sky, all red with the blood of slaughter.'

The clouds wept. Then the drainpipes too were crushed.

At Hiroshima some of those who died did so instantaneously as they were vaporized. We know of their existence only because their shadow was left behind, as the fire-flash scorched the pavement around them. These shadows have become a symbol of the way modern warfare may annihilate us as we go about our business.

There is a similar symbol for Stalin's victims. First, most were blameless. Second, many followed him with a mixture of sincerity and indifference to their fate. Third, they worshipped him. Fourth, he killed them. An eloquent outline of this history was traced by the crushed drainpipes of Moscow in March 1953.

THEY LOVED HIM

The standard view in the West is that information about Stalin is almost completely suppressed in the USSR. For example:

> Even now Mr Gorbachev's talk of 'blank pages' is painfully euphemistic. I have yet to hear a Russian official talk straight about Stalin . . . the massive lie about the past which all Russians are required to keep up, is a cancer that erodes the integrity of a whole people . . .[39]

But the real problem is not what Stalin did. A dramatic moment of my trip was when I fell into conversation with three younger members of a party from Eastern Europe, training in Moscow. The group had asked to be given a talk on the new policies. A Party official, who was in his thirties, was sent from one of the Moscow institutes. He gave a scathing account of the realities of the system and the need for change. Asked about the past he told them that over thirty million people had died in the Soviet Union between 1917 and the outbreak of the war with Germany in 1941. 'Stalin,' he concluded, 'was the greatest criminal in the world.' The group leader was shaken white, while those I spoke to were relieved that they could now debate what happened more truthfully.

Some estimates suggest that perhaps about nineteen million died in the Civil War that followed the revolution, and in the famines that continued through to 1921. Others imply that the toll of collectivization and the purges in the 1930s, when Stalin was in charge, total around ten million rather than fifteen. Some Soviet officials say it is far less. Such a degree of uncertainty is humiliating. The USSR owes to the world, to the memory of the dead, and to itself above all, a detailed accounting of the losses.

This is not the main problem, however. Everyone who wants to know – everyone, that is, who does not wish to stay blind – is aware that Stalin was bad on a monstrous scale.

The trouble is that they loved him.

He was a bad Tzar, and they loved him.

He shattered the peasantry, and still they loved him.

He purged his close colleagues, wrote notes demanding that they be beaten, approved fabricated charges and personally ordered their deaths.

He 'rolled the executions round his lips like berries', in Osip Mandelstam's immortal line (for which he paid with his life) and they adored him.

About one person in twenty was in the camps, yet they wept when he died.

⚘ This is what is difficult to come to terms with.

Recently there was an exchange in the Soviet press. A letter was published from Ivan Karasev, 'I am 57. I work as a driver and I live in Penza.' He thought that mistakes had been inevitable and Khruschev wrong to denounce his predecessor:

> It was not his fault that people idolized him. During the war
> our soldiers attacked the enemy with the cry 'For the
> Motherland, for Stalin!' not because Stalin forced them to
> do so but because the Soviet people respected, loved and
> trusted Stalin very much.

Stalin did a great deal for his people, and the people responded by working hard for their country and for Stalin. We all lived as one large, closely knit family and worked for the good of our country.

Stalin's name must be immortalized in granite, bronze and even gold. That would also be a reward for those who fought for socialism, defended it in the Great Patriotic War, and raised our cities from ruin. We have had socialism in this country for nearly seventy years but have not yet come onto the right path.

The paper then published a long response to the lorry driver by the Soviet historian Alexander Samsonov. He argues (and cites an example from his own experience) that letters to widows of servicemen killed in action, which stated that their husbands died with the words, 'For the motherland, for Stalin!' on their lips were often false. It was Stalin himself who was responsible for the personality cult, he points out. He insists on Stalin's blunders that allowed Hitler to overwhelm the USSR's initial defences, including his execution of the pride of the Red Army's commanders. 'I am convinced,' Samsonov concludes, 'that if Stalin had not committed all those mistakes, the German army would never have reached Leningrad and Moscow.'[40]

The lorry driver's letter is about 500 words, the Academician's reply three times as long. As history, the latter is indubitably superior. But as a reply it fails. For all the stress on the collective rectitude of the party's condemnation of the cult of the personality, the fact is that millions of Soviet workers and mothers did love Stalin. A huge correspondence poured in, which divided fifty-fifty.[41] It is this divide which any reply to

Ivan Karasev must comprehend; any response to him and those who feel the same way about Stalin, must accept what is authentic about their adoration. Karasev was fifteen when the war ended; doubtless his family had participated in its losses. He grew up with the painful victory. He believed. The sincerity was given freely, not by force. It was genuine, not criminal. He loved Stalin. He is right to insist upon this experience. How is it to be explained?

Desparadim

'OUR PARTY RELIES ON
TWO CLASSES'

Stalin was a success. He triumphed over the peasantry, over his opponents, over Hitler. Millions may have died as he smashed his way to victory. Those who lived, built. He oversaw a terrific growth rate economically, alongside the death rate. People (including his wife) committed suicide before him, but there is no record of any determined attempt to assassinate him. Instead, his legacy had an energy that contributed to Khruschev's ebullience even as he denounced his predecessor.

Brezhnev was a failure. His self-glorification was a mockery. He inherited an economy with a growth rate of 9 per cent a year. When he died it was 2 per cent, and the country was in debt. Fast growth can be at the expense of everyone, but this was not a slow down with an ecological or humanitarian purpose. On the contrary, it ensured the worst of both worlds: shortages and waste, lousy harvests and pollution. Brezhnev's regime was more than an economic and social failure. His detente turned into a boycott at the Olympic games. The grandiose 'doctrine' of intervention that began with Czechoslovakia ended in stalemate in Afghanistan.

A profound disenchantment set in. It was a disenchantment that concerned belief. Those who had been educated to regard religion as pernicious superstition and were instead offered belief in Stalin now had nothing to believe in. Children under Brezhnev had even less, they had nothing to be disillusioned with, because they never had the illusions in the first place. A school teacher told me that her most painful duty was to tell her pupils things she knew were false, for example about the Soviet way of life being the best in the world.

'But do they believe you?', I asked.

She shook her head, 'They all know'.

One consequence: a groundswell for religion.

On our first weekend in Moscow we drove the fifty miles to the monastery of Zagorsk. As the approach road curved and dipped down, the glorious golden onion domes appeared, bright in the hot sun. Then the monastery's immense white walls came into sight. They project outwards at the top, to make defence more impregnable, and give the appearance of huge skirts whose hems have been blown inwards by the wind.

The monastery was one of the defensive complexes around Moscow; within its walls today are crowded a cathedral, churches and seminaries. The day we went was the festival of Saint Sergei. Many pilgrims had come, and perhaps almost as many tourists and onlookers like myself. One of our little group went to kiss the tombstone of the saint. The patriarch was there: as he began to leave St Sergei's, the oldest church in Zagorsk, built in the fifteenth century, people pressed forward to see him on the steps.

I joined those who were waiting outside. I was struck by the urban features and style of the worshippers. There was a very Russian woman who looked in her thirties, dressed up in a pink trouser suit; she even had a badge on her lapel that said 'Black Panthers' – an adornment of Anglo-chic. The feel of the crowd was quite contemporary, of town people having a day out.

Suddenly, and the fact that they were so stark in their difference made it doubly shocking, there were two old peasant women, whose physical and spiritual wretchedness seemed appalling, as if they had emerged from Russian serfdom only yesterday.

They were both short, about five foot. One was hunched downwards. The other was thin but with strong forearms, her brown hands much thicker than mine. They wore dark, tatty clothes. Perhaps they were sisters.

The taller had a black scarf over her hair. The shorter had an old, grey, crumbling shawl, made of plain material with no decoration. It covered her completely in the stifling heat, for it was being pulled down hard over her head by her companion, with such force that it bent her body towards the ground as the other held the shawl taut in a vice-like grip of thumb and finger.

A woman in a modern dress told the dominant woman to release her companion, but was snarled off. For a minute or so the other whimpered and trembled, and the crowd backed away from them and their unpleasantness. A young man with a long beard and pious features, wearing a cheap grey suit, could stand it no longer. He argued, at first quietly, then vigorously, saying that the victim should be released. Then he physically tugged away the shawl. The other woman emerged desperately red in the face, trembling with anxiety. Her companion grabbed her, and pulled her downwards, covering her again, arguing with the man as she did so, saying, I presumed, that her companion was not a fit person to set eyes upon the Patriarch.

But the bearded man insisted that the torture stop, and once more pulled away the shawl. The hot, frightened woman who had been beneath it, huddled towards him for protection.

The image of the peasant today is of a wealthy Asian cultivator, or the independent French smallholder, with a large barn, some livestock and implements, a degree of literacy and a telling way with language. Skill, judgement, very hard work, but work that is also rewarding, these are peasant virtues – and realities. Realities that find their predecessors down the ages past. Even in Van Gogh's *Potato Eaters*, the women wear white linen caps. Hardship endured may bear in its impress the effort to overcome it, and thus embody hope, cunning and courage.

But there are also conditions in which the grinding has done its work, in which all that is left is vindictiveness, narrow-minded prejudice, acid despair and snivelling.

Perhaps it is the towns rather than the countryside which generate such an outcome; only the violence of human authority, not nature, could reduce life so severely.

The depth and extent of the division between the 'two Russias' of town and country has determined the character of Russian and then Soviet history. Teodor Shanin emphasizes that:

> In the economic, political, legal, cultural and even visual and linguistic sense (in dress and idiom) the Russian peasants have varied consistently from the non-peasant sections of society. Existentially, every Russian would recognize nearly every peasant at a glance, and adjust his behaviour accordingly.[42]

The contrast I witnessed was testimony to this gulf. Yet in 1987 it also seemed exceptional. To be sure, the large, good-natured religious crowd, was traditional. But it was traditional in a contemporary way. The two women personified another, older, and repellent society.

131

From his earliest study on the development of capitalism in Russia, the search for an alliance between workers and peasants was a central theme of Lenin's tactical arguments and strategic considerations. At the very end of his life he wrote in his Letter to the Congress of 1922, which became known as his Testament: 'Our Party relies on two classes and therefore its instability would be possible and its downfall inevitable if there were no agreement between those two classes.'

Lenin perceived a short term danger: 'a split' between Stalin and Trotsky, 'the two outstanding leaders of the present central Committee'. His major concern was the class division, that was also a division between town and country, that could rend the whole country. Lenin dictated a now famous postscript to the Testament, which begins, 'Stalin is too rude . . .' Stalin, Lenin stated, should be replaced by a General Secretary who is

> more tolerant, more loyal, more polite and more con-
> siderate to the comrades, less capricious, etc. This . . . may
> appear to be a negligible detail. But I think that from the
> standpoint of safeguards against a split . . . it is a detail that
> can assume decisive importance.[43]

There was no such candidate. This absence was no mere detail either. In his autobiographical reflections, Trotsky argues that Lenin wanted to give the succession to him, and would have done so had he lived. Lenin's description belies this: tolerant, polite, considerate to the comrades . . . This is hardly a description of Trotsky.

If there was nobody who could hold together the alliance of outstanding leaders created around Lenin by the revolution, historical materialism would suggest that this was not just a matter of personalities. The first place to seek for an explanation is in the balance of social forces themselves. They were already stretched to breaking point when Lenin declared the NEP, the New Economic Policy, in 1921, which put an end to 'War Communism' and allowed the peasantry to trade. The period of economic expansion that followed is highly regarded today by the reformers in Moscow. But it was also accompanied by an intensification of Party discipline, rather than an extension of democracy, and in the conditions of the time allowed an explosive build up of antagonism between the cities and the rural majority.

Over a hundred and twenty-five years ago, in 1861, the serfs were emancipated. But the internal organization of the Russian peasantry remained relatively unchanged. Only in the course of 1917 did they – the overwhelming majority of the population – finally partition the endless noble estates, to divide their land among themselves. While industry was nationalized, smallholders took possession of the fields; the revolution made by Lenin's 'alliance of workers and peasants' thus paradoxically *intensified* the division between town and country. As it abolished the autocracy which had ruled them both, it unified manufacture but atomized the land.

At the end of the 1920s, after Trotsky was driven into exile, Stalin committed the newly fledged Union of Soviet Socialist Republics to a fundamental transformation, from being an agrarian to becoming an industrial country. The alliance was thrown aside, the countryside was collectivized. The Party proceeded to 'the elimination of the kulaks as a class'. Kulaks was a derogatory term for the better-off peasants.

From the evening that we got off the plane, through the rest of our stay, people were talking about an article by Nikolai Shmelyov in the June issue of *Novy Mir* (which means 'New

133

Times' – it is one of the country's major journals). When he went to the polls in his Moscow district, Gorbachev was asked what he thought about Shmelyov's article. The television news showed him saying he disagreed with some of its conclusions. Not least the author's suggestion that the Soviet economy would benefit from unemployment, 'that is something we are not prepared to accept'. But Gorbachev felt that the analysis in *Novy Mir* 'resembled very closely the actual position'.[44] In his article Shmelyov writes:

> At one time the slogan of the 'liquidation of the kulaks as a class' was proclaimed. What actually happened was the abolition of the peasantry as a class.

Brezhnev was among those directly involved. He had grown up in what he describes as 'a large working-class settlement' of what was to become Dneprodzerzhinsk, where his father worked in the iron-rolling mill. In his brief *Memoirs*, he recalls the four years between 1927 (when he was twenty-one) and 1931:

> I happened to be working in the countryside, creating collective farms – right in the thick of events of the greatest social revolution in the country . . . We land-managers had not only to erase the boundaries, but to unite on the maps all the broken up, individual strips of land into one collective field. This had to be done on a new social, scientific, economic and technical basis . . . While working as a land-manager, I felt myself to be, for the first time, a plenipotentiary of the Soviet regime in the eyes of hundreds of people . . . Together with other komsomoltsy I had confrontations in the fields with kulaks and discussions

with them at rural assemblies. They threatened us with stakes, pitchforks, malicious notes and stones thrown through windows. At one time . . . the kulaks committed a heinous crime. At night they had lain in wait for the tractor driver Peter Dyakov who was asleep in his cabin, poured kerosene over him, and set it on fire . . . ever more decisively and daringly we led the offensive against the hated kulaks.[45]

The hated kulaks who survived were driven into *Kolkhozy* or 'collective farms'. There they were paid only from the residual surplus and had no proper wage. Often they were obliged to undertake forced labour, on roads and hauling timber, equivalent to a *corvée*. They were not entitled to passports and were thus unable to travel: indeed they were forbidden to leave the *kolkhozy* without the manager's permission. Breach of this contract was made a criminal rather than a civil offence.

A producer so strongly fettered and discriminated against could not be efficient. On the contrary, he lost the incentive to exert himself on the job . . . 'We are not our own men, but the *kolkhoz's*', the peasants often repeated. This summed up the whole process. Before, they had been 'their own men'; now they belonged to the *kolkhoz*, but the *kolkhoz* did not belong to them.[46]

Formally gained in 1861, peasant freedom was in reality obtained only in 1917. Ten years later it was annihilated; the peasants were re-cnserfed. Only this time it was an industrial serfdom, imposed after massive resistance left millions dead, a landscape terrorized, its livestock devastated over five years amid 'indescribable confusion'.[47]

Those who protested became 'enemies'. Not only the countryside but most of Soviet culture was crushed. *Pravda* reported that members were being expelled from the Party for saying such things as:

We have no meat because we began to liquidate the kulak before we created a base for meat supply.

Or:

You can only talk about the favourable side of things; if you talk about difficulties you become a Right deviationist and are out of harmony with the decisions of the Party.

One Leningrad Party member stated:

The Party invented sabotage and the people who were shot allegedly for creating hunger were innocent victims. [48]

Pasternak recalled:

In the early 1930s it became fashionable among writers to visit the collective farms and gather material about the new way of life in the villages. I wanted to be like everyone else and also set out on such a trip with the intention of writing a book. But there were no words to express what I saw. There was such inhuman, unimaginable misery, such frightful poverty, that it began to take on an almost abstract quality, as if it were beyond what the conscious mind could absorb. I fell ill and could write nothing for an entire year. [49]

Such recollections remained private. Soon *Pravda* ceased to publish the counter-revolutionary remarks of those who were expelled. Political terror struck the cities in the wake of the horror that had swept the land.

THE STALIN UNITY
OF WILL

I think that collectivization was both a mistake and a failure. And because that couldn't be admitted, every means of intimidation had to be used to make people forget how to think and judge for themselves, to force them to see what wasn't there, and to maintain the contrary of what their eyes told them. Hence the unexampled harshness of the Yezhov terror, and the promulgation of a constitution which was never intended to be applied, and the holding of elections not based on the principle of a free vote.

And when the war broke out, its real horrors, its real dangers, its menace of real death, were a blessing compared with the inhuman power of the lie, a relief because it broke the spell of the dead letter.

It was not only felt by men in your position, in concentration camps, but by everyone without exception, at home and at the front, and they all took a deep breath and flung themselves into the furnace of this deadly, liberating struggle with real joy, with rapture.[50]

Stalin's regime attracted loyalty and devotion. An inspiring industrialization took place: rivers were tamed, electrification installed, heavy goods manufactured. Millions from rural backgrounds became literate, then technically qualified. Muscovites, as the older ones can still tell you, had better conditions than today; they ate sausage while famine stalked the Ukraine.

But I do not believe that this economic improvement, however profound, lies at the heart of the love for Stalin. Life isn't like that. The crucial turning point was the Nazi invasion, as Pasternak argues in the passage above.

In 1941 people embraced the very harshness of Stalin for themselves and together they were victorious. Out of the furnace of invasion and twenty million dead, myriads of disabled, the destruction of one-third of the country's fixed capital assets, and the immediate post-war years of reconstruction that were especially hideous for women, a new people was forged: the Soviet people. The first personification of the Soviet people was the Georgian.

Stalin was no longer 'Little Joe'. Nor was he just the sinister General Secretary, with his slightly withered arm and gleaming eyes. Through being the successful leader in world war he became a kind of God. True, he had mishandled Hitler, to put it mildly. But he remained the country's leader in its ultimate test. Once, John Erickson, the outstanding British historian of the conflict, was ticked off by a Soviet colleague for writing about 'Stalin's war with Germany'. Erickson responded:

> I do not see that formal recognition of Stalin's role as war leader must necessarily diminish any collective achievement . . . action was forthcoming, even to the point of near impossible achievement in the field or in the workshops. When Stalin sent out signals of such terrifying import as: 'I demand more. This is my last warning', 'more' usually materialized.[51]

Khruschev attacked Stalin's war record, especially the way he executed the Chiefs of Staff and allowed himself to be surprised by the German invasion on 22 June 1941, when there was every reason not to be. The Soviet General, and later dissident, Grigorenko argues that Khruschev's criticism of Stalin at the 20th Congress in 1956, 'is on the level of small town gossip'. 'I can and do hate Stalin with all the fibres of my soul', Grigorenko wrote in his memoirs:

> I know that he brought my people death, torment, suffering, famine and slavery. But I cannot help seeing that the brilliant offensive operations of Soviet troops are models of military art . . . no one will ever imagine that they were prepared and carried out without Stalin's participation or against his will.

Furthermore, Grigorenko argues, Stalin, 'as commander-in-chief, had no equal either among our allies or among our enemies. To the present moment, Europe is the way Stalin left it.' What was Stalin's strength?

> After he had got over his confusion and panic at the beginning of the war, Stalin not only understood the necessity for military specialists, but he learned also to listen to them and respect their opinions. At the same time he remained involved in operations and strategic activities. His participation can be sensed everywhere. On each operation lies the shadow of his mind. All were carried out under his inhuman standard: 'Don't spare the men!'[52]

Throughout the war, Vasily Grossman reported from the front for the army newspaper *Red Star*. Afterwards, he became an esteemed writer. In 1961, he completed *Life and Fate*, a monumental novel centred on the battle of Stalingrad, and submitted it for publication. It was confiscated. He was summoned to see Suslov himself. In his role as the USSR's ideologist-in-chief Suslov told the author to his face that his manuscript would not be published 'for two to three hundred years' (an extraordinary mis-estimate).[53]

Thus Grossman was hardly a Stalinist. Nor at the time of the conflict did his actual reports from the front drip with praise for his country's leader. On the contrary. In his collection, *The Years of War*, published immediately after 1945, there is only one such reference. It concludes an essay about 1944 called 'How Victory is Forged':

> Our material strength, the tremendous crushing power of our artillery fire, of our tanks and of our aircraft . . . is a magnificent expression of the creative effort of the entire Soviet people . . . This creative effort, inspired by the Stalin type of strategy and welded by the Stalin unity of will, is the pledge of our victory.

This may have been an insertion demanded by his publishers, but there are two telling phrases we should note: 'The Stalin unity of will' and 'The entire Soviet people'.

Millions gave themselves to a unity personified in Stalin as they fought for the survival of their society and its peoples against the onslaught of Nazi extermination. It was called 'The Great Patriotic War', and most western commentaries make much of the way Stalin abolished the Communist International and raised the Patriarch of old Russia from oblivion.

But it was *Soviet* patriotism that rallied the people, the Red flag not the Russian one. This Soviet patriotism may not have been too kind to the smaller nationalities of the USSR, but nor was it to the larger one. It may not have been formally democratic, but it was mass based and by the end drew upon an overwhelming loyalty. It may have been defensive, but it was also international in its conception and allied itself with Britain, America and the exiled French.

The paradox is that while Stalin personally was a murderer, what he personified was not the genocidal murderousness of a Hitler. Stalin built universities where there had been none before, while Hitler destroyed Europe's finest intelligentsia. Soviet patriotism is quite the contrary of Russophile slavism: it proclaims the equality not the superiority of peoples, just to take one, rather important, example.

If Khruschev underestimated the link between Soviet identity and Stalin, Brezhnev abused it. A generation came to adulthood in a cataclysm that in every way was a *baptism* of fire; that is, it gave them their name and their existence, as a world power. Brezhnev exploited the fact that they could hardly say 'no' to their own identity.

The intensity of the wartime birth of the Soviet people has left a formidable generation gap. The reproduction of Soviet patriotism continues, and often takes the War as its symbol. In a genuine and quiet way, couples who are married go to the local war memorial, on which the bride places her bouquet. Then they pose for a photograph. In the big cities in summer there may be photographers waiting, with arm-bands to show that they are registered. I watched a best-man shoo them away so that he could make his own record with the family camera, of the bride, in white, leaning forward, one hand in the groom's, the other holding the flowers she is about to place before the perpetual flame.

A look at the way that the British people similarly dedicated themselves to Churchill may help Anglo-Saxons to understand the roots of Soviet patriotism. On 18 June 1940, Churchill addressed the House of Commons after Hitler's armies had swept into France and the British forces had been hastily evacuated from Dunkirk. It was a long assessment of the dire situation. The Prime Minister ended by saying:

> I expect that the battle of Britain is about to begin. Upon the battle depends the survival of Christian civilization. Upon it depends our own British life, and the long continuity of our institutions and our Empire. The whole fury and might of the enemy must very soon be turned upon us. Hitler knows that he will have to break us in this Island or lose the war . . . Let us therefore brace ourselves to our duty, and so bear ourselves that, if the British Empire and its Commonwealth last for a thousand years, men will still say, 'This was their finest hour'.

Many who were young at that time still insist that it *was* 'Britain's finest hour', perhaps without realizing that this means that nothing that follows can be so good again. Only recently, Michael Foot, who led the Labour Party from 1980 to 1983, looked back to 1940 and described

> the nature of British patriotism, during that dazzling summer when the whole future of our country appeared to be at stake, when we might so nearly have been crushed as a people . . . I remember London too, how the sun blazed more brilliantly each day, how the parks, indeed the whole city, had never looked more lovely, how the people of London, especially those most hard hit in the East End, went about their business, how it truly was, as Churchill said, our finest hour. All of us who had the good fortune to live through those times had a special instruction in the meaning of patriotism.[54]

It is inconceivable that a Soviet of the same generation as Foot could write about the war with such idyllic nostalgia. For Churchill was wrong, the 'fury and might' of Hitler turned eastward. By invading the Soviet Union, Hitler 'brought Britain reprieve from a situation that appeared hopeless in the eyes of most people outside her own insular boundaries'.[55]

But nor did German conscripts turn against Hitler, even after his designs were clearly turning their country into a killing ground. In the 1960s the German youth movement was strongly 'anti-authoritarian' because it expressed the anguish of a generation that sought to come to terms with the fact that its parents had been fascists. But they had some advantages: Hitler had been defeated, his genocidal programme was explicit, the cut-off date of 1945 was definitive. In the Soviet Union Stalin is a more ambiguous figure. He was not the greatest criminal in the world, Hitler was, and he defeated Hitler. Stalin lived for nearly another ten years, during which time his God-like status as 'the good father' was really drummed home. Stalinists stayed at their posts after he died. It is therefore very difficult for the Soviets to come to terms with his legacy: the 'Stalin unity of will' that he demanded, and which the Nazis made necessary, Soviet people accepted – although it imprisoned them. In a way, it was the price paid by one half of the larger European continent for the liberation of the other.

The process of 'de-Stalinization' is not therefore a simple matter of exorcism of wrongs, or publication of facts. These are necessary, but far from sufficient. Stalin's central position in Soviet life goes back to the War – a war with a dual legacy. It created a modern sense of shared citizenship for the peoples of the fifteen Republics of the USSR, that draws upon popular loyalty, the ideals of education and improvement, the willingness to endure hardship for a just cause, a sense of the collective good and, not least, an aspiration for alliance with the West.

But at the same time the total centralization of the war, and its ruthless personification, intensified by Stalin to help cover over his crimes, drew upon the traditions of Tsarism and the Russian Empire as the prison house of nations. It left a modern state machine whose sole capacity was limited to its 'unity of will'. Stalin's mortmain, 'Don't spare the men!', reverberates as the standing order of Soviet life. Today, time and effort are squandered rather than blood – but the 'Stalin type of strategy' lives on.

The revolutionaries of perestroika may draw their international self-confidence, and their belief in the capacities of the Soviet people, from the achievements of the War against fascism. Yet to succeed they must also overthrow the War's other legacy.

DREGS OF HUMANITY

The Stalin 'unity of will' had two faces. One, the shining outward example: the face of the people, of their united effort, their common purpose, their own determination, in each of countless individuals, as they fought and fought with staggering persistence. The other is the dark, inward looking face, distrustful, spying, punishing: imposing unity through fear. It was not just a matter of military, that is, of hard if necessary discipline. On the contrary, its evil power was established before the war, when it took as its victims most of the Soviet military and political leadership.

> In 1937, new facts came to light regarding the fiendish crimes of the Bukharin-Trotsky gang. The trial of Pyatakov, Radek and others, and the trial of Tukhachevsky, Yakir and others ... showed that ... these dregs of humanity ... had set out to destroy the Party and Soviet state ...
>
> These Whiteguard insects forgot that the real masters of the Soviet country were the Soviet people, and that the rykovs, bukharins, zinovievs and kamenevs were only temporary employees of the state, which could at any moment sweep them out from its offices as so much useless rubbish.

These contemptible lackeys of the fascists forgot that the Soviet people had only to move a finger, and not a trace of them would be left.

The Soviet court sentenced the Bukharin-Trotsky fiends to be shot.

The People's Commissariat of Internal Affairs carried out the sentence.

The Soviet people approved the annihilation of the Bukharin-Trotsky gang and passed on to next business.

And the next business was to prepare for the election of the Supreme Soviet of the USSR and to carry it out in an organized way.

The Party threw all its strength into the preparations for the elections . . .

They were something more than elections; they were a great holiday celebrating the triumph of the Soviet people, a demonstration of the great friendship of the peoples of the USSR . . .

One can think of others ways to demonstrate friendship (that word again). This passage is from the official History of the Communist Party of the Soviet Union, overseen by Stalin and known as *The Short Course*. Published in 1938 it became the bible of the world Communist movement, 'It was without doubt the world's most successful historical compendium'. Twelve million copies in Russian, along with two million in other languages, were printed immediately in the USSR, where it had been serialized in *Pravda*. It was the basic textbook not only for all Soviet children, students and cadre, but also for militants around the world. Within ten years there had been 200 editions in 62 languages, a total of at least 34 million.

The operation was unprecedented in the international workers movement. The distribution of *The Short Course* dwarfed the circulation of the *Communist Manifesto* . . . Only Mao Tse Tung's *Red Book* invites quantitative comparison.[56]

Thus did the world learn to marvel at the great holiday of Stalin's democratic franchise. With the dregs and vermin expunged, *The Short Course* cheered the way that

90,000,000 persons, by their unanimous vote, confirmed the victory of Socialism in the USSR.

'YOU DON'T UNDERSTAND BECAUSE YOU ARE A FREE MAN'

On mid-summer Sunday – the longest day of the year – I woke to the strange echo of amplified music. It droned incessantly through my hotel window from the direction of Red Square. The Soviet Union was holding elections.

Across the country tens of thousands of candidates were about to be elected to local and municipal soviets. Since 1937 it had been a shoo-in, with only one aspirant presented by 'the bloc of the Party and non-Party masses'. Now there was change in the air, as well as stirring tunes. As an experiment, in some 76 districts, 47 cities, 87 settlements and 859 rural Soviets nearly three-quarters of a century of proletarian democracy had led to – hold your breath, there really was something to celebrate – a choice between more than one candidate.

I live in a kingdom in which the throwing of democratic stones is unwise. Only the week before these Soviet style local elections, six out of ten British voters had cast their ballots against Mrs Thatcher. Yet, in the comfort of a pleasant dacha south of Moscow, I had watched the Soviet TV news show her disliked accomplice Norman Tebbit presenting Thatcher with a bunch of roses as she regained power with an absolute majority. Elections are strange things.

Especially ones with single candidates. Perhaps because they are now an endangered species, Moscow's brought out the ecologist in me. I wanted to learn about them before they became extinct. How do they work? What are the mechanisms that produce regular endorsements of 97, 98 and even 99 per cent in favour of what is already a foregone conclusion?

Sergei began to explain. It was about ten days beforehand. In the middle he turned to his wife and, still speaking in English, commented that a friend who was to oversee the local ballot was still unclear about what he should do. But I lost track of what they were saying. I asked him to explain again but still we seemed to get in a muddle. 'I don't understand your English', I concluded.

'You don't understand,' he paused for emphasis, 'because you are a free man. It means you *cannot* believe what I am saying.'

I tried harder. We went through it again. When people vote they come in and collect a ballot paper. This has the candidate's name on it. A positive vote is easy. You simply fold up the paper and put it in the box. Inevitably, there are people who do not vote. The question, then, when the poll closes, is what to do with the unused ballot slips. Should you just pick them up and shove them in with the others? Thus, you do not really need to count them at all. But so far, and this is what I had been unable to follow, his friend has received no instructions one way or the other. Perhaps he will be told that the boxes should not be stuffed, and he must count the real turnout. So that even if there is only one candidate, people's alienation from the process will be registered.

Will it happen, won't it happen, is it just a rumour? Such is politics in Moscow.

The day after the election my feeling was that most people

had gone to the polls anyway. Not that they are obliged to by law, but Soviet duty is hard to evade.

The way it works is this. You take your passport to the polling station where your name and address is ticked off the register. This gives you your ballot paper. So far not much difference from the West where your claim to a vote is also marked against a copy of the electoral register. Then you cast your vote. If it is 'for' the candidate you just drop it in the urn. If you *don't* wish to vote for the candidate you have to go into a booth and cross out his or her name completely. Thus it is perfectly obvious who is voting against, especially as the booths often do not have curtains.

Why stick out like a sore thumb?

'Of course, I voted,' she said the next day. 'Because why make things hard for the people in the polling station? The sooner you vote, the quicker they can go home, and next year it might be my turn to do the task. And if you don't vote then maybe the Party person at work has to come and ask you, why as a good Soviet citizen you didn't. They are embarrassed, you are embarrassed, it just makes life more awkward.'

Especially with some candidates. The last public appearance of Chernenko, Gorbachev's geriatric predecessor, was at the polling booth in February 1984. The televised conversation between him and the old Moscow boss Grishin was transmitted for posterity.

GRISHIN: We must express our satisfaction to you that you were elected unanimously in the Kuibyshev district.
CHERNENKO: Thank you, thank you.
GRISHIN: I don't remember exactly, but roughly one hundred and thirty thousand voters . . .

LOCAL OFFICIAL: One hundred and thirty-six thousand.

GRISHIN: One hundred and thirty-six thousand voted precisely for you. This testifies to your tremendous prestige among the working people, all the working people of course. Any other constituency would certainly have voted the same way.[57]

It certainly would have.

On the day itself I drove round Moscow with a friend looking for a record he wanted to send to a relative in London. We parked outside the polling station just off Kalinin Prospect. Red flags on a warm day. A group of four women with red arm-bands walked across to the nearby tower block. 'They are going to ask people to come and vote.'

As we drove back we passed a friend of his, a director. We all went to have an ice-cream. 'Has he voted?' I asked. 'Of course.'

'Does he know who for?' The question was translated, my ironic touch lost in the process. He shrugged his shoulders rolled his eyes and they both laughed. 'How should they know?' Such questions! Foreigners!

'Did you vote?' I asked Sergei, when we met again after the election.

'In some constituencies there are now, as you know, more than one candidate. But here there were just three candidates for three posts, two regional deputies and a judge. We did not have a choice, so I voted against them. It used to be dangerous (he saw a look of alarm cross my face) in Stalin's time. But today I suppose not. Perhaps I am naïve. Yes, they could see that I was crossing out all the names.'

Ivan is in his thirties. We were sitting in his flat talking about rock and roll. Had he voted? 'My mother did it for me.'

'Your mother!'

They lived in the same apartment. He was going to get married and was searching desperately for new accommodation. But here was an advantage to multi-occupancy I'd not expected.

'Yes, she took my passport as well as hers, gets two ballot slips and puts them both in. That way, everyone is satisfied. They are introducing more than one candidate. If there is a choice for the voters then there will be some campaigning, so that we know what they stand for and why. I hope very much this happens. Otherwise there is no point in elections at all.'

As he said this I thought of a Polish colleague I'd talked with before coming to Moscow. While condemning Slav nationalism he said that unlike the Czechs and his own people, the Russians had no tradition of democracy and were incapable of the necessary individual independence of mind and attitude. 'As for multi-candidate elections,' he waved his long fingers with contempt, 'we have had those in Poland for years, they make no difference whatsoever.'

When such public cynicism becomes an official 'No' vote, as in the Polish referendum at the end of November 1987, then even these regimes may be seeking an authentic relationship with their people. But the example shows that in the USSR too, the leadership is playing with fire. Perhaps it has to, to fan the spirit of initiative and self-confidence in its peoples. But while my little sample dismisses the single candidate elections as a harmless rite that goes back so far no one can remember anything different, it is attracted to the idea of choice – of a real vote. The theatre of single candidates is one thing. The distance between reality and fact is so great, the pretence so brazen, that it is accepted for what it is: a ritual. If officialdom changes the system, however, only to make it seem like a choice without in fact delivering one, then Soviet pride will find this harder to swallow. The Kremlin's standing will diminish accordingly.

· My feeling seems borne out by a survey of 3,400 voters in twelve regions, carried out after the elections I witnessed. It was published in *Sovyetskaya Rossiya*, and showed growing public interest in reform. On the basis of their sample, the pollsters recommended that candidates 'put forward real plat- forms and proposals for what they intended to do once in office', for in none of the twelve experimental regions did a single local paper 'report on what the deputies hoped to achieve in the future'.[58]

Yet a contorted, pseudo-democracy could well happen. The official Soviet news analysis of the 21 June 1987 elections reported this, for example:

> During the elections the strongest 'fight for votes' unfold- ed in multi-mandate constituencies, as it had been expect- ed, where 90,000 seats were claimed by about 120,000 candidates. About a thousand of them did not get into the deputy's corps because they received less than half of all votes. Those who passed this threshold were divided into two categories. The candidates who got the biggest number of votes (depending upon the number of deputy's mandates) have become full-fledged deputies of Soviets, whereas others have received a status of 'reserve depu- ties'.[59]

Which is quite a brain teaser even if you are not 'a free man': one hundred and twenty thousand candidates compete for ninety thousand seats and only one thousand of them lose . . . Fortunately a back issue of *Moscow News* explains the new system. It reported on a trial election in the Lukhovitsky District of the Moscow region held in April to pave the way for the wider experiment of June. Over the whole district the old constituencies were amalgamated into much larger ones. These would return three, four or five deputies. In each enlarged constituency, voters have one vote *more* than the number of candidates they are supposed to return, i.e. they can vote for four people in a three-candidate constituency, five in a four-member one, etc. The top three, or four, get elected. Those who 'get less than fifty per cent' (and don't ask me 'exactly fifty per cent of what?') are eliminated. The rest become reserve deputies.

What in hell is a reserve deputy? *Moscow News* explains:

> The reserve will be used if something happens to one of the 'main' deputies – he might fall gravely ill, move to some other place, prove not to be up to the duties of a deputy and so forth.[60]

And so forth, indeed. *Who*, in such a case, decides which substitute reserve to 'use', or whether an elected, but apparently not so certainly elected candidate, has 'proved' not to be sufficiently . . . well, sufficiently so forth?

The cunning of electors should not be underestimated. But this system of multi-candidate choice bears in advance all the signs of another charade, if more elaborate. Furthermore, while the old system ensures a Party ratification of candidates beforehand, the new system invites Communist Party interference retrospectively. It may be less objectionable, but it invites more objections.

In one report on the elections, Alexander Guber wrote about the new multi-candidate districts of 1987:

The voters did not mechanically fulfil their civic duty, but actually elected those whom they considered worthy and who, in their view, would decide not only state problems, but also questions of concern to the inhabitants of the given street, district or city.[61]

Guber does not cite any district by name. Nor does he add that, however worthy, candidates were only elected 'and so forth'.

So how should the Soviets hold their elections? If anyone were to ask me, they should have simple constituencies that return one candidate, either through a single transferable vote or by the elementary means of the one with most wins. That way people know whom they vote for and, more important, whom they are voting against.

You might object that the second of these is the same system of first-past-the-post elections that makes a mockery of general elections in Britain. But you cannot have nationally based proportional representation, without nationally competing parties. In the Soviet Union, the soviets (literally councils), whether local, regional or national, do not generate Party power. On the contrary. At present they are merely a function of it. The major question that leads on from elections Soviet style is: *can* there be more than one Party?

A PESSIMIST

Speaking in slow English, a pessimist in Moscow told me:

Yes, we are rich.

Perhaps we are the richest country in the world.

So what is wrong?
    People don't work.

In order to put this right:
    we must pay people to work.

In order to pay them:
    we must stop the people who stop the payment.

And to stop *them* . . .
    We must get rid of people who run the system
    by making speeches and having everything.

THE BIG SURPRISE

A Russian said to a friend, 'Well, if you had the power what would you do?' His friend paused, thought hard, and replied, 'I'd resign the next day.'

A Moscow joke

Elections to local Soviets and to the Supreme Soviet in the USSR only symbolize a commitment to democracy. The instrument that governs the electoral process, which vets and selects candidates, issues orders about whether or not ballot boxes should be stuffed, and writes the speeches, is the Communist Party. The country cannot be more democratic than the Party, unless perhaps the Party allows or encourages it to be so. The internal and public life of the Party is thus the crucial area for the future of glasnost. Should reconstruction fail here, it is hardly likely to succeed elsewhere. The Party declares itself to be the vanguard of society and where it leads the Soviet Union will go. Brezhnev led Party life into a morass, the country followed. If the Party now calls for perestroika, it is hardly unreasonable for the country to step aside and say, 'After you, my dear.'

Democracy *inside* the Party! The notion would be scorned by most people in the West (and not just the West). We have been

157

brought up to think that the Soviets have captive minds. But we may ourselves be captivated by the image of the utterly imprisoned other; more particularly by an image of the jailer ideology that would also deprive us of freedom: Communism and its sinister cadres. ·

For those who think like this, the puzzle about Moscow today is that the attempt at reform challenges their stereotype. From within the contemptible and despised ranks of the Party itself has emerged an indubitably brave, self-confident and spirited opposition, led by people dedicated to making the Soviet Union more honest, and who endorse their own sort of pluralism. Those Soviet intellectuals who managed to retain creativity as well as scepticism over the last twenty years, have welcomed the change and provided some immediate support, thus salvaging the country's reputation from the fattened bunch of clowns and time-servers who have clogged Soviet culture now for many years. This is apparent because their voices are public, in cinema and architecture unions, for example. But whatever their influence, they do not have the power to be decisive. Power resides in the Party.

I asked a senior Party member what he thought the country might be like after reform. 'We do not have a model. We are *fed up* with models', he replied. 'We need people to have and then use their own initiative.' This is new for Party talk, as he conceded. 'If people showed fresh thinking in the past it could get them killed, so it's not so easy for them to change in this respect.' Such remarks have made him among the most hated men in Moscow for many older Party members. They will have his guts for garters if they can. Perhaps they will, we can't presume the outcome. What is clear is that there are now profound arguments right across the board taking place between Soviet Communists Party members themselves.

I found myself asking three questions about this in Moscow:

- What exactly is 'the Party'?
- How come there are such coherent reformers within it; where have they been all these years?
- What must they do to convince people that their talk will produce lasting change?

And I came up with three provisional answers.

FIRST ANSWER:
THE ESTABLISHMENT

Instead of bothering with perestroika, the Soviet Communists could follow a Western example and promulgate the following changes, and establish:

1. As head of State the senior member of the Gromyko family, who signs all legislation into law, heads the national church, and provides the country with a symbol supposedly 'above' politics, but who (just in case) can be made to abdicate.

2. A Party Senate consisting of the male heads of families that have been in the Party since 1920 alongside individuals appointed for life by the Party. This completely non-elected Senate to supervise and if necessary veto all legislation.

3. A lower house of members of the Party whose different factions can campaign for election whenever the majority of them decides, but who, for all their speeches about the local people they represent, are under discipline from their faction boss.

4. A permanent, secretive and self-selecting administrative wing of the Party in the Ministries and the Judiciary, 95 per cent of whom are recruited from two Party universities, which themselves take most of their students from a few elite Party schools.

5. A military command drawn from a couple of training

colleges that recruit from the same elite Party schools.

6. A smattering of the brightest 'outsiders' who have proved themselves to be reliable and 'realistic' Party material.

7. No written constitution at all, because the Party 'knows best' and will therefore be able 'to adapt'.

If the Kremlin announced to the world that henceforth it was going to organize the political system of the USSR along these lines, and thus it was now a democracy, why the world would die laughing. A completely unelected second chamber! A deliberately secretive, self-selecting, permanent senior administrative network that would run circles around elected figures whom it didn't like! No written constitution! It is patently obvious that the whole thing would be a gigantic fix, a means whereby the Party would continue to run things as it chose.

Should the Kremlin respond that it had modelled itself closely on the British system, then the world would reply, 'That's Britain's problem, don't try and pull the wool over our eyes!'

This fanciful comparison – which Germans in their attempt to control the imagination might term a *Gedenkenexperiment* – has a serious point. First, it helps us to see that the Communist Party of the Soviet Union (or CPSU) is not at all a party in the Western sense. It is not a small grouping that specializes in advocacy. Rather it *is* the country's Establishment.

In some provincial cities 'the Party' is, from all accounts, an open conspiracy of connections that decides who gets what jobs. But overall, the analogy with a mafia is misleading, even if there are gangster networks within it. My contact in the British multinational, who is the director of the group's Soviet bloc sales, tried to describe his contradictory feelings about the

Soviet colleagues he dealt with across the table. They are, he told me, his intellectual superiors though culturally more narrow and less experienced. They are frightened of taking decisions, 'You can feel them backing off.' Then he lent across the arm of his chair:

> They are very well trained and their education is excellent, you know. And they really believe in their system. It is an elite system and they are the children of the elite. Almost like our public schools.

The analogy works to a surprising extent. There is a specific sort of English corruption, difficult for foreigners to discern. It is not monetary or thuggish in the continental and American way. It is a much more deep set and social phenomenon, in which words do not quite mean what they say. Behind all the fine talk of an open society in the United Kingdom, there is closure. Beneath the style of benevolence there is, with a few outstanding exceptions, contempt. Not unlike the Soviet elite, the British one is a privileged, self-co-opting group. It demands from its members a similar repression of individuality and tacit conformism, known as 'good form'. It dominates the political system. What does it represent? Itself. 'The club' or 'the Establishment'. Although, thanks to Mrs Thatcher, change is in the air, it is still true that if you want to get on in London you need to be on good terms with, preferably to have been born into, the Party – I mean the Establishment.

The *nomenklatura* of the USSR is the term for the ranks of those who hold official posts. It is a graded system of around 500,000 major positions, each accompanied by its related privileges. Most, but not all, of the *nomenklatura* are in the Party. The Party, however, not only predominates within the *nomenklatura*, it controls the selection of appointments to it and the various promotions through it, while it also surrounds the *nomenklatura*, in every institution and zone. The doorman who is in the Party cell has some kind of say in the appointment of an institute's director, even if the latter is part of the *nomenklatura* and the doorman is not. It is hardly a constructive relationship, for the Party is not an open democracy. But if the cell is mobilized to fire the existing director, then the doorman could have a role. The nineteen million Party members constitute a different kind of Establishment from the British one.

Another significant divergence between the formal Establishment of the Soviet Union and the informal Establishment of the UK, resides in their relationship to the rest of the country and its activities. Britain has a well-endowed, if relatively powerless, civil society (a crucial term that I will discuss below) while the Soviet Union does not.

Despite such important differences, a rough and ready parallel can be drawn. In Britain there is freedom, but there is also rule from above. A form of rule which is organized by a quite subtle Establishment symbolized by the crown. Its network embraces both of the major political parties but extends well beyond them.

The Party-Establishment of the Soviet Union equally embodies the country's social, political and economic order. It is therefore inconceivable that the reformers will seek to declare a multi-Party system in the USSR. The idea is absurd.

But nor would such a move make sense in terms of a comparison with the West. The equivalent to the CPSU in the United States is not the Republican or Democratic Party but the combined Houses of Congress and the White House along with all the Departments of State. Western-style regimes do not offer their people a choice between alternative political orders, even if they offer some choice *within* their given system.

SECOND ANSWER:
NOWHERE ELSE TO GO

Gorbachev's election took five votes. He had a majority of one. This showed that the Party-Establishment is no longer a one-man band. Accounts suggest that the small Politburo was evenly balanced and it took the combined authority of Gromyko and the insistence of Chebrikov (the head of the KGB who wanted a clean General Secretary) to defeat Grishin. The top administrators of the Central Committee apparatus waited for the outcome. Talking to western journalists at the Chautauqua conference in New York State, Leonid Dobrokhotov described the scene.

Reformers like himself had been uncertain of Mikhail Gorbachev; presumably they wondered if he was just a fast moving careerist. Also Chernenko was evidently attempting to push him aside. According to one account, Chernenko knew he was ill and was thinking of retiring to ensure a Brezhnevite succession.[62] Rather than toe the line, however, Gorbachev made a hard hitting speech in December 1984. He attacked the economic slowdown, saying it had begun in the seventies. He derided attempts 'to squeeze new phenomena into the procrustean bed of moribund conceptions', and called for 'deep changes in the economy and the entire society'.[63]

It was only then, Dobrokhotov said, that he and his like-minded colleagues realized that if Gorbachev were elected 'there would be great changes' and decided to throw in their lot with him.

If this is true, then significant bodies of opinion and influence had debated about what direction the leadership should take. It wasn't just a matter of personalities. When Chernenko died in March 1985:

> The Central Committee apparatchiks were assembled in the waiting rooms . . . there was a high state of tension: a good deal of nervous pacing up and down and chain-smoking went on . . . Boris Stukalin came in and announced dryly, 'Comrades, the new General Secretary is Comrade Gorbachev.' Half of the Central Committee functionaries . . . almost leapt with joy; the other half were scarcely able to conceal their disappointment.[64]

This is life at the top, of course. Even so it describes the co-existence of strongly opposed views. The reporter compares it to the election of a new Pope. A good analogy, although Pope Mikhail told the Party at its 27th Congress in 1986 that it should free itself from the 'infallibility complex'.[65]

Negative factors – the state of the economy, corruption, the fact that the USSR was on the edge of falling irrevocably behind Western societies – forced open the way for the reformers. The shrewder elements of the old guard had to turn to them. Grishin, who seems to have been somewhere between Mayor Daley and Al Capone (to take Nixon's analogy further) was not a credible alternative to Gorbachev, even if one disregarded the fact that he would have been the fourth consecutive General Secretary in his seventies. In the very nature of things, Al Capone does not have a political programme.

Yet for the old to be replaced by the new, there has to be a new guard waiting and ready. Where did it come from? That anti-Stalinists existed outside the Party is understandable enough. Of course there was external opposition to the Party's direction under Brezhnev. But how could opposition survive within the very heart and belly of the beast?

Like the Establishment of any modern society, the Soviet Party-Establishment is not monolithic, and it is becoming less so thanks to new generations who are completely urban in their experience, global in their tastes and responsive to technically advanced production. Khruschev's assault on Stalin showed that even those drenched in blood, and at the centre of what was indeed a totalitarian machine, could denounce its crimes and rehabilitate its victims.

But Khruschev remained a despot, if a despot with a human face. Eventually his despotism became much too human, erratic, whimsical and even 'harebrained', to use the official term of criticism levelled against him. The Brezhnev-Suslov team that deposed him installed what has been termed 'Ordinary Stalinism'. One of its chief characteristics was that cadres were only expected to *behave* themselves ideologically. Private opinions were not searched out or exposed. Votes had to be unanimous, but hearts could carry on beating to their own rhythms.

The generations inspired or disturbed by Khruschev's revelations could thus discuss among themselves; despise Brezhnev's senility; draft tough economic analyses (for their own drawers) and read *samizdat* documents such as the Medvedev-Sakharov-Turchin appeal for democracy, all without being driven out of the Party. During the terror you could be arrested for a chance remark, or because you were denounced by someone jealous of your success, or because a contact of years back was now under suspicion. There was no knowing why you might be among the next victims. The regime installed after 1965 may have frowned on liberalization, as we have seen. Centralism was insisted upon, any open breaking of ranks was forbidden. But survival within the Party could be combined with scepticism over its direction, without fear for your life.

And where else could the survivors go? While it is important not to view the Party through the eyes of dissidents famous in the West, they can still provide us with a glimpse of the acute problems suffered by honest and loyal Party members behind their closed doors in the USSR. This is Rudolf Bahro, author of *The Alternative*, who was imprisoned in East Germany, talking about the many years he spent as an active member of the East German Party:

> The most important thing that I learnt was that the Party really consists of two parties, the same as the two that emerged in Czechoslovakia in 1967-68. One sticks to the status quo, adopting a basically authoritarian position; while the other favours deep reforms, seeking out discussion and giving rational answers to awkward questions. I was convinced that the second of these would eventually win through, but my residual Party solidarity and my belief in open debate still held me back from seeing the necessary struggle in fully antagonist terms . . . I still did not realize what an impediment the Party apparatus was to the progress of socialism.[66]

Jorge Semprun has given us a compelling story of a militant

in a western Communist party. Although difficult for the uninitiated, it is one of the century's finest pieces of political literature. And it can tell us something about the inner tensions of the Soviet experience today.

As a young Spanish Communist Semprun joined the French resistance when the Germans occupied France. He was arrested by the Gestapo and sent to the concentration camp at Buchenwald. Afterwards he returned to France, became a member of the Spanish CP's small Central Committee, and an organizer of its clandestine network in Madrid. He took the political name of Federico Sanchez.

In *The Autobiography of Federico Sanchez*, Semprun recalls the Slansky trials in Czechoslovakia in 1952 – the last great Stalinist show trial – at which one of those who 'confessed' to being a Gestapo agent was Josef Frank. Frank was then executed. He too had been a prisoner in Buchenwald, and a member of the camp's Communist network. Semprun explains how he knew that Frank could not have been a double-agent. Indeed, sixteen years after his ashes were scattered, Frank was posthumously cleared of all charges. But in 1952 Semprun did not protest Frank's innocence: 'I kept quiet, sacrificing the truth on the altar of the Absolute Spirit, which among us was called the Party Spirit.'[67] He knew, he kept quiet, and more than that, when Stalin died a year later he mourned Stalin. Semprun/ Sanchez wrote a poem. 'I did not write it because I was ordered to: it was something that came spontaneously from the innermost depths of my alienated consciousness.' A taste is enough:

Impossible to imagine having read,

in plain, simple words that he is dead . . .

The working class is an orphan . . .

that world won and defended,

from Shanghai to Berlin,
happier each day, made vaster
by the hand of Stalin . . .

Perhaps because he was an underground organizer active on Spanish soil, Semprun had a grasp of the country's realities. Along with Fernando Claudin, he argued that an authentic capitalist development of Spain had taken place under the Franco dictatorship. A new strategy was demanded to take account of this, and the old slogans about a general strike had to be discarded. The leadership sought to silence them; in effect they were expelled in 1964. Semprun felt that the same commitment to what he calls 'Communist freedom' which once took him into the Party now led him out.[68]

Semprun's account demonstrates that those who loved Stalin when young did not necessarily lose their sense of truth or commitment to a purpose larger than their own careers. But the Spanish Party was in opposition and its life was highly confined. To leave it meant a chance to enter the real world. Communists in the USSR who joined the CPSU of their own free will, and who also found themselves trying to insist upon contemporary realities in the face of the Brezhnevites, had almost no equivalent way out. Few wanted just to walk away from their country. Nor, for such good Communists, did leaving the Party provide an exit to a renewed freedom. Highly confined though it was they actually had more space to manoeuvre within it than outside.

Condemned to proceed by the millimetre in the largest country on earth, life for them seems to have slowed right down. When they talk about the 'years of stagnation' there is a personal sense of loss. In an interview with the British Communist Monty Johnstone, Fedor Burlatsky, an influential commentator for *Literaturnaya Gazeta*, said in response to a question about the introduction of multi-candidate elections:

> From 1953–60, I published many articles about the development of democracy. And thirty years ago I proposed that we must do something of this kind – to have maybe a list of candidates . . . You know, I personally am an optimist – a biological optimist – I have believed in reform for maybe thirty-five years . . .[69]

THIRD ANSWER:
PROCEED IN PUBLIC

Can the momentum for reform prove so irresistible that its impact will change forever the way the USSR is ruled? There is much talk about Gorbachev being yet another figure in the long history of Moscow's enlightened despots. Although they achieved much in their time, Russia's benevolent emperors never managed to break the machinery of absolutism they inherited, and in their wake the system reverted to type.

Today, the key question is whether the despotic hold of the Party can be transformed into a democratic one. Rule in Russia is bound to remain 'from above' for decades to come, but the form of rule from above can become democratic in important ways, as the capitalist democracies have shown. The Party-Establishment of the Soviet Union is already diverse and even pluralistic, full of differences and debates. Yet its discussions remain closed. The Soviet citizen does not know what choices are placed before the leaders, and learns of the outcome only after decisions are made.

If the Kremlin is to drag the USSR towards the levels of democracy in the West, it needs to open up the decisive formal proceedings of the Party to public scrutiny. Under Khrushchev the crucial plenary meetings of the Central Committee were published. Under Brezhnev this was stopped. The reason given was that people would be more frank if they spoke in private. Of course, the opposite was true. The Party was able to indulge in an irresponsible refusal of reality for years because its main policy proceedings were held in camera. The secrecy that cut them off from the world gave its senior participants an inflated sense of their own importance. Acolytes could describe Brezhnev as the world's leading statesman safe in the knowledge that colleagues would not hold them up to ridicule.

Apparently Gorbachev has said that he would be happy for Plenum proceedings to be published, so that all can see for themselves who are the opponents of reform. Such an attitude is not reassuring. It links 'openness' to suppression. It treats publication as a form of threat, a means of silencing rather than allowing disagreement.

A young, patriotic Russian, keen to see Gorbachev succeed, told me there were impassable limits:

They will never allow criticism of the leaders personally. One could never say on TV about a senior Politburo member, 'In my view in this respect he is wrong,' even politely, and expect to appear again.

You can see why. If neither senior Party members themselves nor their supporters are allowed to make such utterances in public, however diplomatically, naturally they will find it intolerable if others exercise such a right.

At the same time, while the artifice of the monolithic leadership may provide defence, it invites total attack. Any criticism of one member of the Politburo becomes an attack on all. After which it is only a short step to becoming an enemy of socialism.

But if formal Party sessions, especially the determining

plenary meetings of the Central Committee, are opened by law to public observation and the media, then glasnost would indeed begin to turn into democracy.

As any Western politician can tell the Kremlin leaders, such openness during debates over basic policy will provide them with a powerful new means of manipulating and dominating public opinion, even while they also have to take greater account of it – it is a development that can strengthen not weaken the State's support. Indeed, as we in the West know all too well, the most massive barrage of completely justified criticism need make not an iota of difference to the policies of strong leaders. But the fact that we have the right to make them – and not just over coffee – gives us a means whereby we can moderate official action. Democracy will never be secured in the Soviet Union until – prior to their decision – the principle debates of the Party are revealed to those whom it rules.

The Yeltsin affair dramatised this problem. As an alternate (i.e. non-voting) member of the Politburo, and head of the Moscow Party, it fell to Yeltsin to open the proceedings of the 350 strong Central Committee Plenum, just prior to the celebrations of the 70th anniversary of the revolution. The Plenum's main stated purpose was to approve final arrangements for the celebrations, including Mikhail Gorbachev's historic, televised address which would survey the seventy years of Soviet history. At this sensitive moment, Boris Yeltsin, an outspoken advocate of reform and a Gorbachev appointee, apparently launched an assault on those of his colleagues who were in his view obstructing perestroika. According to Gorbachev, Yeltsin 'went so far as to say that perestroika did next to nothing for the people', and that the Party leadership 'lacked revolutionary ardour'.

In his subsequent account of the Plenum (for we do not have Yeltsin's) Gorbachev also said:

> Of course, the fact that a member of the Central Committee criticized the Politburo, the Secretariat and individual persons at the Plenary Meeting should not be considered as something extraordinary. It is a normal thing. We all agree here that there must be no areas in the Party closed to criticism and there must be no individuals immune from criticism. We shall continue to encourage criticism and self-criticism at all levels.
>
> But this case is different. At the critical political moment when the Central Committee concentrated on fundamental problems of theory and practice of our development, Comrade Yeltsin tried to divert the Plenary Meeting's work to other things by declaring his special position on a number of issues.

As a result, the Central Committee discussed Yeltsin's intervention. After twenty-six members had taken the floor, the Meeting was unanimous in 'qualifying his statement as politically wrong'.

What Gorbachev meant by saying that Yeltsin's accusations came at a 'critical political moment . . . of our development', was that the Committee was due to scrutinize the General Secretary's speech – including his characterization of the role of Stalin, the nature of collectivization, the position of Khruschev – before it went out live to the Soviet people. According to Gorbachev, the Central Committee – the majority of whom were appointed under Brezhnev – 'approved the main tenets of the report', and we may therefore speculate that it moderated certain aspects. Quite apart from any other consideration, Yeltsin's timing was dreadful.

Soviet Freedom

After the Central Committee session, foreign correspondents were informed of the disagreement and told that Yeltsin's intervention would be discussed at a special meeting of the Moscow City Party when the anniversary celebrations were completed. The Soviet Union's own newspapers were instructed not to report this, generating massive rumours – at least in Moscow. At this stage the Kremlin proved more adept at handling international than domestic opinion.

The proceedings of the post-celebration Moscow City Party meeting were reported in full in *Pravda* on 13 November 1987. They were opened by Mikhail Gorbachev, who gave a description of what had happened at the Central Committee, told how he had personally asked Boris Yeltsin to withdraw an offer to resign made in the summer, and to postpone a debate about perestroika in the capital until later in the year. The General Secretary's introduction hardly invited those present to support their local chief, who had anyway been imposed on them from the centre.

Having adopted high-sounding statements and promises from the very beginning which were largely nourished by his inordinate ambition and fondness for staying in the limelight, Comrade Yeltsin let it go and slacked off control over the city Party organization and the work with personnel.

And thus the same Moscow City party organization that had been asked to consider, in secret, the future of Comrade Grishin, after reports of criminal investigations had been read out to it, was now asked, this time on the record, to consider the resignation of his successor, Comrade Yeltsin. Twenty-three members spoke; Yeltsin replied, concluding:

I must say that I cannot refute any of this criticism. And not because I must make a show of repenting, but because, as you understand, as a Communist I have lost the political face of a leader. I am very guilty before the Moscow City Party Organization, I am very guilty before the City Party Committee, before you, before the Bureau and, of course, before Mikhail Gorbachev whose prestige is so high in our organization, in our country, and throughout the world.

Then Gorbachev summed up, saying that the meeting had been difficult but instructive, that some of the speeches gave off 'such a strong odour of naphthalene . . . that you become sick', that 'I personally hold this matter close to my heart. I have had more than one straight, frank and sincere private conversation with Boris Nikolayevich Yeltsin . . . I would like to support those comrades who spoke about the positive aspects of Yeltsin's work . . . our path is not easy . . .' and so on.

The capitalist press had a field day. It might have drawn a parallel between Yeltsin's pathetic admission and the ludicrous *mea culpas* of American Presidential candidates, as they swear their loyalty to their wives and the moral values of their society, while expressing sorrow at the lapses that oblige them to withdraw from seeking their country's highest office.

Instead, it delighted in the assault on Yeltsin and his humiliation by comparing it with the Moscow show trials of the 1930s. The analogy is quite grotesque, but here it is in a lead editorial from *The Times*:

Glasnost is not what we have been led to believe. It is rather the party's one-sided use of the official media for its own ends, and only that. Similar openness was shown during the early show trials of the 1930s. Then, often respected leaders were indicted for their alleged failings – in full view of Western reporters, and the details were published in *Pravda*. Now, as then, the official reason for making the details public was 'democratization' – a desire to involve people and keep them on the Party's side against the enemy.

The Moscow show trials were a form of murder. When you accuse people of murder it is usually best to be familiar with the evidence. But there is little sign that the author of this accusation has considered the process which had just taken place. It certainly is one that can be criticized, but it was neither murderous nor was it staged like a Stalinist trial. On the contrary, it offered an opportunity to hear the voices of senior Party officials speaking spontaneously, and some interesting exchanges took place of a kind rarely published between ranking cadres in the East.

The first speaker stated that Yeltsin was fond of publicity rather than action, and that his resignation should be accepted. The second, from the City Soviet Executive Committee, said, 'We were not bold enough to speak out earlier', and then complained about Yeltsin's meeting with the right-wing Pamyat Society.

He ceded them one position after another. And to whom? To hysterical people and members of the Black Hundred.

A few speakers later, it was the turn of A.N.Nikolayev, First Secretary of the Baumansky District, who said:

It is sacrilege even to cast a shadow of doubt that Muscovites can have any other stand than the stand of the Central Committee. This is a tremendous or, if you wish, a Party crime.

Do I smell naphthalene? After all, some Muscovites are in Pamyat. He was followed by I.N.Konyukhova, a women who levelled the one charge Yeltsin specifically denied:

> You, Boris Nikolayevich, unfortunately, are not fond of either Moscow or Muscovites.

The next speaker complained of the cruel way Yeltsin dismissed people. The one after, said that, despite his business qualities, Yeltsin 'has one very negative feature – mistrust of his colleagues'. He then attacked the Bureau of the City Party Committee for, in effect, encouraging Yeltsin rather than resisting his suspicions.

V.V.Skitev, a member of the aforesaid Bureau, then spoke: 'I must admit', he said:

> that working as a department head under Boris Niko-layevich was torture, you know ... I don't wish to remove the responsibility for what happened from myself. But it was very difficult work.

Skitev's plea for sympathy does not seem tremendously convincing and he was immediately reminded of his own vulnerability by the next speaker, A.M.Larionov, who described how Yeltsin

> replaced 22 district Party committee secretaries, some-times simply persecuting the comrades. A person would be called away from his or her vacation a week before it ends, and be told that there is to be a talk on the problems of the district. Instead of that you begin to be made, in turn, to run around in circles as if in a dark room and be blamed for the most unexpected things. By the way,

Comrade V.V. Skitev has just spoken here, but it was precisely he who went in for all that. Maybe he was forced to do it, I don't know, but he didn't muster the courage to object to it.

More speakers followed, one of whom read out an instruction from Yeltsin to a district committee First Secretary holding him personally responsible for the daily control over the supply of fruit and vegetables. A.S. Yeliseyev, Rector of a Technical High School, said that he felt complicity in Yeltsin's guilt because although he had taken part in many Moscow City Plenary Meetings:

I have not heard anything like what we've heard today. Anything even half or three times less sharp. Somewhere we are beginning to lose adherence to our principles. Let us gain the courage to speak in time and then we shall avoid making such mistakes. This is the result of the long neglect of the standards of Party life.

He was immediately followed, however, by Yu. A. Belyakov, the Second Secretary of the City Committee (Yeltsin was the First Secretary). He was one of only two people to refer to Gorbachev by name. On behalf of the Bureau, Belyakov declared even more flattering and complete support for the Central Committee resolution, and went on:

Comrade Yeltsin's statement at the Plenary meeting came as a total surprise for us . . . Never has the Moscow Party organization had any differences with the general line and practical actions of the Party Central Committee . . . This blow was dealt on the eve of the 70th anniversary of the October Revolution . . . our exactingness towards the

First Secretary was patently insufficient (a wonderful formulation, he should be invited to Whitehall) ... Perestroika continues ...

In short, moth-balls. An interesting intervention by
V. V. Vinogradov came next. He immediately criticized the
Second Secretary for saying that Yeltsin's outburst came as a
surprise,

> I think that this is not quite so. An explosion after all was
> ripening, and it was based on Comrade Yeltsin's
> arrogance, toughness, lack of firmness and his inability to
> listen to people.

To prove that Second Secretary Belyakov indeed knew the
explosion was coming, Vinogradov alleged that his personal
district had been 'overturned':

> My patience ran out and I went to the Second Secretary,
> Comrade Belyakov and frankly told him, 'either dismiss
> me or stop the executions'. They stopped ... Boris Niko-
> layevich lost touch with us – moreover, he has not been in
> the same rank with us. He kind of used to fly above us ...

And with that, Boris Nikolayevich Yeltsin came crashing to
the ground. At any rate, he was reduced to being a Minister for
Construction.

It seems that Yeltsin showed signs of Khruschevite
impetuosity, and combined a similar brilliant populism with
tactical blundering. Without doubt one of the reasons that he
infuriated Party leaders is that he criticized their privileges and
said the truth without mincing his words. Evidently, he also
found himself out of his depth.

At his London press conference, Professor Abel Aganbagyan said that figures like Yeltsin can be dangerous to perestroika because they talk beautifully, draw people to them but do not withstand the test of power by turning policy into deeds. Ministers get fired for less in the West; Yeltsin's removal is not in itself a matter of principle.

But if the Kremlin wishes to convince us of the unfeigned character of its democracy, the method of his removal must be queried. Yeltsin was powerful and popular. If what he chose to say before the Central Committee was rubbish, people should be allowed to judge him for themselves, just as (and more to the point) they should hear with their own ears his spontaneous condemnation by his most senior colleagues. For the crucial point is that while the Moscow City Party meeting from which I have just quoted shows evidence of some genuine political life, it was nonetheless a put-up job. It may not have been controlled, but its outcome was known in advance.

On this question Aganbagyan followed the present Party line. Central Committee plenary meetings will not be open. The first justification for this is that inner-party meetings in the West are not published either. A second justification is that 'these meetings are intended for people who are taking decisions'.

Now this second argument is a real one. It touches on a point that is distinctive about the Soviet system, and to which I'll return, namely that its top figures are not politicians in the Western sense but are administrators. And executive meetings in the West – from the boards of large companies, to cabinet meetings – are never placed on the public record. Far from it. Secrecy is regarded as a matter of right and leaks are even seen as treason.

However, Aganbagyan's first argument is spurious. The comparison with Western parties does not hold, as we have seen. In the Soviet Union the Party-Establishment is everything. If there is no glasnost when its major policy directives are being decided, then sovereignty is sealed from the people and they cannot be considered proper citizens of their own country.

Nor do Central Committee meetings take decisions at a practical level, even if their membership consists of practical decision makers. The Plenums lay down the general line. They decide policy, not practice. Under public scrutiny, of course, Central Committee proceedings would often be delphic and polite, disagreements muted. Doubtless 'security issues' would remain under wraps. Caucuses would meet beforehand. But major questions of contention would obtain a public form of expression where it really matters.

When major issues are openly debated 'from above', then – and only then – can there be genuine debate 'from below'. The reformers want democracy so that economic reconstruction while governed by Party leaders is activated by the people themselves. This combination of popular action and strategic guidance can hardly develop if the Soviet people are forbidden access to Central Committee debates. If the leadership cannot take this elementary risk, what does it mean? It means that it cannot trust itself before the population of the USSR. But this is the crucial relationship, that between citizens and Party, which Gorbachev and his supporters say is essential for perestroika to succeed in the Soviet Union.

Finally, criticisms of the General Secretary himself which are now possible in a Central Committee Plenum, will go on the public record, whether they are deserved or not. This is the key comparison that has to be made with the procedures of capitalist democracy, where *lèse-majesté* is not illegal. Only when this happens will tumble down the keystone of the 'Stalin type of strategy, the Stalin unity of will'. Only when the General Secretary can be argued with openly by his peers will the long shadow of the sacred Tsar, or 'little father', be lifted from Russian soil, and the fatal, imperial enchantment of the ruler as representative of God on Earth be dispelled.

CIVIL SOCIETY

In an unduly critical assessment of Gorbachev, soon after he came to power, the Hungarian philosophers Agnes Heller and Ference Feher argued that reform of the Party is much less significant than encouraging 'autonomous' activity in society.[70] They concede that the two changes need not be incompatible, but insist that the latter is much more important. For them what matters is life outside the Party and the State.

But the character, and the degree of self-determination in the life of any society, is linked umbilically to the political culture within its regime. If democracy is to flourish in factories and localities and among special interest groups, there has to be democracy within the State.

When it was reported that Yeltsin expressed his guilt before the unanimous opinion of his peers, people in the street shivered. Either he should have been allowed to stick to his views – however wrongheaded – or those long critical of him should have made their opinions known earlier. Given that Yeltsin was outspoken, his denouement makes free speech everywhere seem like a trap. The shiver was a palpable expression of the relationship between political life outside and inside the State.

The changes being attempted in the Soviet Union today are as difficult as they are momentous. There is no simple, technical solution to its problems. I have suggested that the Party should be seen as a vast, institutionalized Establishment. There is plenty of evidence to show that this Party-Establishment has a vigorous – and harsh! – internal life (before one even begins to consider regional and national differences in an organization whose membership of nineteen million is larger than the population of many countries). If these differences are given due public expression, so that the Party's policy decisions belong to the public domain, it might be possible to break the closure which is essential to despotism. As it is, the way the Yeltsin affair was handled shows the unresolved nature of the reforms: its publicity was a measure of both openness and closure.

For democracy to flourish outside the doors of the Kremlin, its citizens should be aware that differences have an accepted stability within. To achieve such a transformation is harder than to write about it. Even so, it is not simple to analyse. The idea of political space outside the State should not be taken for granted. Categories like 'public opinion' and 'politicians' are too narrow to elucidate the processes of modern power. There is a more sophisticated contrast, that between the State and what is referred to by an honourable if still little-known concept, civil society, a distinction which also seems to inform the Hungarians' polemic against Gorbachev.

THEIR SYSTEM AND OURS

END, the organization for European Nuclear Disarmament, held an international convention in Coventry in July 1987. Large public sessions took place in the cathedral, rebuilt beside the ruins of the historic one destroyed by German bombing. One such session had a panel of three official Soviet delegates. Afghanistan was raised. The head of the delegation gave the official line, that Moscow wished to withdraw its forces. They were only in Kabul, he said, because American interference undermined a peaceful settlement. Then his colleague, Galina Sidorova, also responded. Her performance was that of a tough, svelte, fashionably dressed journalist. She works for *New Times*, the official foreign language weekly and she didn't seem to be giving anything away. This time she answered personally,

> I know that there is a treaty on Afghanistan. But in my view Soviet soldiers should not perish in a far country in peace time.

The audience gasped. She went on to say that there was no need for demonstrations against the war because everyone was aware of the feeling of Soviet public opinion. She then described the film, *Is It Easy To Be Young?*, which had swept the Moscow cinemas earlier in the year, and is, among other things, a moving and well-made anti-war film. The third member of the panel added that there could be a demonstration, but it would also march on the American Embassy. (Later, a Moscow opinion poll showed more than half its respondents against the war and only a quarter in favour, while Sakharov has written to *Moscow News*, 6 December 1987, saying withdrawal 'brooks no delay'.)

This was a very remarkable performance from an official panel, quite apart from their responses to other questions. However, the session did not receive a single line in the British press, or a moment of coverage on television or radio. Why? What Sidorova said was news. But she said it at a meeting convened by END which is considered too 'unofficial' for its affairs to be granted news coverage. The British Establishment, in its wondrous ways, dislikes the idea of nuclear disarmers becoming influential. It does not wish the END platform to be perceived as thoughtful, let alone important. END is free to mount such an event, and hundreds of people were in the cathedral, but the few million who would have been interested to learn about it, did not.

The reality of a free press in the West can bend to the reality of authority, even when this is not exercised through edicts or censorship. Northern Ireland presents an interesting example. According to the 1984 *Report on British Social Attitudes*, 58 per cent of British voters think that the best long term policy for Northern Ireland would be for it to reunify with the rest of Ireland, and 59 per cent of Britons believe that there should be a complete withdrawal of British troops (38 per cent feel this strongly). An impressive body of opinion about an issue that concerns the integrity of the United Kingdom.

Only one major national newspaper endorses such policies,

though quietly, and I do not recall a single television pro-gramme that has allowed such a perspective a forceful airing during peak viewing. This is bad news for Galina Sidorova. It means that the war in Afghanistan may continue for years despite Soviet public opinion. If the English can do it, so can the Russians, even if they need to be more skilful and diminish their losses.

In both countries public opinions exist that are distinct from and even contrary to official policy. In both countries such opinions may be ignored. In Britain, however, autonomous organizations exist dedicated to influencing both public opinion and State policy. Organizations such as END can even hold large international conferences, without any question of approval or permission from the authorities: this is our free-dom and our right. Such conferences, however, may be com-pletely ignored. That is also the name of the game. To exercise influence outside the official system is possible – but hard.

Very hard, but without this possibility an essential element of the real freedom we enjoy in the West would be lost. It was natural, therefore, that when a delegation from END went to Moscow just before the Coventry convention, one of its con-cerns was to see how far glasnost and perestroika would allow free space for independent organizations like itself to try to influence the direction of affairs.

Two of its members, Mary Kaldor and Jonathan Steele, met with Yegor Yakovlev, the editor of *Moscow News*, whose paper has been in the forefront of glasnost. They discussed the dif-ference between the Khruschev reforms and today's. Yakovlev argued that in 1956 there had been severe criticism of Stalin personally, but little about the system. Now the attack was directed at the way the institutions worked rather than personal scapegoats. The two westerners wondered if democracy really had ripened over the last thirty years and asked whether civil society had expanded. Yakovlev's interpreter

> was unable to translate the term 'civil society' – neither he nor Yakovlev was familiar with the concept. They seemed puzzled by our arguments about autonomous political activity and said that we were imposing Western conceptions onto Soviet society.[71]

This incomprehension is full of irony and interest. The concept of civil society as used in Moscow in 1987 by the representatives of END, was developed by the leader of the Italian Communist Party, Antonio Gramsci, after he himself had returned from Moscow in the 1920s. Though dating back to the eighteenth century, when the idea of the citizen was developed, its use as a socialist term derives from Marx, who counterposed civil society to the State in France. Gramsci, imprisoned by Mussolini and writing his difficult but subsequently acclaimed notebooks behind bars, was concerned with the contrast between the European and Russian history, a divergence so fundamental it meant Lenin's insurrectionary strategy could not be applied to the West:

> In Russia the State was everything, civil society was primordial and gelatinous; in the West, there was a proper relation between State and civil society, and when the State trembled a sturdy structure of civil society was at once revealed.[72]

Gramsci went on to suggest that Western societies had a depth and complexity to them, thanks to their civil society, which meant that they would not fall to a dramatic revolutionary assault. Thus when Yakovlev suggested that to talk about 'civil society' was to impose Western criteria on Russia, he hit the mark but, understandably perhaps, missed the point.

There are real difficulties about the concept (especially now that national structures are being overwhelmed by international ones). Nonetheless, in the West a political space exists outside official state processes and parties, a space in which 'public opinion' can play its own role and have its own influence. Freedom to travel is linked to this, for example, as it gives people the authority to discuss for themselves what it is like elsewhere.

But to *oppose* civil society to the State is misleading. Whether parliamentary or presidential, western states seek to organize and orchestrate the broad and multifarious political culture around them. Likewise, in any country the strength of autonomous political movements, such as the Greens, depends on their constitutional rights and practical ability to alter legislation and shift the balance of power.

The character of a country's civil society is defined only in part therefore by the independence of organizations, whether religious, educational, political or social. What matters as much if not more is the ability of such institutions and networks to influence national policy. It is the nature of the relationship between them that defines the character of both civil society and the State.

If this is so, we can see that in terms of Gramsci's concept things have taken a new twist in Russia. On the one hand civil society is still, to use his wonderful term, primordial and gelatinous. It exists: societies of model aeroplane enthusiasts have their autonomy. But they suffer from it. For it is not influential autonomy, and the attempt to become influential has hitherto been banned.

On the other hand, as if in compensation, the Party has become overdeveloped and ubiquitous. The Party-Establishment that holds state power in its hands is immensely large, powerful and deeply entrenched. Too much so: Stalin's Unity has grown obese. A Muscovite related to me, with a sense of awe, that he had heard that in Budapest a local party organization might have just two or three full-time members whose tasks were ideological. Whereas in Moscow, he complained, each local party branch has tens of full-timers checking up on this, that and everything, usually knowing less about it than the managers or officials they oversee. In his view the Party had become an administrative impediment to the functioning of the system, not its vanguard.

Nor is the Party of the Soviet Union just a matter of its own mass of full-timers; the whole structure of institutional power, from factories to apartment blocks, is Party-organized. The police too are relatively efficient and even better informed. Born out of revolution, and at the head of a vast country whose population is often instinctively anarchist, the Party is all too sensitive about any challenge to its authority. *Its* state power is well and truly defended in depth. That which has been suppressed outside itself, it has now had to generate from within. And inside its bloated body there exists a clumsy understudy for civil society and public opinion.

An interesting sign of this was the sudden fashion for the term 'political culture' that swept into Soviet terminology after 1969. The British Soviet specialist Archie Brown has traced the way it appeared in both political speeches and academic discussion. For Brezhnev (who talked about 'raising the political culture of the workers') and for the 1980 *Concise Political Dictionary* (which indicates the 'regulative' function of political culture), the term is unitary. But while those in authority deployed the concept to project their official attitudes on to the population, the more sophisticated social scientists and commentators used it as a term free of bourgeois taint, that enabled them to discuss different political beliefs and commitment in society at large. In 1980, in Sverdlovsk, there was even a special conference – The Political Culture of Developed Socialism – attended by 1,100 scholars and officials: evidence of the enormous effort to deny, and yet come to terms with, civil society.[73]

Effective autonomy in a modern society means not local autarchy and isolation – there is plenty of that in the Soviet Union today around the kitchen tables. It means expressing differences while remaining in association with the larger society, being able to influence it and react freely to its influence and development. Similarly, democratization within the State needs autonomous action and support within civil society. The two thrive hand in hand. To be democratic each needs the other.

An argument on such lines was developed in *New Socialist* by Raymond Williams, a leading thinker on the left in Britain, who argued:

A socialist economy does need a general plan, but there is no socialist reason why this has to be monopolist. Instead of one state planning group there could be alternative state planning centres, offering different analyses and proposals . . . for public discussion and decision . . . Older socialists had a simple equation for planning – rationality plus public interest. This led often to the arrogance of monopoly. For it is a matter of everyday experience that rational people arrive at different conclusions and that the public interest is not singular but is a complex and interactive network of *different* real interests. A sharing plan begins from this acknowledgement of *diversity* . . .[74]

The Soviet Union is a long way from qualitative change of this calibre. But in their calls for more democracy, multi-candidate elections, a widening of choice, the need for democracy, the importance of factory elections, the mastery of the working people and so on, the new leaders of the CPSU are attempting to create their own civil society in the Soviet Union. This is a measure of their ambition.

Which brings us to another important difference between the Soviet system and the West's. Capitalism has generated its specialist operators: professional politicians. Their image is as rulers of the State on behalf of the people. But their actual role is rather to 'handle' civil society on behalf of the already existing regime. They are thus a peculiar breed, different in kind from the figures who constitute the Politburo. The rulers in the Kremlin are not publicity conscious speechifiers – they are an administrative group, the heads of the actual Departments of State. In Western Europe their equivalents are the shadowy figures in the civil service, who carry out but (supposedly) do not make policy.

Instead, policy creation is the responsibility of figures who 'run' (or in Britain 'stand') for office. Western politics ensure thereby an arms length, or two, of *distance* between public opinion and the functioning of the State. Disagreements between them are open, but most politicians are anyway quite powerless; their arguments often hot air, a smokescreen that hides the machinery of power from the scrutiny of the public.

The moment that some top politicians actually get their hands on real decision making, for example in Cabinet meetings, their proceedings become secret.

To put it another way, in the West politicians are the brokers between civil society and the State. They sanitize the pressures of civil society and protect state policy from its influence, functioning to weaken rather than strengthen the direct impact of public opinion, especially on security issues. At the same time politicians constantly measure that opinion, and if it looks as if it might become irresistible, they will insist upon changes in the regime. Finally, some politicians protect the rights of civil society from the agencies of the State. This is a rather crude description of their role, which may in exceptional circumstances be creative and far-sighted. But in today's mass democracies, the legal separation of powers has also become a pliable hierarchy of control.

So although it sounds easy to say that Plenary meetings of the Central Committee should be made public, it should be remembered that nowhere in the West do the chiefs of the defence staff, or the security forces, or the country's central bankers find themselves voting on the record. Like administrators everywhere, they are terrified of democratic scrutiny.

Thanks above all to Lenin, the Soviet Union does not have western style politicians. This reduces the flexibility of its leadership, but in the long run could provide an opportunity for the society. Politicians, for all their blatant faults, are preferable to administrators. Especially those who keep a tight hand. Ask anyone who has lived under a military regime. Even when disagreements do occur they remain sealed off and unresolved: a closed system leads to stalemate and immobilism. But a system that is both administrative and democratic would be something new. The USSR faces the dreadful possibility of becoming more democratic (if not more free) than Britain and France, perhaps even than America. Should the Party-Establishment ever manage to conduct its proceedings in public, its debates and their outcome will naturally be deflected by public opinion. Then, the absence of western-style parties might bring citizens closer to those who are taking the actual decisions and could give people greater influence over their own lives, than in the major countries of the West. This is one reason why, for all their sympathetic interest in Gorbachev's reforms, many in the chancelleries of capitalism hope that the Kremlin will fail to shake off its despotism.

They may not have long to wait. Gorbachev faces two sorts of problem. There is an intrinsic contradiction in his approach: not only does the system which demands reform resist it; he must use that very system to carry through his programme. The Party seeks to strengthen the economy. To do so it has to diminish its own role; to succeed, Gorbachev must both renew the Party and reduce its influence. If a genuine civil society is a precondition for the renewal of the USSR, a drastic programme of slimming must be approved by a majority of Party members themselves.

This would be difficult enough in the best of circumstances. It has to be carried through against considerable opposition. An opposition which is complex and ubiquitous, outside as well as within the Party ranks.

It is also hidden, in part deliberately, in part because it has yet to come alive. Strikes, boycotts and other protests are likely and natural. How they might be exploited can hardly be predicted. So although I am very interested in the opposition to glasnost and perestroika, the discussion of it that follows must necessarily be fragmentary, impressionistic and speculative.

THREE ADVANTAGES

'When she was here, I said to your Margaret Thatcher, "Have you seen the second film in *Star Wars?*" She just nodded, but that is where we are at: *The Empire Strikes Back*. For the first time in my life I'm involved in a real fight. And believe me, they know how to fight.'

I took notes as he continued:

'They have three advantages. We are for abstract things such as more openness and democracy, whereas they are fighting for concrete things, I mean their privileges.

'Second, like Brezhnev used to, they speak of "We Soviet Communists", or "We Russian people", always in the plural. We have fought against the cult of the personality and its crimes. But at the same time, we are real people with real personalities. Gorbachev uses "I" and talks about his opinion. But the plural language appeals to the bottom, like Le Pen's in France. Brezhnev was popular. He stole our country, but people recognized themselves in him. They too would like to have lots of medals and ribbons, diamonds and cars, just like him. Whereas Gorbachev is even against drink. They come home and want their half litre of vodka and say, "I'm a real Russian man, all my life I've had drink". Gorbachev is incomprehensible to them.

'The third thing is that they are afraid of change. If you

speak with people, everyone is unhappy and fed up. But if we say, OK let's get rid of the old way and build afresh, they say, "Good or bad, but we live". They all have their little hole in the wall and their little tube of oxygen.'

A MAGIC PASSPORT

The importance of privileged access to good quality food, clothes and vacations cannot be overestimated in the conduct of the mass of older Party officials. The key reason they and the bureaucrats cling to their jobs like medals pinned to a veteran (which allows him to jump to the head of the line when shopping) is that they may lose access to the perks of their ministry, enterprise or establishment, when they retire. Such perks are more valuable then roubles.

At the same time it seems to the ordinary Soviet that the people who are helping themselves to the decent things in life are the very same people stopping everyone else from earning good money and obtaining those same things. Yet the Party has no retirement age whatever. The vanguard suffers literally from arteriosclerosis. Above all it desires warm holidays and no need to stand in line.

Why not, Nikolai said with a sudden laugh, over some rare vodka, close the special shops and cancel the privileges to all Party members and *nomenklatura* unless they have retired. Let them jump without pain. If they want to involve themselves with perestroika, well and good, but they must set an example and join everyone else in the struggle for goods. If not – and who can blame them for keeping the pattern of a lifetime? – they can keep that to which they are accustomed. Should the relationship between retirement and access to the special distribution of supplies be reversed, the number of the privileged won't rise. And by making it hurt more to stay at your post than leave, members of the old guard could be bought off. Indeed, this would probably cost the economy less in the long run than the damage they do by staying at their posts.

I know, however, that in the sober light of day, he would rile at the possibility of what he regards as the semi-competents being rewarded. He wants them *punished*. But the delightful, if momentary speculation, led on to the story of his relative.

One day, in circumstances that Nikolai declined to describe in detail but which he insisted were not improper, his cousin noticed that a stranger had dropped his passport. It was a red passport, full size and not the little card-sized wallet for Party membership. On the front it stated it was issued by the Central Committee. The cousin had been wanting to buy some foodstuffs for his mother who was in hospital. He kept the passport. Then he went to a large food store, showed it and asked to see the manager. He flashed the passport at the manager, who immediately sold him some excellent supplies that were not available for the public. No one dared check the photograph in the passport! Later, he was stopped by the police when driving and drunk – a very serious crime in the USSR even before the clamp-down on vodka. He showed the officer his new passport, and drove away. A close friend wanted very much to go on holiday to the Ukraine, but could not get a train. Nikolai's cousin lent him the magic passport, and he got a perfect seat without trouble. Never once had it been opened. How we laughed as the story progressed.

It is little wonder that everyone is against egalitarianism, at least until they are all issued with similarly wonderful passports.

The story says a lot about how those who govern the Soviet Union are cut off from its conditions. There is a revealing passage in Gorbachev's book *Perestroika*, concerning his walk-about, in the summer of 1986, when he talked with people in Krasnodar:

> What a substantive conversation it was, what problems people raised! I was really pleased to see them so zealously supporting the Central Committee line. And then I realized how bitter the people are . . .

In my experience, it is impossible to go to the Soviet Union for even a week without hearing how bitter people are. That a senior Party member with exceptional perspicacity has to become General Secretary in order to be able to break through the barrier of officialdom to realize this, is an astounding confirmation of the effectiveness of the elite cocoon.

The story of the magic passport brought home to me the massive human scale of the resistance. Hundreds of thousands of officials want to keep their jobs, in municipalities, in agro-industrial centres, as Party full-timers, as people who check up on those who check up. Quite understandably, they do not want perestroika for themselves.

At one stormy meeting, Sergei told me, he pressed for perestroika in his work place. He was asked to the Party cell to explain himself. 'Gorbachev has called it a revolution,' he told the comrades, 'and every revolution is met by a counter-revolution.' An older member agreed, and stated bluntly, 'I am a counter-revolutionary.'

In May 1987 Anatoli Strelyanyi, an editor of *Novi Mir*, had a hair-raising discussion with the Komsomol *aktiv* at the Moscow State University. Strelyanyi declared dramatically,

'There are already two parties in the Party.' And he argued for the rapid acceleration of reform:

> The revolutionary nature of perestroika resides in the fact that the people should have freedom . . . The opponents of perestroika . . . have a remarkable feel for developments . . . Administrators and bureaucrats are against a free press and for preliminary censorship. They are afraid of freedom, and they have us by the throat . . .

He concluded on an even more apocalyptic note, with an image that was doing the rounds in Moscow the following month: 'You can't cross an abyss in two steps. We are standing before an abyss.' Such declarations may belong to a national tradition of impatience that has caused as many problems in Russian history as sloth and conservatism: the best way to cross an abyss is to build a bridge . . . At one point Strelyani was asked, 'What is the social base for perestroika?' – the Marxist way of saying, 'Who is for it?' He replied:

> Gorbachev is being slow about expanding the social base for perestroika, and this will lead to the defeat of our cause and of Gorbachev himself. It is necessary to take sides openly, from the top to the bottom. The social base of perestroika consists of: highly qualified workers, parts of the scientific-technological intelligentsia; parts of the creative humanitarian intelligentsia; and parts of the lower-level Party apparatus and economic managers.[75]

Weak though the sum of such forces may be, the reformers have momentum on their side, and if they can can keep the conservatives off balance, the latter, without a political rallying cry, may find it hard to accumulate their numerically stronger support.

Why are the conservative forces so strong? If their weakness is that Brezhnevism was a failure – economically, ideologically, socially, scientifically and politically – their strength is that the Brezhnevites themselves did very well, thank you. They may have allowed their opponents to survive, but for their part they did a great deal better and multiplied. There was considerable artificial and some real growth through Brezhnev's two decades, and its administrators took the lion's share. There is thus an enormous vested interest in the recent past and the monolithic way of doing things.

Tatyana Zaslavskaya, the economist who drafted an early assessment of the crisis on the Soviet economy, does not think that the reforms could go any faster:

> The old saying, 'measure seven times before you cut' is more than applicable to a large country. We need a certain period of preparation, and you can't cut that short for the sake of adventurism.

But she regards the new legislation as inadequate, even compromised, because the new laws

> are prepared at a lower level in the central bureaucracies. Their influence can cause deradicalization of the reforms, I mean the State Planning Committee, the State Committee on Prices, the State Committee on Labour, the State Committee for Science and Technology, the Ministry of Finance, the State Bank and the big industrial ministries. The biggest problem is that the professional knowledge is all in the hands of people who occupy these posts. They don't take an open position against perestroika. They say they are doing their best. (She laughs)[76]

BIRDS OF A FEATHER

Overall, the reform programme is a powerful package. Economically, it demands self-financing of enterprises, use of market forces, and dismantling of the command economy. Legally, it seeks to establish greater rights and safeguards for citizens. Politically, it is pushing openness in the media and democracy in elections. Internationally, it aims to shift Soviet strategy to sufficient deterrence – and disarmament – alongside an important accord with China. Morally, it is an attempt to make the Soviet Union an honest place. Psychologically, it wishes to stimulate initiative. Scientifically, it is supposed to encourage freedom for research. Domestically, it is committed to more housing and better health. Agriculturally, without which nothing else will stabilize, it aims to allow those who farm the land to take command of it so that it may yield the surplus that should easily be forthcoming.

Such a sweeping assault is bound to create fierce resistance. Yet while the sheer breadth of the reforms extends opposition, it may make them harder to oppose. The more strongly Gorbachev unifies his programme and also makes different parts inviting to different groups, the less likely they may be to combine against him. Gorbachev's and Schevadnardze's diplomatic success strengthens their political position internally. To remove them now that the INF treaty is signed risks alienating the world community – not just the newspaper readers of Moscow. The *obkom* First Secretaries, the key regional bosses who make up a significant section in the Central Committee, are said to dislike glasnost. They do not want their affairs looked into or publicized. But they are enthusiastic about the economic measures that decentralize decision making and weaken the power of the Moscow ministries over their zones. This distinction points to the crucial question: since all want economic change, but the more conservative wish to back-pedal on political change, can these two aspects be separated?

There are at least three wings to the opposition, each belongs to a different species even if all are hostile to 'western' freedoms. There are the pterodactyls, the corrupt dealers in office and supplies, as old as ages past; there are the ostriches of orthodoxy, with their lovely feathers and their inability to fly; and there are the ominous great skuas of Russian nationalism.

The first group has been routed since the last years of Brezhnev. The *'nomenklatura* revolution' instigated and invigilated by Andropov after he replaced Brezhnev laid the basis for Gorbachev's victory over Grishin. The backing of the KGB (itself transformed by Andropov) was essential to the initial cleansing of the Soviet *apparat*. The old corruption seems broken. The real resistance to change will come from the other wings.

The 'Suslovites', for want of a better word, the ostriches of orthodoxy, are relatively clean and believe in the righteousness of the Party. They present the clearest immediate challenge. They hold leading positions within the Party and the military. Their bureaucratic mentality appeals to *nomenklatura* who want a quiet life with a bit of travel, and to the lower bureaucracies and suspicious provincials. They take comfort in passive reluctance to get the reforms to work. Their credo appeals to those who dislike risks.

This tendency within the Party faces two problems. Its leaders are not blind to the need for change in the economy; they too desire much higher levels of efficiency and a faster rate of development. Their model is East Germany – a centralized, orthodox socialism that works. (Well, it works much better than the USSR, but perhaps that is because the Soviets are not Germans.) They desire deep perestroika but a very shallow glasnost. So they cannot oppose all the changes in an outright fashion. The orthodox tendency could certainly win power, especially if the KGB supports it actively (I'll come to the KGB). But the second problem faced by those who want to slow down democratization while intensifying economic reform, is that they have to move soon, although their perspective is still incoherent. For a process is underway that becomes more difficult to reverse by the season.

For example, I asked an English colleague about a Soviet official with whom she had negotiated. She dismissed what I thought was his rather creative and imaginative style. 'He told me that it took him a year to understand that Gorbachev wanted him to think for himself,' she laughed. 'He is completely a man of the apparatus, if they tell him to stop thinking for himself, he will.' I doubt this. It will be true of some, but not all. Ian McEwan, the English writer, has argued that glasnost is a 'permission'. Not only is it easier to grant a permission than withdraw it, it becomes steadily harder to withdraw it over time. As people succeed in the effort of thinking for themselves, they will become increasingly reluctant to relinquish such a gain. The longer people 'learn' democracy, the harder it is to stop them from keeping it. It is far from impossible, mind. It is just that the more you wait, the greater the force needed to reverse such a change.

So the time for the old guard to defeat Gorbachev is now. This year or next, at any rate before 1990. Now is the time when he may still be overthrown by those older than himself, the 'honest monoliths'. At present they are bending to the assault of the new men that Gorbachev leads. Are they bending all the better to recuperate and lash back, like a strong reed that is rooted in its place; or are they finally being bent out of the way?

One key figure in their struggle is Yegor Ligachev, generally held to be the leading 'hard-liner'. Born in 1920 – he is just over ten years older than Gorbachev – he spent eighteen years in Tomsk, Siberia, after he fell foul of Brezhnev, and was brought back to Moscow by Andropov. He is

> known to be uncompromising, with a strong character and unfaltering convictions, and not reluctant to express his views ... He tried, for example, to expel some Moscow *raikom* secretaries who were linked to corruption cases ... without getting Grishin's permission.[77]

In his recent statement, *Activating the Human factor – the Main Source of Acceleration*, Ligachev signals his low-key attitude towards glasnost:

> Some people understand openness in a lop-sided way, as the exposure of shortcomings and their eradication. Openness is also popularization and affirmation of what is advanced and progressive.[78]

And he went on to insist that openness must 'encourage the

sprouts of the new', but without any stress on the need for open argument. By contrast, this is something advocated with respect to science by Ligachev's politburo colleague, Alexander Yakovlev, who argues:

> We cannot endure an official monopoly of the truth – a situation in which the last word in the work of thought belongs not to truth but to the office . . . Science can develop only in the process of constructive discussions and clashes of opinions . . . it should be realized that no one has a monopoly of the truth, either in formulating new questions or in providing answers to them.[79]

Ligachev too stresses the need for individuals to become aware of themselves as an 'active personality'. But he takes a relatively uncritical approach towards Stalin's economic strategy. When emphasizing the need 'to activate the human factor' he criticizes as inadequate for today the 'kind of technological determinism, which was *quite justifiable* when the country was building the material and technical foundations . . .' (my emphasis).[80]

In these muted debates a central issue is encoded in 'the role of the individual'. Although he discusses agriculture at length, Ligachev declines to mention the high productivity of private plots. Early in 1987 he asserted that 'individualism' is among 'phenomena alien to socialism',[81] an attitude that has its roots in more virulent times (the word 'alien' being another alarm signal). The following, for example, was the sort of thing published in the *Literaturnaya Gazeta* back in the 1950s:

> The socialist revolution has eliminated the question of freedom for creative work . . . What sort of reasons can

anybody have in our socialist conditions to pine for 'freedom of creativity'? . . . The reason can only be sought in philistine individualism, a mortal sickness distinguishable from the plague perhaps only in that outbreaks still occur. Anybody who feels himself restricted by his part in the common cause should look deep within his own heart: he will probably find a wretched individualist lurking there.[82]

In July 1987, by way of contrast, *Izvestia* quoted Lenin's view that, 'One should not see an intrigue in those who think differently, but value individuals who think and act for themselves.[83]

In public all Soviet leaders smile upon the dignity of the individual, and frown only upon the 'ism'. One need not be obsessed by Kremlinology to grasp that an absolutely fundamental disagreement is registered in the superficially reconcilable shades of emphasis; a basic antagonism that must be won or lost, on which there cannot be a compromise in the long run. Either socialists have their right to argue different points of view in public or they do not. I say socialists to get round the problem (for the moment!) of the question of the expression of 'anti-socialist' views.

It may be true that there is little experience of granting legitimacy to the existence of perspectives opposed to one's own. Dmitri Likhachev, the eminent Soviet philologist, interviewed in a recent *Literaturnaya Gazeta*, argued:

I believe that glasnost is a poor substitute for democracy. When we enjoy all the fruits of democracy we will not want to replace a free exchange of opinions by settling accounts and exposing one another ... we must learn democracy, learn to be more considerate of listening to dissenting opinions. We must learn to listen to both sides with equal impartiality.[84]

But what if the other side does not agree that there should even *be* an equal exchange of views? Before you can argue about Stalin, say, you need to agree that disagreement about such a central matter is legitimate. Some feel that there can only be one correct view, the Party must draw this up in private and then publish its conclusions so that everyone knows what to think, or at least what they have to say. Others accept that radically different analyses and assessments of the Stalin period can co-exist in the open among Party members and let the best argument win – not by command but thanks to its quality.

There is therefore a clear, fundamental point of disagreement in principle between the logic of reform and orthodox resistance to it. It concerns the nature of Soviet politics itself. Either debate on major topics should be free or conclusions should be pre-ordained. For glasnost to retain its credibility over the next few years, politically it needs to move towards a situation in which people exercise a legal right to say what they wish to say, and scientifically, in terms of research and publication, it must do so.

Such a development will challenge at least two Soviet generations – and one-quarter of the million-strong Moscow Region Communist Party is over sixty. Either the orthodox break the political momentum gathering behind the reforms or they will be obliged to retire in favour of those who insist that an open exchange of views is essential to progress. Totally different attitudes lie behind these positions. As life throws up contention after contention, one view or the other will prevail. One of the problems about writing a book like this at such a time is that even as it moves towards publication the two sides of this historic conflict are gathering their forces.

RUSSIAN
FUNDAMENTALISM

Even if Gorbachev is assassinated, as many fear, the system is unlikely to default back to a mild despotism for very long. It did this once when Chernenko, barely able to sustain a speech, was made General Secretary after Andropov's brief tenure. The ostriches of orthodoxy were content with a mildly belligerent military posture and domestic oppression, but nothing too drastic. The stability of such a regime masked its growing incredibility. To return to it would be to say goodbye to most Soviet science. And the young?

The danger is just as likely to come from the third wing of the opposition, the arctic skuas of the black side of Russia. Suppose the reformers continue for some years but then fall into difficulties, perhaps because of further economic dislocations; chaos in the Ukraine; aggression from the West; a reactor blow-out in Czechoslovakia, followed by uprisings in Eastern Europe; disaster in Afghanistan – you can make up your own blood-curdling agenda. If the reforms falter after seven or eight years, then a new opposition could get underway, utilizing the conditions of greater freedom and partial democracy to gather force. It had already begun to do so under Brezhnev when in every possible case non-political means were used to silence awkward problems or opponents. Towards the end few bothered even with the façade. Behind it, within the Party, the more intelligent and internationally aware swung towards reform. In the country, kept in ignorance, people fell back on traditional values and prejudices.

In their assault on this legacy the new men in the Kremlin seek to repoliticize their society, and to do so systematically and institutionally. This is their strength. To displace them in the 1990s may require a similar kind of strength – an equal ideological coherence.

A down-the-line anti-Gorbachev programme of the future will be one that is explicitly anti-western, trenchantly anti-democratic, cogently opposed to individualism and consumerism. The more Gorbachev moves the USSR towards democracy, the more ferocious and despotic will be the political line of those who aim to crush democracy.

Such an ideology already exists in the USSR. It is traditional, anti-semitic, pan-slavic nationalism – or Russian fundamentalism. Some already see Solzhenitsyn as the Russian Ayatollah, in exile in America, just as Khomeni waited for years in Iraq before he was eventually called to lead Iran against the pagan-bourgeois world.

Another Russian exaggeration, of course. Yet there are more than traces of evidence to justify such concern. *Pamyat* (which means memory) is one of the more coherent of the new groups testing the water of glasnost in Moscow today, and it propagates a resentful right-wing Russian traditionalism. Memory is certainly called for: the land of the *Protocols of Zion* later authored the Stalin Constitution, fabrications of a different kind but both born of autocracy.

To take another example: Natan Eidelman wrote a private letter of concern to Viktor Astafiev, author of *The Sad Detective*,

213

and got back a blast of vicious invective, which has now circulated in samizdat. Some extracts:

Dear Natan Yakovlevich!
You cannot imagine what delight your letter gave me . . . Every national renaissance, and even more so the Russian, has its opponents and enemies . . . and to your bitter letter, not simply overflowing with malevolence but boiling over with the pus of Jewish high-intellectual arrogance (your usual 'poking fun'), I'll not answer with ill-will . . . As you see, we Russians have not yet lost our memory and we are still a *Great People*. Killing us amounts to but little. And we have yet to be overthrown. I send you my greetings. And may Most-Gracious God enlighten your soul![85]

This seems to be one little peak in a range of prejudice. Alexander Yanov, writing in the West, has already insisted on the strength of what he terms 'The Imperial Russian Idea'.[86] Panslavism, in his view, lurks not only outside, but is also a strong current within the Party, that dates back to the appeal for patriotic unity during the Second World War.

Belligerence feeds those who desire orthodoxy in any country. Could this be especially true of the USSR, as it seeks to keep together its huge extent, and its dozens of internal nations? Gorbachev and the reformers show signs of underestimating indigenous nationalism, both Russian and non-Russian. As modernizers they see such phenomena as a product of backwardness, which will dissolve with the successful implantation of economic growth and democracy. In fact, the traditionalism of figures like Khomeni, to take an extreme example, is misleading. He is an intensely contemporary figure: the first Ayatollah to blast apart an oil terminal with a Red Chinese missile (that was guided by American technology). Nationalism, even chauvinism, is not the opposite of development but its accomplice.

STRIKE?

It was not called a strike. But all the buses stopped at Chekhov, and few could get to work. 'Black Monday', the head of the bus depot called it, in September 1987. A wonderful irony that the first decent report on a Soviet work stoppage should come from Chekhov, a small city 70 km from Moscow, where the playwright once stayed. Perhaps one day they will build a suitably small memorial there, to the problems of perestroika.

The Chekhov strike – er, sorry, I mean incident – was a tiny revelation of the volcanic pressures likely to be released by reform. Far more important than black reaction, at the moment, is sheer economic frustration. As has often happened in the past, those who introduce change release anger, anger accumulated by the bad old previous way of doing things. Thus the new is punished by the pent-up fury of the old. Through such revenge the past may ensure that it is not overcome, as leaders panic and reform is reversed.

Moscow News (20 September 1987) carried a report by Yuri Teplyakov on 'The Chekhov Incident'. Here are some of the players, speaking for themselves:

VYACHESLAV ARKHIPOV (Head of City Transport): It is outrageous. What happens if tomorrow the doctors of the maternity hospital do not come to work? Or something else like this happens? . . . Now everything is back to normal. But I don't understand one thing. The drivers are guilty but their chief was punished instead of them.

VICTOR TROFIMOV (Chief of the Bus depot): I came to the garage and saw people standing there, buses in place. Silence reigned. I asked what was the matter, why weren't they on their way? They held out the calculation sheets . . . Someone shouted, 'What are you knocking our heads together for?' I understood everything immediately.

We had just introduced a new system of remuneration. Team contract plus collective responsibility . . . The bonus fund is now a common one . . . Everything is done, so to say, in the spirit of perestroika. The day before the incident the collective agreement was discussed. Not a single question was asked . . . I'll be frank, many of them lost in real earnings but the administration has nothing to do with it. They must work better, must not live as they did in the past but be in step with the times.

NIKOLAI KOMKOV (Team leader, worked in garage for eighteen years): There is nothing new in teaching a person to behave graciously. But how can you work with poor equipment? In order to earn well under the existing labour remuneration one must fulfil ideally all operating schedules, all points. Ideally! How can they be fulfilled when most of our buses are like tanks after battle? Their average age is that of my grandmother. Now one part goes wrong, now another. Suppose a young man gets work at the garage. He is given an old bus and has a hard time with it. He spends one hour on the route and one day repairing the bus. What will his earnings be, if some amount is not taken from another and given to him? But what is the fault of the other? No violations, no late arrivals, but he gets less. Once again we have legal wage levelling. Now, it seems as if it is from below. The administration seems to stand aloof. It is very convenient for them: it is not their worry if someone comes and complains of low earnings and demands a normal bus. Colleagues will not let him die of hunger, we will share. And we do share, it is our moral obligation.

Nobody in our garage asks how you live and get along in such conditions. A driver leaves the house early in the morning, drinks a quick glass of tea; on the route there is no suitable place to have dinner, in cafés prices are exorbitant. At the terminal there is nowhere to have a rest. But the main problem is the apartment. It is impossible to get one from the garage, even theoretically. I think that the dispute was probably not about money. This was just what triggered it.

VIKTOR VORONIN (City vice-chair in charge of transport): Three days ago such a thing could be regarded as sabotage. There was talk in the street: people have been demoralized with this democracy. But this is what is lacking. In his heart Trofimov does not consider himself guilty, he did everything according to the instructions . . . he was told to introduce a team contract with collective responsibility. But he did not take into account that the bus garage is a specific enterprise . . . the buses are different and, therefore, working conditions are unequal . . . It is not a shop of a machine building plant where everyone works side by side.

It seems to me that we must not make everyone fit into the same pattern even if that pattern looks good. Or rather it can't be done right away. I understand that the time calls for acceleration. But acceleration must not be mixed with haste and fuss . . . and we must not idealize people particularly as apathy about change has been inculcated in us for decades.

NIKOLAI SOLYANKIN (driver, worked in garage for seventeen

years): No, it is not the usual thing in our garage to take account of the opinions of ordinary people. Therefore, at meetings workers usually keep silent. What's the good of talking? When the new remuneration system was being discussed there were no questions. But as we see, there *were* questions. If anyone had talked to people heart-to-heart in advance, everything would have been all right. This is what actually happened when the chiefs from Moscow descended out of the blue . . . Now a council of work collectives has been set up . . . Promises were given to organize conditions for rest on the routes. Maybe our hopeless housing problem too will finally get moving.

VIKTOR TROFIMOV: Of course, that day taught me a tough lesson. It was a black Monday, indeed. For quite a long time we grappled with the new system. It looks as if we did not violate anything but now there is no making head or tail of it. The people's reaction to it proved to be quite unexpected for us. Really, every person is a problem . . .

A SAD TALE

'Every person is a problem.' A sociologist in Moscow told me a story about his life which was perhaps the saddest of the tales that I heard about the last few years in the Soviet Union.

He and his colleagues had many discussions about what people really thought. So at the end of the seventies he decided to conduct his own poll. Over three summers and at every other moment that he had a break, he went hiking and camping across the country, to get a wide geographical spread for his sample. He never told anyone what he was doing, of course, both because he feared it might change their answers and in case it would be reported. Instead, he fell into conversations with people on trains or in hostels, in circumstances where they talked in a relaxed way, as so many Soviets will do if you give them the chance to complain. In this way he accumulated a sample of nearly eighty in-depth interviews.

Out of the eighty, only two people were relatively content with their lot, and felt that they were well off. All the others had many complaints about their superiors, their conditions, their bosses, corruption, the local Party secretaries, and so forth. The two who did not have any complaints, he told me with a thin smile, were both part of the black economy. One (male) was an underground businessman and the other (female) worked in a hotel where foreigners stayed.

He considered something else his most important finding: no one was happy yet everyone thought the system was the best.

Although they were overwhelmingly critical of their own conditions and situation, all – and he emphasized 'all' – thought that the Soviet system itself was a good one, and that their problems were exceptional. Deeply critical of their own fate, they have suffered for the system and do not wish to lose faith in it, he argued.

His conclusion was that many people would not believe the critical assessments that glasnost has made available, they will not accept the General Secretary's overall criticism. Another possibility, is that finally they will generalize from their own conditions to society as a whole, and then turn against it harshly. Just at the moment when, after seventy years, there really is the prospect of a socialism worth believing in the USSR, the population may finally stop believing in their government altogether.

The tale took another twist when I asked what he had done with all his years of private research.

'Last month a very close colleague who knew about it suggested that these days it might be published in *Novy Mir*. So I tried to find the manuscript and the material. But I had hidden it too well. In my concern to ensure that the KGB never got it, I am now no longer sure where it is myself.'

But the KGB knows. Not about this little investigation, perhaps, but it conducts its own. It knows the general conditions, what people think of them, and how explosive the reforms could be. It is its task to contain the reaction and to police the dangerous transition.

WHO ARRESTS WHOM?

Power is two-sided. It allows you to do things, and to stop things from being done. Negative power sets the limits to positive power. Ultimately therefore, power depends on the question of who can arrest whom.

The KGB is respected and it is up to date. It has played a crucial role in the changes so far; without it Gorbachev would never have got where he is today. So will the KGB support democracy?

The Soviet Union is huge, its police force even more so. Just as the USSR seems more centralized than it actually is, so there are a baffling number of different sorts of ordinary and special police, regional and national. We think of the KGB as spies and agents – as the CIA rather than the FBI. It is both, a complex not a simple organization, with different branches, foreign and domestic, gathering political, economic and scientific intelligence as well as military, alongside its actual police and surveillance work.

We were walking through central Moscow. I asked him – he was a young man in his twenties – why there was change.

The whole state was rotten, it was even hard for the KGB when you have to investigate Brezhnev's daughter *as well* as dissidents and spies and ordinary criminals. Really, it was quite tough for them.

I took the opportunity to ask him what he thought about the KGB.

They want Andropov's programme, discipline, order, honesty, they want to clean up the state. Glasnost makes life more complicated for them and means that they have to be more subtle. But the KGB is definitely more advanced than other institutions. It has more prestige than the Army which is corrupt and has a big drinking problem, or the Ministry of Finance or of Culture – the KGB are more realistic, smarter and more effective.

I witnessed the police in action for myself, in the early hours of one morning. I was with a British correspondent, who had taken me to a party – we drove out in his Saab – where we listened to a young singer, said to be a second Vysotsky or 'the singing Dostoyesvky'. He reminded me of Jim Morrison of the Doors.

Afterwards, we crowded into the lift to descend the seven storeys to the ground (it only takes three people in one of the lifts of a modern Moscow apartment block to make it crowded). We went up to the Saab. It was one o'clock in the morning, a dark night, stars in the sky, some curtained room lights from the high-rise. Only an occasional street-lamp could be glimpsed through the overgrown area between the blocks. It was some way from the road. I was just about to put my hand on the handle of the front passenger door when I realized that the window was shattered. At the same moment, from his side of the car, the owner saw the glass across the seats. Soviet vandalism!

We noticed a torch. Two ordinary policemen approached us. They came up, said they had seen a damaged foreign car and had summoned help.

I could only follow one part of the discussion between the

owner and these ordinary police. They asked if the car was locked. He told them that by turning the key in the driver's door, all the doors locked and he demonstrated the gimmick. With a twist of his wrist all four doors locked with a satisfying multiple clunk that carried through the night.

'Ahhh, tekhnologiya,' whispered one of the policemen to himself.

A jeep drove up, with two armed police in darker uniforms in the front. *Four* plain-clothes men appeared from the back, and after a while the jeep drove off.

I was very grateful to the hooligan who, it turned out, had catapulted a small steel ball through the window and stolen a packet of cigarettes from the glove box. Thanks to him I saw the four KGBers.

One was about thirty, dark complexion, medium height and with a black beard. He had very sharp eyes, memorized our faces, wore jeans. As the taking of details proceeded, those still left at the party had come down. The host asked me if I had any cigarettes to give the police. I'd none. Then the singing Dostoyevsky, with his long hair, single ear-ring, and reeking of drink, asked the dark KGBer with the beard if *he* had a cigarette, and took one off him. Our plain-clothed friend of the night was not in the slightest fazed.

The second plain-clothes man was a bit older, had a light raincoat and carried a plastic *avoska* or shopping bag. He appeared so ordinary, that even when you looked straight at him, it was hard to notice any distinguishing characteristics.

The third, the youngest, was also the tallest. Very tall, not someone you would like to get into a fight with. He carried a radio and kept out of the way.

The fourth, the oldest, probably in his mid-thirties, was

small, had receding hair and was the chief. He wore a short leather jacket and asked most of the questions. At one point, he turned, and as his jacket shifted I caught sight of a holster.

A single headlight appeared at the end of the dark avenue and approached at speed. It seemed odd. I was suddenly reminded of Hanoi, where trucks drive on one headlight only. But it was a motorbike with sidecar that came to a halt. As if in a strange modernist drama, there was a policeman sitting side-saddle across the sidecar, inside which there sat a crumpled drunk. The motor-bike police had a word with the chief, and then the ensemble drove off into the darkness – the drunk groaning.

The police-work was completed, details taken; it took forty-five minutes. Apparently the chief pointed out that if you do leave expensive foreign cars in the middle of a housing estate then these things can happen. The owner protested, I was impressed by his command of Russian. We all brushed the glass off the seats. The four plain-clothes men wandered away, glancing casually at the other cars, looking like four youngish men out rather late.

When I related this story on my return, people in London said, 'If only we had such service when our cars get vandalized.' But their cars do not have the equivalent of a diplomatic number plate (vehicles numbers in the USSR are issued by occupation; every foreign correspondent's car starts with the letter K.). All the same, I was impressed. What their exact status was, I never ascertained. But they were not caricature cops with fat faces and piggy eyes. They didn't have the aura of men who were badly paid, or ignorant; instead they appeared well trained and modern. Above all, it seemed to me, they could have melted into a crowd if there was 'trouble', where they could spot a 'ringleader' and chat up the locals. If the first task of good policing is to be informed, and to have a feel for realities on the ground, then my midnight observation of the four led me to think that they and their organization would pass.

What their organization makes of the information it gathers is not for me to say. The KGB is not Stalinist in the extreme sense. On the contrary, Andropov, who was a quarter Jewish and was apparently close to being arrested himself in the late 1940s,[87] has ensured that the obvious first lesson of terror is inculcated into the senior ranks. Namely, that the executioners get executed. Those who implement terror usually become its victims. At least three leaders of the KGB were shot.

In *Tass is Authorized to Announce*, an semi-official KGB thriller that became a Soviet best-seller and TV mini-series, the neighbour of the key suspect whom the KGB think might be a double-agent is approached for his co-operation. He is reluctant. 'It's a relapse of the sickness of '37, Comrade General. That way you can haul anyone in as a spy.'[88]

As a good police force the KGB is against terror, but does it still favour ordinary Stalinism? Does it have the subtlety needed to handle glasnost and democracy? A recent speech by Chebrikov, its chief, in which he said:

We have among us, and here one must speak plainly, people with alien ideas who are even openly hostile to socialism

does not inspire complete confidence. The churches are full of people with non-socialist ideas. Perhaps he had *Pamyat* in mind. Perhaps he is in favour of limits on anti-semitic reaction, so as all the better to allow freedom to flourish within the law. Or perhaps not. Given the cruel history, in which millions have suffered as well as benefited in the name of Soviet socialism, the victims too have a right to speak plainly.

This touches on a crucial aspect of reform in the Soviet Union. The law. It is necessary to rectify the hitherto abysmal lack of practical legislation. There is a standard joke about this – I was told it three times. A man goes to his lawyer and asks, 'Do I have the right to . . .' His lawyer interrupts him: 'Yes.' The man starts again, 'Look, I have a problem and I want to know if I have the right to . . .' Before he can finish the lawyer says 'Yes, yes, you *have* the right.' The man gets angry, 'But can I say to you what it is?' 'No,' says the lawyer.

'You see,' said the second person who told it to me, to make sure I got the point, 'with us everything is legal but nothing is permitted.'

The issue has now entered more serious forms of circulation. In April 1987 there was a discussion about the new economic legislation concerning individual enterprise on the TV programme *Dialog*. One of the commentators said, 'If the law did not prohibit a particular activity, then it was OK.' Others disagreed, and said that positive approval was always necessary for any new venture.[89]   A cardinal principle is involved. In August 1987 in Moscow, there was a meeting of forty-seven unofficial clubs.[90] Afterwards, some of the participants discussed the experience with Gennady Zhavoronkov of *Moscow News*. Pavlovsky from The Club for Social Initiatives said, 'There is a very good democratic rule – whatever is not banned is permitted.'[91] Alexander Yakovlev, the influential Politburo member, also addressed the need for law in his 1987 pamphlet:

So far the Law of Individual Labour Activity seems to be the only operating law dominated by the whatever-is-not-banned-is-permitted principle. But, as before, it is widely assumed that anything which is not referred to in the law is forbidden.[92]

Gorbachev addressed this issue directly in his book. So much so, in fact, that the passage on page 108 may prove to be historic:

Experience has demonstrated that what we need is not a total legislative regulation of diversified phenomena of social life, but sound rationality, and constant fostering of and support for the worker, workforce and all forms of popular initiative. Let's strictly observe the principle: everything which is not prohibited by law is allowed.

There may be a long way to go, to strict observance of this principle, but its forthright avowal marks a qualitative step away from dictatorship. In terms of the well-known distinction, the Soviet Union has long boasted of the way it provides its people with freedom from hunger, unemployment, illiteracy etc; now it may also provide them with the freedom to do things of their own accord.

The immediate issues, however, are not legal rights or philosophical distinctions. Most Soviets, tired of speeches, are concerned with what's in the *avoska*. As one woman said to me, 'Yes, yes, people are talking now, that's true, but life doesn't change.'

PRICES

Life will change, however, as prices start to rise. This is a dramatic danger point. In his Murmansk speech in September 1987, Gorbachev compared the price of Soviet bread to that in other countries. It costs 5.5 times as much in the USA, 4.9 times as much in West Germany, and in part this is a measure of wasteful and massive subsidies in the USSR. Gorbachev said that the old system must go in such a way that it will 'not affect the living standards of the population'. But the population regards such assurances with suspicion. They want their cheap bread and they know foreigners earn much more. Few believe that wages will rise continuously to compensate for more expensive food. Their official money incomes are already a joke. The prospect of getting a little bit more is hardly inviting. The new incentives will need to be really significant, so that those who earn them can buy with ease on the free market. Otherwise, to take measures that make stealing harder, and then remove subsidies and raise state prices, is to risk people generalizing their complaints with a vengeance.

General price rises could thus provoke 'incidents' graver than Chekhov's. Incidents that will make it even harder for the KGB than the old corruption. Incidents which may go a lot further than talk. Incidents in which people act in ways that are definitely not permitted.

As they read the danger signs, especially in the provincial cities, where conditions are dire and ordinary commodities such as butter are rationed, the KGB might well be persuaded that order must come before change.

Prices and incomes brings to mind the jewellery shop in the Arbat.

The Arbat is part of the old quarter of Moscow, and in one of the streets that is still preserved there is a long pedestrian shopping mall, which has better quality shops. One sells rings, brooches and other jewellery. Young couples go there to see what they can afford. Naturally, I looked in. As you go along the counter the stones and their settings get more pricey. At the top, to my astonishment, there are diamond bracelets and necklaces for well over 10,000 roubles, in a country where (officially) a good salary is 300 a month.

I asked one of Nella's friends about the place. It is possible for individuals on special royalties to have huge sums, and nowadays you have to provide evidence that you have obtained such money legally. But in fact the shop advertises the successful existence of an alternative economy.

On one occasion it did so with a twist. A couple of young men came in who wanted to buy an expensive necklace for their sister, or so they said. They looked at the very best on offer and liked one for nearly 20,000 roubles. They asked to have it out and to see it in its beautiful box, and decided to buy it. So they went to the cashier to pay. Cheques have only just been introduced in Soviet Russia on an experimental basis. Then, they simply had to pay in cash, which they did. The cashier saw immediately that the notes were an obvious forgery. She pretended to accept the money but signalled to the assistant to call the police.

The police came almost at once, swiftly arrested the two men, took the forged currency and the necklace and congratulated the cashier for her vigilance. Then they bundled the villains and the incriminating evidence out of the shop.

About five minutes later the real police arrived.

EASTERN EUROPE

For him socialism is not serious. He has money, and a fine apartment in central Moscow. He regards it as ridiculous that he should pay a mere twenty roubles a month for rent and heat – 'For all this', said with a wave of his arm – the contemptuous beneficiary. It had lots of western technology. He rents a dacha, his wife has no need to work. He has the vitality of a free marketeer. If he could have his way he would dismantle all restrictions – with a slavic warmth, though, rather than a British or Germanic coldness. Now, he is trying to establish a co-operative to make use of his evident skills at dealing and marketing. Shrewd, determined and disbelieving, he, at least, could make perestroika work – and help the Soviet economy become more efficient. He enjoyed the irony.

I'd not expected to meet such a person. He is not a dissident, yet he loathes the system.

'If we don't change we are ruined. In the West you have the contrast of rich and poor neighbours. It causes problems. Now we will have them. Capitalism separates people from each other. I've seen it. It makes them struggle for prosperity. But all we have is a narrow, bureaucratic class that passes by in black cars. Your Churchill,' he added with delight, 'once said that capitalism was the most horrid form of society in the world, but he didn't know anything better'.

'America has the same disease as us. Imperialism. They suppose themselves to be better than the whole world, and that everyone should be like them. We have a saying: "Which is the bigger dwarf?" Of course, we think that we are bigger.'

Which led to Afghanistan: 'We should withdraw immediately.' And Eastern Europe: 'You know, most of it was always part of Russia.'

I realized that part of him was built out of the same brick as the Kremlin. Not least, because of the Second World War.

'Today, youngsters make jokes about the War. For example, there was a small child weeping at the grave of the unknown soldier. The people around were concerned. "Why are you weeping here when you are so young?" they asked, "Because my mother says that my father was an unknown soldier".' Simultaneously, he chuckled and shook his head with disapproval. 'I was here in Moscow as a boy. I saw the red fires on the horizon and heard the guns through the night. My brother died at the front. For me, it was not a joke and it is not one today.'

Russia, a victim? The Tartars, the Poles, the Swedes and the French etc. all got to Moscow. Well, the Romans conquered Britain. In my view it all belongs to another age. But the Nazis are part of living memory; they and their allies from Hungary and Romania. So far as the ordinary Russian is concerned, if the Poles get in the way of their control over Germany, then that's tough on the Poles – after all, the Poles would give the Russians no quarter if they had the chance.

Crude stuff, but it is the stuff in a lot of heads. In many ways my friend shares a view of the Kremlin common in the West. He regards Russian ambitions in the Third World as 'imperialist'. He would welcome the experimental introduction of capitalism in Hungary, or the agreed neutralization of central Europe. But he, who is by no means a supporter of the Soviet system, would never, for one second, support any move by the USSR to withdraw strategic control over Eastern Europe, if that risked a new Germany that might once again pose a threat to his land and his city.

'How can anyone talk about any sort of freedom in Russia?' I was asked after I returned, by a Dutch colleague. 'They occupy the countries of Eastern Europe. They should start by letting them be free.'

I told him about this contradictory discussion in Moscow. 'And what about America?' I added, 'How can a country which is free enough to hold the Irangate hearings continue to fund terrorists who kill families and burn down community buildings in Nicaragua?'

'Don't ask me, I don't understand it!' he exclaimed.

Big powers rarely believe that they should be obliged to treat others as they themselves demand to be treated.

But the strains on the Soviet dwarf – without and within – are more intense than those experienced by its Yankee rival, even after the crash of October 1987.

IN THE BALANCE

Add it all up, and what is the balance? If the USSR is taken in isolation, the ingrained, Russian influence makes it hard to foresee how Gorbachev and the reformers can succeed, as there are so many ways in which the bottom line of tradition could break them. There seems to be insufficient will, knowledge or democratic instinct for the political reforms to triumph, if they are based upon indigenous resources alone.

The same public opinion poll of a thousand Muscovites that found over half against the war in Afghanistan and only a quarter in favour, asked whether dissidents should be amnestied from prison and exile. Forty-two per cent *disapproved* of the idea; only 27 per cent were for their release (31 per cent had no views). [93] And this is Moscow, which is far more relaxed or, if you like, advanced in its views than Minsk.

The few overt critics of the regime who remain incarcerated are hardly a threat to the Kremlin. But to deprive a single person of freedom merely for their views, intimidates everybody. This is elementary. It seems that it has yet to be grasped by the Soviet public, many of whose older members regard public disagreement with military disapproval, as treason.

Perhaps also the vastness of the country means the possibility of vast disorder. The centre may have a terror of discord and break-up. A recent CIA report to the Joint Congressional

Committee Hearings on Gorbachev's new policies went so far as to claim that:

> The fear of public disorder is central to the Russian character.[94]

Those who look upon the USSR as Russia in this fashion see little reason to hope that the reforms will succeed. Glasnost and perestroika increase the strain because they are embraced at a different pace in different countries and regions. The response in the Baltic Republics has been swift, in the Muslim ones slow; Romania is alarmed, in Siberia they are sceptical. The logic of perestroika suggests that the Soviet empire should become a commonwealth. But the international tension sparked in the short run could damage all prospect of reform.

Within this unpredictable multinational situation, and working back along the list evoked in the previous sections, the prices question looms over everything, because it threatens to unite the whole population against perestroika. Next, perhaps, industrial resistance may become widespread as rationalization intensifies. The Kremlin might then fall back on technocratic authoritarianism. There remains the potential for a more violent opposition to democratization, pan-slavism. Its prejudices may well have penetrated the Party, sections of which despise what they regard as Western-style changes. Then there are the ostriches of orthodoxy, whose bureaucratic mentality has advanced many of them far up the state apparatus, and rewarded them with special shops. They see no reason to take their heads out of the golden sand.

But the Union of Soviet Socialist Republics cannot be taken on its own. World forces influence the internal evolution of the USSR, just as it has an influence on the world. The Party intelligentsia are more aware of this, perhaps, because better travelled and more widely informed, than the sardonic intellectuals without passports. The latter look to the West, but their sense of powerlessness often leads them to exaggerate the purely Russian character of what is happening. They see contrasts not connections. Yet connections with the outside world, in particular the example of America and the lure of youth culture, encourage reform in the Soviet Union.

THE TWO
FUNDAMENTAL FORCES

Before I went to Moscow I wanted to know if the Soviets thought of themselves as Europeans or were becoming, as I feared, more like Americans. I presumed it was much better to be European, to belong to the European socialist tradition, with its culture of sophisticated and serious debate. To become like the Americans meant to get fat (or superficial), crude, oppressive even, and to lose a sense of international solidarity.

I had to rethink – or rather abandon my prejudice.

Ivan is plump, and well travelled in both the West and the Third World. He works for a museum and speaks good English. He is probably in his late thirties. We didn't meet for long, but he made an impression.

'I like Americans,' he told me 'I feel at ease with them. They are like us – we understand each other in our souls. The French, if I may say so, are snobs.'

He gave me a significant look, which seemed to imply that the English were also included in this description . . .

I knew exactly what he meant!

In a rivalry of long duration, enemies take on each other's character. As they size up their opponent, each is impressed by the strengths of the other, adjusts to meet them, and thereby becomes like the hated opponent.

The historic enemy of the Soviet Union was Nazi Germany; Hitler and Stalin helped to form each other. The subsequent enemy of the Soviet Union was the USA. The companionship of Brezhnev and Nixon followed. They had a lot in common: the similarity in their power plays, their loathing for public argument, contempt for the press, desire for centralized domination, exercise of global force, love of secret diplomacy and penchant for military parades.

The twinning process with Nixon also confirmed in the minds of the Kremlin leadership a long-standing Soviet prejudice about US public opinion. Namely, their view that it was a chimera.

Soviet leaders failed to understand the autonomous nature of US civil society, or its capacity to affect state policy despite the policy of the state.

Instead they projected their own form of power onto their enemy. This stemmed from their experience in Europe, where talk about German opinion, or the British public, was indeed largely spurious – a function of the regime more than an influence upon it.

They also manipulated their own peace movements, and mass Communist Parties outside the USSR, often cynically subordinating them to auxiliary status in the short-term foreign policy of Moscow. The price of such control was, over the years, the expulsion, defection, desertion or simply exhaustion of most of the talented. The Kremlin failed to comprehend this. Instead, it was Communist orthodoxy to regard western opinion that was critical of Soviet domestic and foreign policies as CIA-inspired and controlled. This applied particularly to independent movements on the Left. Historically, their own domination of Stalinist opinion in the West confirmed the

Kremlin in its belief that all opinion in capitalist countries was regulated and supervised behind the scenes.

Finally, there is a tradition of vulgar Marxism which views the class societies of capitalism as a pure apparatus of exploitation. A recent example can be found in a book published by Alexander Yakovlev during the Chernenko period. Party politics in America is described as 'a well-developed way to confuse the masses, a method used in pursuing the fundamental policies of the ruling forces'. Later, it asks, 'Were there any essential changes to be observed during the 1970s and in the early 1980s?' and answers, 'There were none.' (The word 'essential' is an important device in this kind of non-think. One can argue that there have been no *essential* changes of any kind.) The book continues in this vein. There is 'nothing' really new about American aggressiveness, it claims. When the USA drew up scenarios for the unprovoked use of nuclear weapons against the USSR after 1945 (as it did), these plans are described as 'old-hat' because they are just like Hitler's 'schemes'.[95] In other words, imperialist aggression hasn't changed since the birth of Soviet power.

But it has changed. Modern American power is radically different from Nazi deployment. In particular, US public opinion is a real force. The new men in the Kremlin may have learnt this. The crucial events that impressed the present generation of foreign policy specialists, now exercising influence in the Soviet Union, seem to have been the anti-Vietnam war movement followed by Watergate. If the Soviet system had also been able to apply the law to Brezhnev and his staff, when Nixon was removed, the standard of living in the USSR today might be 20 per cent higher than it is, perhaps even more.

As well as being enviable, Watergate demonstrated that the American system had an ingenious flexibility, a capacity to recover and renew itself. Furthermore, it made evident the peaceful instincts in US popular attitudes as well as the bellicose ones. Instincts that can be turned against the USSR on issues such as human rights or the invasion of Afghanistan, as well as against US intervention in Vietnam or Nicaragua. Responses, therefore, which have to be doubly attended to.

I once saw a Soviet official admit, in a television interview, that for many years he and his colleagues thought talk about public opinion in America was just propaganda. Then they realized that US leaders took public opinion very seriously indeed. 'If they took it seriously', the official said, 'we thought perhaps we should too'.

Slowly, the Soviets learnt that the animal of US opinion, while dangerous, has a head of its own. It can be attracted, appealed to and convinced, once the ways of the media have been mastered. Churchill was one of the first foreign statesmen to grasp this with sensitivity, thanks perhaps to his American mother. His Fulton speech of 1946 which announced the existence of 'The Iron Curtain' and in effect the cold war between an Atlantic partnership and the Soviet bloc, was a masterful mobilization of US public opinion.

It was far from being a foregone conclusion. US hostility to the British Empire dates back to American independence. Support for a besieged island was one thing; helping to reconstitute its world influence and colonies after 1945 quite another. A large population descended from Ireland and deeply intransigent to the British meant that a vocal base of hostile opinion had to be overcome. Helped by Stalin's brief invasion of northern Iran, the English pioneered the kind of persuasion later developed by the Jewish lobby for Israel. That the administration of President Truman co-operated is not in doubt. The point is that they had to work for it, and could not take US public opinion for granted. Washington feared a resurgence of isolationism, and desired endorsement for its global 'endeavour' just as much as London feared US anti-colonialism. They – the US and the UK leaders – succeeded. As Fraser Harbutt concludes in his brilliant analysis, 'the trap was successfully sprung and the two fundamental forces – American opinion and the Soviet leadership – were brought into final confrontation'.[96]

What will happen if the two fundamental forces begin to co-operate?

There were signs at the summit in Washington at the end of 1987 that this might happen. The personal popularity of Gorbachev in the States could prove ephemeral. But a more lasting shift in the perception of the USSR may take place. The Soviet leaders played their role with skill. They refused to celebrate American values, or act as a publicity machine for the American way of life during their televised trip. (Unlike Deng Xiaoping who put on a Stetson hat when he visited Texas.) Yet they emulated the Chinese success in overcoming a pathological popular hatred that dates back to the 1940s.

Gorbachev told news executives that the Soviet Union was 'the world's second ranking power', a refusal to claim equality that surprised many. Yet such a statement of the obvious benefits the Soviets. For their artificial claim to equality with America cost them a lot during the Cold War – it made them seem more threatening, made their country's poverty and restrictions less legitimate, and was anyway a form of bragging that inspired an immediate loss of confidence.

At the same time Gorbachev bristled over questions about human rights, and told his hosts that the Soviet way of life was not on trial before them.

To gain the confidence of the American people, however, the Kremlin must demonstrate confidence in its own people. Glasnost is about relations with the West as well internal affairs. It is a prerequisite not only for the Soviet economic and political composure but also for a new sort of international confidence – different to secret negotiating across a table, thick hands on each others' knees.

The democracy that Gorbachev desires is perceived as a strength by the Kremlin reformers domestically, to invigorate economic reform, and strategically, because they have learnt that it is one of the strengths of their enemy.

They seem to have learnt this at a personal level also. Leading Soviets have found in the US a style of politics at once powerful and unsnobbish. If it is blunt, they like that. If it is tough and cunning, it is also plebian in tongue and enjoys doing business. The Communist elite have learnt a special sort of democracy in America from its politicians and their staffs – a democracy of power. They find a certain ease there, which the European mandarin tradition cannot offer them. It is not the European peace movement nor the sophisticated vanity of the *Quai d'Orsay*, but the frankness of capitalist representatives in Washington that has educated them in the advantages of the free airing of differences.

The world is more relaxed as a result. Identification with Americans is progressive and emancipating for the Soviets, clogged as they are by bureaucracy, suspiciousness and an ideology that seems to know best. This may be a two-edged matter for the rest of the world. American civil society is the most healthy there is, in any large country, yet much of it has been pulverized by the US media. US state power includes a capacity for subjecting the highest officers of the land to special investigation, but it also throws up a continuous stream of senior officials whose legal and financial affairs require legal prosecution.

Nonetheless, my initial presumption was confounded. I came to the conclusion that socialism has to be freed of its European elitism if it is ever to fly popular colours – and that the spirit of America will help.

THE ROLE OF ROCK

And sing what you want
And not just what is allowed
We have a right to yell
Televisor

Many Soviet Party leaders, particularly the reformers, have been favorably impressed by American-style capitalist democracy, its vigour, capacity to renew itself and even its legal formality – all admirable qualities compared to the cramped resentments and insider routines of European elite traditions. Were this the sole influence on the Kremlin of the US example, perestroika would indeed be nothing more than a re-run of an old Russian story: an enlightened leadership seeking to impose cosmopolitan values – values that the tens of millions whom they rule regard as foreign.

'Gorbachev should declare a generation gap.'

Everyone round the table laughed. I laughed at the idea that even the generation gap needed to be state policy before it could become reality.

But it is a reality, one that's easy to see in the big cities of Leningrad and Moscow. The great majority of young people under thirty, those born since Khruschev's first speech exposing

Stalin in 1956, are urban men and women. They have grown up to the rhythm of the high-rise, the atom, the countryside as an idea. They move to the sound of the city – to steal the title of Charlie Gillett's pioneering account of the rise of rock and roll – and that sound too originated in the painful energy of the United States.

Rock came slowly to the Soviet Union. But it came. Now, even a book has appeared on it in English; 'The first', as its author says in the preface, 'because there are no other such books even here in Russia'.

Artemy Troitsky's *Back in the USSR* begins with the late fifties, when a tiny handful of young Russians listened to Glen Miller rather than Elvis, and were pilloried as 'parrots'. They were known as *stilyagi*, after the Russian word for style:

> The most important thing is this: the stilyagi were the first effort at a youth sub-culture, the first group of offbeat 'monkeys' and 'parakeets' striving to separate themselves from the grey respectable world of ordinary 'grown-up' life.[97]

Troitsky then tells of how the first wave of Soviet youth culture was obsessed with western songs and dress. The Beatles had an overwhelming impact, he thinks because their melodic inspiration attracts the Russian ear.

> The generation gap (we call it 'the problem of fathers and children') highlighted by the stilyagi . . . began to widen in response to the Beatles. The cherished and fostered 'communality' of cultural identity suddenly started breaking up. Now it was not just an isolated gang of hipsters but an enormous mass of the "children" who said goodbye to arias

and operettas, athletic marches, tearjerker romances and other formalistic popular music and surrendered to the power of alien electric rhythms.[98]

Early in 1968 the first article to praise rather than excoriate the Beatles appeared in the Soviet press. Greeted as a victory it proved a false concession. Officialdom did what it could to stifle the new sounds. Between 1973 and 1982, for example, the Moscow branch of the songwriters section of the Union of Composers admitted no new members. As with so much that was talented in the Brezhnev years, rock was marginalized but not physically stamped out.

The first disco opened in Moscow in 1972. Later, Time Machine led the development of native language lyrics and toured Siberia. *Komsomolskaya Pravda*, the official youth paper, published a harsh attack on the group and their music. According to Troitsky, about a quarter of a million youngsters bombarded the paper with letters of protest – a decisive and irreversible expression of public opinion, however youthful.

Then Boris Grebenschikov's Aquarium took the lead, in Troitsky's estimation, to set the tone for the new decade, which was opened by the 1980 festival at Tbilisi. Neither proscribed nor prevented, rock had become native and unstoppable. The way had been pioneered by Vladimir Vysotsky, the folk-hero balladeer, whose singing crossed the generations, and who died in 1980.

Bureaucrats regarded him with apprehension, but couldn't ignore his universal popularity. Vysotsky was subject to the same hazy, duplicitous attitude as were the rock groups before 1980 – no formal ban, but no official support.[99]

Vysotsky tapes were everywhere (a friend of mine who learnt Russian in London in 1976 was given one as part of her course). In the USSR, groups followed the bard. Prevented from issuing their music through Melodiya, the monopoly record company, first bootleg recordings circulated, then more professionally made *magizdats*, recorded on imported kit, spread rock throughout the length of non-Islamic USSR. Discos ensured multiple listening to multiple copies. Little wonder that the old intelligentsia, with its hand-typed samizdats, pinched its lips at the new sound of the people.

One of the bravest and most esteemed, Dmitri Likhachev, said in a recent interview:

> Regrettably, modern popular art is largely banal, vulgar, publicity-oriented, and dominated by crude sex. Such forms of popular art should be combatted. Music that dulls human minds poisons the artistic atmosphere no less than the use of drugs. [100]

Admittedly, when you are over eighty it becomes harder to differentiate between varieties of electric noise, and no one denies that much of rock is trash, while most pop is a soporific. But the intensity and attraction of rock stems from its capacity for innovation. Charlie Gillett argued at the end of the sixties:

> Rock 'n' roll took so many people by surprise in 1956 because ... popular music, it had been assumed, was entertainment, and entertainment was escape, which necessarily meant sentimental pleasantries ... But rock 'n' roll singers treated popular music as a medium for self-expression. [101]

But the great days are probably over, he concluded, thanks to commercial exploitation.

Yet they were not over and the argument continues to this day: 'The potent idea that pop music can be about something more than mere entertainment has remained and deepened,' claimed David Widgery in 1985, pointing to Band Aid in particular.[102] Two years on, Maxim Manuilsky and Nikolai Meinert carefully summarize recent sociological analysis of Soviet tapes, 'by some of our well-known rock groups and discs by various pop ensembles':

> The latter show relatively little variety in mood. Rock is more varied. All of 76 per cent of pop pieces turn on romance, which accounts for only a quarter of rock output. On the other hand, nearly half of all rock compositions have a bearing on social and moral issues, which applies to only 4 per cent of pop songs.[103]

It's a good thing these heavy phrases appeared in *New Times* and not *Rolling Stone*, or it might have put an end to rock altogether.

The authors observe that in the USSR, 'Sociological opinion polls show that today rock is firmly top of the list in the musical sympathies of youth'. As they struggle to reassure their worried senior editors, Manuilsky and Meinert argue that rock:

> represents no uniform position, but rather covers every possible youth stance, from global humanism to physical aggressiveness, from active compassion to passive consumerism.

This is the point: the role of rock is resistance to uniformity.

The important argument is not, therefore, the one that dates from the sixties, as to whether rock is more than entertainment. Some is, most is not. Just as most paintings are rubbish, while some are quite good and a few painters seem to change the way we see our world, so most rock music is debris, yet one or two groups and their singers can shape the feelings of a generation. Rock is not exceptional in this sense.

The older generation find it hard to see beyond the intensity of individual expression and collective experience at rock concerts that are flashed on their television screens. They shudder at the image. The shudder is about order, hence law and order, hence politics. They regard it as poison.

But when the fascist National Front began to march against the black communities of Britain in the mid-seventies, Rock Against Racism helped to mobilize an opposition that overwhelmed the Front. Widgery, who was one of the organizers, recalls:

> On one level Rock Against Racism was an orthodox, anti-racist campaign utilizing pop music to kick political slogans into the vernacular. But on another level it was a jailbreak. We aimed to rescue the energy of Russian revolutionary art, surrealism and rock and roll from the galleries, the advertising agencies and the record companies and use them again to change reality, as had always been intended. And to have a party in the process.[104]

The orthodox Marxists, including his own Socialist Workers Party (followers of Rosa Luxembourg, now as important, or as unimportant, as the Communist Party in Britain) also shuddered. You can't keep discipline, you see, at a party with a small 'p'. The idea of the vanguard with the correct political line withers before the amplifiers of a ghetto blaster.

It is not the music but its natural pluralism. The culture of rock is the pleasure it takes in differences, however modish, violent or occasionally inhuman; its refusal of singular models of behaviour; the inventiveness of its styles; its search for authentic expression . . . it is hardly surprising that the conservatives dislike it intensely. At the end of 1987, the Party orthodox and the Russian Orthodox Church joined hands. Seventy-nine-year-old Archbishop Mikhail of Vologda and Velikoustyng was given the columns of *Pravda* to denounce television, the degeneration of the young and rock and roll:

> You do not have to be a composer to feel disgust at the wild whining, howling, banging and crackling and at the entire cacophony that violates human hearing and the human soul.

Like life rock music can take any form. It is not inherently progressive. England now has 'white power' music, with its own magazine that advertises 'Hitler was Right' T-shirts.[105] Eventually, I've no doubt, there will be Russian *metalisti* singing in praise of the Black Hundreds. But while there can be fascist rock, rock itself is anti-fascist. It is quite capable of mobilizing inhuman and collective violence, spasmodically. But its restless search for the novel is inherently anti-authoritarian, and it is inimical to the uniformity of militarism.

Most important of all, the rhythms of rock originated in black music – and are at this moment being refreshed by African groups. Its weird, sometimes wonderful sounds have been shaped across frontiers by different races. It is the music of a culture more genuinely international, and thus – despite the Archbishop's disgust – more human than anything the

Communist movement has yet produced. The role of rock is the shared celebration of differences. Which is why its arrival in the USSR is so significant.

THE SIXTIES COME TO
THE SOVIET UNION

The Communists in Moscow suffer from a painful ideological problem. If their system is so much better than the West's, why has it fallen so rapidly behind, whether in terms of diet or compact discs, over the last twenty years? Theirs is supposed to be the way of the future. Why has it seemed like a force from the past?

The question of 'backwardness' has a long history in Russia and many Soviets today still tend to see their predicament in terms of national tradition, rather than international history. Moscow, however, is not so backward, and hasn't been for a long time. Its rulers defeated Napoleon and participated as a great power in the nineteenth-century European settlement, which thereafter always included Russia in its state-system.

And to what did it lead? The First World War, followed by the rise of Fascism in Italy and Nazism in Germany. The British and French encouraged and invested in this barbarism, and then appeased it at Munich. Stalin did not pioneer treating with Hitler to partition other countries. Chamberlain, the British Prime Minister, did. Stalin copied the British example. It was the West, for Germany was the pride of continental culture, that orchestrated the Holocaust. It was the East that brought it to an end.

The Soviets defeated Hitler. Soviet lives (and, to be fair, American dollars) saved Europe. We have our freedom thanks to those who shouted 'For the motherland! For Stalin!' as they died. Even if these were not the actual words on their lips, we must nevertheless recognize the effort made by the men and women of the USSR. They, almost alone, broke the might of Hitler's army and died in their millions to emancipate the continent from the SS.

The Second World War – not the revolution and not the thirties – is easily recognized as the moment that legitimized the present regime in Moscow. It was then that the Soviet Union demonstrated its superiority to Tsarism (which had led the country to defeat in 1914) and won itself international recognition. Victory in 1945 made it a charter member and veto-holder in the United Nations.

The Second World War is thus the starting point for any discussion of the West's present relations with the USSR. Our hands were not clean with respect to the rise of Hitler, nor were they decisive in crushing him. Historically, the West has little right to presume moral superiority or superior intelligence.

This simple and important truth has a empty echo, however, when it is used by Soviet officials to excuse the present. They say, 'Our system caught up with yours, was strong enough to crush Nazi Germany, but the price was so great that we suffer still. Eventually our moral superiority will turn into an economic one, and then you will see that our way is best.'

There is something immoral about this exploitation of the past, especially when it suppresses the appalling human record of Stalinism itself.

There is another way of looking at what happened. And it is not just a matter of scholarly history but of how we perceive what is happening now. The Soviet system was conceived through the revolutionary response to Russia's defeat in the First World War – the first sustained international mass slaughter of millions – and gained adulthood through its costly victory in the Second. The incredible importance in Moscow today of arguments over the past are attempts to make sense of this crucial time. Furthermore, such arguments are lodged in the very centre of the regime's projection of itself. Lenin argued the now orthodox interpretation of events that gave him power. There are three aspects to his theory of the Great War of 1914-18. First, its moving force was capitalism. Second, the riches of capital were used to buy off the masses and persuade them to slaughter each other. Third, capitalism had thus reached its final stage: it had ceased to emancipate society from its feudal bonds, instead it now thrust people into barbarism. Thus, only socialism could provide a progressive development for humanity.

At the end of his book *The Persistence of the Old Regime*, Arno Mayer argues that the societies that dragged Europe into catastrophe in 1914 were *all* dominated by 'old regimes' – monarchies of landed and aristocratic interests. Even France, though republican in name, in fact remained Bonapartist in its form:

> It would take the two World Wars and the Holocaust, or the Thirty Years War of the twentieth century, finally to dislodge and exorcise the feudal and aristocratic presumption from Europe's civil and political societies.

Mayer wrote too soon. The British Monarchy and House of Lords are not without a touch of the old presumption. Less obviously, but more important, there remains today more than the shadow of feudal privileges in those special shops reserved for a hierarchy of ranks within the *nomenklatura* of the USSR . . .

But I am jumping ahead. The implications of such a thesis are momentous for any understanding of Russian history – and our own. According to Lenin, writing at the time, 'the struggle of the British and French bourgeoisie is aimed at the seizure of the German colonies, and the ruining of a rival nation, whose economic development has been more rapid.'[106] A good attempt was made to ruin Germany (although one that had to be moderated due to the presence of the Bolshevik menace). Its colonies were seized. The first aspect of Lenin's argument was at least partially true.

But where he was wrong is more important. At the outset of international hostilities in 1914, Lenin expressed his 'feeling of the most bitter disappointment' about the failure of the European socialist parties to condemn the war. Instead, they betrayed their class as they enlisted under imperial banners. Lenin pilloried the 'British and French bourgeoisie' for 'hood-winking' their toiling masses into believing that they were fighting for freedom against German militarism, while all the time they were financing Russian Tsarism, 'the most reactionary and barbarous monarchy in Europe'. The millions who rallied to the flag were dupes of capital, labour aristocrats; 'workers-turned bourgeois' who became, in his italics, 'the real *agents of the bourgeoisie in the working-class movement*, the labour lieutenants of the capitalist class, real vehicles of reformism and chauvinism.'[107]

This explanation is inherently improbable – that so many should die in such numbers while being untrue to themselves. In 1912 the Socialist International declared itself against the forthcoming war, at a special gathering in Basle. Lenin often cited its words two years before against its deeds, when across Europe the influential deputies of socialism voted for war credits. This reversal was not just a matter of hypocrisy or cash. More powerful historic forces were at work than bourgeois hoodwinking, as workers everywhere marched towards the trenches.

The third aspect of Lenin's original analysis on the outbreak of war was not borne out at all. He explained:

> Since Russia is the most backward and has not yet completed its bourgeois revolution, it still remains [our] task
> . . . to achieve the three fundamental conditions for consistent democratic reform: a democratic republic (with complete equality and self-determination for all nations), confiscation of the landed estates, and an eight hour working day. But in all the advanced (i.e. European) countries the war has placed on the order of the day the slogan of socialist revolution.[108]

Reality reversed this expectation. While Western Europe witnessed the development of democratic republics – and even then a faltering one – Russia proceeded to a socialist revolution.

Perhaps it was the theory, not reality, that was the wrong way round. Perhaps it was not a war of capital, at least not primarily. In Britain, Norman Angell wrote *The Great Illusion* to argue that international war between the European powers would be too costly to contemplate. He argued the rational banker's case. Lord Esher responded with the remark that Angell 'assumed that the businessman's point of view would prevail over the warrior's'.[109] It didn't. A dominant political segment of the elite had interests other than those of commerce even while it benefited from its revenues. This generated a tension which was registered even in the Basle proclamation of the Socialist International embraced by Lenin. The Great War was being prepared, the Basle Manifesto declared: 'for the sake of the capitalists' profits and the ambitions of dynasties'. Profits there may have been in wars, but 'the ambitions of dynasties' can hardly be viewed as the highest form of capitalism.

The Great War was a war between old regimes, between imperial governments each seeking to protect itself, not because they were untouched by capitalism but because they had been transformed by it and the industrialization it had made possible. Imperialism – the creation of colonies across the world – was less a function of the profit motive than a means by which the old regimes sought to contain, control and govern through external expansion the threatening internal force of industry and banking. It was as if these new forces, in the form of railways, machine guns, newspapers, the telegraph, expanded to the point of explosion the old forms encrusted with imperial honours.

Such an interpretation reverses Lenin's description of the place of capital in early twentieth century Europe. He argued:

From the liberator of nations, which it was in the struggle against feudalism, capitalism in its imperialist stage has turned into the greatest oppressor of nations. Formally progressive, capitalism has become reactionary . . .[110]

The alternative, he went on, was for mankind either to adopt socialism or suffer decades of 'armed struggle' for the sake of

the artificial preservation of capitalism by means of colonies, monopolies, privileges and national oppression of every kind.

In fact, the regimes of colonialism and privilege were not being used to preserve capitalism artificially. The elites were using capitalism artificially to preserve their old regimes. Lenin liked to disparage the hypocrisy of the money-makers. At one point he refers to German capitalists as 'this bourgeoisie which servilely grovels to the Prussian Junkers, headed by Wilhelm II'. Unwittingly, perhaps, this description acknowledges the domination of the warriors.

It follows, on Lenin's own terms, that capitalism had not reached its highest stage. Not only had it the capacity to develop economically, it was far from coming into its own politically. It retained considerable progressive potential. Capitalism had still to wrest Europe's states free from the leadership of elites whose rule was organized around feudal values.

The First World War was not primarily a conflict for markets, but a war between old regimes fighting to preserve themselves under new conditions. Therefore, the masses who fought and died in it were not duped by commercial interests. Mobilization was inspired by princes from the past to preserve belief in their own God-given authority. However ludicrous this may seem now, or seemed to Lenin then, it was not hypocrisy or hoodwinking, but an authentic, passionate atavism, for which millions died in the names of their fathers.

Around ten million men were killed (1.8 from Germany, 1.7 from Russia, 1.4 from France, just under a million from the UK) and nearly twenty million wounded, almost half from Germany and Russia alone.[111] Many millions more were mobilized, at the fronts and in the factories, the lives of their families transformed. What was the spirit that sustained these huge efforts and sacrifice? One could begin the answer today by considering the motives of those in the trenches that separate the armies of Iraq and Iran.

I have a copy of *King Alfred's Book*, which I bought cheap (there were three copies) at a local second-hand book stall. It was published by the *Daily Telegraph* at Christmas 1914 as a tribute to Belgium as personified by its King. The German decision to invade France through Belgium had, formally, taken Britain into the War. The book aims to 'invoke the world's sympathy . . . for the gallant little nation'. A nation 'desiring only to be left alone that she might pursue the arts of peace (and the) historic heritage of freedom and all the spiritual traditions of her race'. A tradition which included her notorious colony that was the heart of darkness: the Congo. This goes unmentioned in the parade of contributions from the Archbishops and Earls; 'India will never rest till Belgium's wrongs have been avenged' pledges the Viceroy himself, Lord Hardinge, his face untouched by the pink blush of shame, not to speak of native brown. There is even an endorsement of the eugenicist Sir James Barr, MD, LLD:

> As one of those who do not look upon war as an unmixed evil, and who think that it is sometimes well for a nation to be purified by fire, I feel confident that a fine race like the Belgians, who have shown their survival value . . .

It is little wonder that those who saw further, like Lenin or Bertrand Russell, were nauseated. (The latter wrote on the war's outbreak. 'I seem to feel . . . all the shouting . . . Emperors at balconies appealing to God, solemn words of duty and sacrifice to cover red murder and rage. It seems as if one must go mad or join the madmen.'[112])

Why did they fight? In *August 1914* Solzhenitsyn describes

the thoughts that go through the head of Colonel Vorotyntsev as he seeks to persuade the six ranks – the remaining half – of the Eastland Regiment to cover the retreat of their army at Tannenberg:

> What was he to say to them?.. There was no point in using words like 'honour' – the concept was an incomprehensible piece of aristocratic fiddle-faddle; still less would he impress them by talking about their 'obligation to Russia's allies'. Should he invite them to sacrifice themselves in the name of their Little Father, the Tsar? They understood that . . . but to Vorotyntsev . . . it would be sheer hypocrisy to invoke him. God then? The name of God would touch a chord in them. But . . . would be blasphemous . . . One last appeal remained – their fatherland. This was a concept that did mean something to Vorotyntsev, but he realized that it did not mean much to *them* – their 'fatherland' scarcely extended beyond their local district . . . [113]

In the West these concepts kept their meaning, despite the carnage. It was only political defeat, not losses, that made them ring hollow, until the stalemate of the War's end. Notions of honour, race and fatherland were codes for a way of life that had at one and the same time been convulsed, yet gained tremendous self-confidence and material improvement over the previous century.

The argument extends much further if both world wars are seen as a single, thirty-year conflict, in Europe at least. Where the crowns fell in the first round, provincial men of the people placed them on their own heads as they reproduced the old order in plebian form. In November 1922, Mustapha Kemal dismissed the shattered Sultanate to become Ataturk – Father of the Turks – while later that month Mussolini was declared dictator, although he retained the Italian King. Ten years later an Austrian who had served as a private on the Western Front took the part of the Kaiser in Berlin, and a Georgian (who was summoned for service while a political deportee but whose deformed arm made him unfit for duty[114]) took the role of the Tsar within the Kremlin.

Hitler was explicit about his aims from the beginning, his ferocious anti-semitism an amplified version of the belief in race common to imperial consciousness throughout Europe before 1914. Stalin discovered his role, having tried different ones, as he zig-zagged pragmatically in the wake of the revolution, sure only of his personal hunger for power. In 1931, as he swung behind forced collectivization and massive industrialization, Stalin argued:

> We refuse to be beaten! One feature of the history of old Russia was the continual beatings she suffered for falling behind, for her backwardness. She was beaten by the Mongol Khans. She was beaten by the Turkish bey. She was beaten by the Swedish feudal lords. She was beaten by the Polish and Lithuanian gentry. She was beaten by the British and French capitalists. She was beaten by the Japanese barons. All beat her – for her backwardness . . .

This overt identification with imperial history and the will to do better was cited with prominence in *The Short Course*.[115] Everyone knew that Stalin had placed himself in the tradition of the Tsars.

Thus, in defeated empires, new dictatorships arose rapidly from the stalemate of 1918 to challenge its verdict. Their leaders were from a generation formed by the first round of the conflict. And they had to play out their roles within what remained of an imperial world order, soon made highly competitive by the crash of 1929 and subsequent depression (which we can now see as a consequence of the premature globalization of capital, not its artificial preservation).

This renewal, or reactionary modernization of the vanquished, was to shatter the earlier victors. France was overrun in weeks, which led in turn to a traumatic mobilization in the United Kingdom. Britain's response was internally benign for two reasons – never invaded, its old monarchy remained intact, and it drew upon external sources, in particular American finance, borrowing upon the future to secure its position. Nonetheless, an immense conservative rallying took place, personalized by Churchill, who declared that he had not become His Majesty's first minister in order to oversee the dismantling of the British Empire.[116]

Stalin's regime should not, therefore, be seen exclusively as an episode within Russian history. On the contrary, it was the Russian/Soviet variant of a continental process. The struggles within British politics across the thirty years that culminated in Churchill were over how to reinforce and reinvigorate the British Empire. Likewise Hitler sought to gain the European dominance that had eluded the Kaiser (and the Hapsburgs). For France it was de Gaulle (also deeply marked by the First World War, in which he was taken prisoner), who came to personify his country's response during the Second. Because of France's early defeat in 1940, he only took full powers in the fifties as the torture and killing in Algeria brought France's post-war crisis to a head. For his part he sought a Napoleonic reconstruction of continental Europe under the guidance of Paris. From

Moscow to London, leaders and followers remained deeply imbued with a belief in the truth and mission of their imperial legacy.

The paradox of Soviet socialism is that it did not counter this process but trumped it. Its collectivization of the countryside made the Kremlin by far the largest autocratic landlord. Industrialization was implemented on a scale that put the rest of Europe to shame. A massive educational and training programme accelerated development, rapidly promoting the first Soviet generation, even if it did so by Russian methods. Moscow produced the most advanced of the continent's revolutionalized *old* regimes. It was the most revolutionary and the most successful. Nonetheless it remained the old in a new form. In this way at least, socialism demonstrated a superiority over capitalism.

One country stands apart from this process: the United States. It entered both the First and Second World Wars not in order to preserve its ruling structures or to challenge a settlement that had undermined them, but for markets and profit. The lack of an inherited warrior-imperial tradition makes the American soldier wasteful and poorly led. Masses of soldiers will *not* die for the profit of others, even when they have benefited hugely from surplus extracted by their country from the rest of the world. In relative terms, America's losses were slight, its gains enormous. For the US the war years after 1941 meant full employment, a real increase in the standard of living for many and a more than two-fold increase in gross domestic product. Its overwhelming supremacy then placed it in an imperial situation through sheer economic dominance after 1945, even though at first it disarmed its military.

Two questions follow. If the First World War in Europe was

created by 'old regimes' and generated recharged varieties of the same that brought about the Second, and even extended beyond it, when did these come to an end?

The answer for Western Europe is in 1968. The student/ worker rising, which in effect brought down de Gaulle, removed more than a father-figure from the scene. It also confirmed the predominance of 'Americanization' over the old national politics of Germany, Italy and Britain. The previously chauvinist and militarist cultures of Europe were dissolved by the sound of the city, as European colonialism came to end.

The second question concerns the USA. Why didn't its imperial power turn it into an old regime? The answer again is that code year, 1968. Not that US dominance ceased then, but its Vietnam war can be seen as an attempt to impose outside the Americas regimes of its own liking – i.e. to turn the whole Third World into its colonial sphere. The public decision to withdraw was taken in 1968. President Johnson's inability to stand for re-election, in the aftermath of the Vietnamese Tet offensive, symbolized the public collapse of the US ambition to become a classical Empire.

True, it was followed by a covert attempt to reverse the verdict, and install an American world order through Metternich-style, secret diplomacy and balance of power politics, orchestrated by Nixon and Kissinger. At home they were frustrated by 'student bums' (Nixon's term) and a domestic political system which, designed to resist absolutism, drove Nixon from office with Watergate. Unable to asphyxiate the sixties in the United States, the two American statesmen collaborated with Brezhnev abroad, as we've seen, to help ensure his efforts were more successful in the USSR. Ceausescu's

Romania, Nixon's most favoured country in the Warsaw Pact, stands as a symbol of this repugnant detente between the Kremlin and the White House. At the time of writing, the days of the Romanian regime seem numbered. Its downfall may confirm the arrival of the new epoch, in the East.

'The French way to America', argued Regis Debray, 'passed through May '68 . . . 1968 was the moment when the world-market informed the nation-state that its services were no longer required ("too small to solve the big problems and too big to solve the small")'.[117]

1968 was not just the way to America for the countries of Western Europe. It was also the moment when the USA began to dissolve into the international economic and cultural system it had originated, as it found itself unable to replace European-style colonial power by its own direct rule.

To recap: the old regimes – whose time is by no means completely over – consisted of a heady and dangerous amal-gam. Highly centralized, invariably personalized, they utilized the hierarchy of traditional values and command over indus-trial forces. Their global predominance was shattered by their internecine conflicts – by Europe's thirty-year civil war – and the nationalist assault upon their colonies worldwide. Domes-tically, their political cultures lasted until their dominance ebbed decisively with 1968, overwhelmed by a new tide that had been gathering since 1945.

Economically, this meant the rise of multinational over national capital; within the elite, a shift (long underway) from those who lived in country houses to those who merely have a house in the country;[118] intellectually, the extension of higher education to large numbers and the end of its especially pri-vileged status; culturally, the termination of deference – in particular TV and rock and roll ensured the extension of a powerful popular culture no longer controlled by the values of church and state; militarily, the intensification of military technology reinforced a decline in militarism and 'male' values; sexually, effective contraception and the transformation of work dissolved the rigidity of lower-class family life; internationally, the end of colonialism tended to free the advanced countries from some of their obsessions with national identity. In short, an Americanization began in Western Europe that often improved upon America itself. The process demonstrated that capitalism had retained a further round of progressive energy.

Now if the Soviet experience is once more included in the global picture, its exceptional trajectory stands out. The decade after Stalin's death saw a liberation from his terror and a marked improvement in living standards. But the achievement of sputnik and the humiliation of the Cuban missile crisis determined the Kremlin to match America as a great power and to realize a global rather than a European status. In the summer of 1968, at the very moment when Western Europe rid itself of the long cultural nightmare that had twice thrust the whole world into war, Brezhnev voted for the suppression of the Eastern May. The Prague Spring was crushed.

The Soviets can argue that their use of force in East Berlin in 1953 and in Budapest in 1956 was necessary to preserve their own hard-fought military success in 1945. But the 1968 reforms in Czechoslovakia were introduced by a loyal Communist, himself brought up in Moscow, who had no intention of leaving the Warsaw Pact. Dubcek introduced humanitarian reforms from above, that might have set an example for socialists everywhere. His overthrow was a straightforward act of colonialism. It was followed by the reversal of economic reforms within the USSR, the suppression of de-Stalinization, the asphyxiation of youth culture and a cult of national Communism. These moves were to culminate at the end of the seventies with Brezhnev seeking an accord with Washington for joint military action against China, and the actual invasion of Afghanistan. In this way, two decades ago the Soviet bloc moved in the opposite direction to capitalist society. As the latter internationalized itself, Brezhnev's USSR became a system of city bosses and bigger rockets – a shadow of a shadow of an old regime.

But within it, the imported factories and cassette decks, the huge new apartment blocks, the white goods – including the ones that didn't work, the cars and planes, and even the modernized party functionaries, now citizens of the world thanks to detente – generated the basis for this regime's eventual transformation. Despite itself, it absorbed the pulse of freedom that emanated from its new chief enemy – no longer Nazi Germany but the United States. In his assessment of his own country, Debray wrote (and one can almost substitute 'USSR' for 'France'):

In 1968 there were two Frances: an industrial and technological France, and a social and institutional France . . . The cleavage became excessive, French society became anti-economic . . . In general, decisions are more effective when the level at which decisions are taken is brought as close as possible to the level at which they are applied. The macro can only function with the aid of the micro. Above a given level of industrial gigantism productivity begins to decline, and small organizations become more profitable

... The France of *oui papa, oui patron, oui chérie*, was ordered out of the way so that the France of software and supermarkets, of news and planning, of know-how and brain-storming could show off its viability. This spring-cleaning felt like a liberation and, *in effect*, it was one.

If, and it remains a big if, the current changes succeed and forms of democracy take root in the USSR, future commentators will ask, not how it could happen, but why it took so long. The USSR did not retain so many elements of an old regime simply because Stalinism reinforced rule from above so effectively. That was only a part of it. The Soviet Union was the only European country positively to win territory in 1945, the traditional goal of Empire. The advantages of socialism led to a victory that allowed it artificially to preserve its old regime where capitalism failed to do this. The key to Russia's present backwardness lies not so much in the losses, massive though they were, or the devastation of invasion, scorched earth and counter-invasion – the standard explanation of official guides. The price of the war for Moscow was its success. It gained territory as territorial control became a burden. Its defensive emplacements in Eastern Europe were a trap that held its regime in forms of despotism now doomed to archaism.

Most Westerners who travel to the Soviet Union are struck by aspects of its backwardness, 'shops like the late 1940s', 'road traffic like the 1950s', while rockets blast into space. I encountered a different kind of recognition. When a rock fan complained to me 'Rock and roll should be about rebellion not entertainment', my eyes pricked with nostalgia. The music really has arrived if its commercialization undercuts its brave progenitors. When I watched *Is It Easy To Be Young?* with its

269

mixture of sincerity, agony and hostility to the war, I felt for the new generation, one with which, although in my forties, I could easily identify. The sixties have arrived in the USSR.

Later in the summer of 1987 a conference of independent, unofficial clubs took place in Moscow, the first for more than fifty years. They said that anyone could join them provided that they accepted the 'Three Nyets': No to violence and the propaganda of violence; No to ideas of national or racial exclusiveness; No to claims of a monopoly of the truth in opposition to other peoples' right to search for it themselves.[119] This is pure sixties; the three Nyets would have been welcomed across the campuses of the Western world twenty years ago.

A TWENTY-YEAR
DIFFERENCE

'The sixties come to the Soviet Union' – perhaps this is just a slick version of the convergence thesis, which says that modernization will make the USA and the USSR more alike. Capitalism and communism can be considered two paths of development towards a similar destination, determined by technology and basic human nature rather than ownership. Despite the present differences in their respective social systems, runs the argument, in the long run they are bound to converge.

I mused about this question a lot. The welcome influence of America's democratic spirit – rock, free speech and due process – on the USSR, may not mean the two countries will converge. The new Kremlin leaders insist that more democracy means more socialism, and they could be correct. English Tories have suggested to the contrary that Gorbachev's stress on money relations, incentives and people standing on their own feet is Thatcherism or even monetarism. There is indeed a shared hostility towards the corporate state: Thatcher's assault on Labour's style of centralism and Gorbachev's on Stalin's, are both attacks upon the monolithic tradition of the old working class movement. But one is from the right, the other from the left.

Thus at the same time that Mrs Thatcher's government proposes to charge people who need to have their eyes tested (something that the British Health Service will do free once a year), the Soviets consider introducing free preventative health checks for everyone. The day Mrs Thatcher demands that factory managers should be elected by the workforce is the day that Mr Gorbachev should be considered a Tory.

How, then, can we understand the strange combination of sharp political differences and real similarities? The answer is that both the British Prime Minister and the Soviet General Secretary are in their different ways products of the sixties. The signs of the sixties were not exclusively left wing. They were radical, so far as the old regimes were concerned; they were against established authority (referred to in the UK as consensus). But such radicalism can be reactionary as well as progressive.[120]

So to take the decade of the sixties as shorthand for no more than student protests, collective meetings and anarchist audacity is a mistake. James Bond personified those years just as much as psychedelia.

This is not the place to discuss the interesting consequences of what then happened in the West. The point that concerns my argument is: only the notorious political and cultural outburst of the late sixties turned into a protest against consumerism. The icon of Che Guevara, who was executed in cold blood on the instructions of the CIA in October 1967, is one symbol of its values. Debray (who missed the Paris rising because he was in a Bolivian jail after having seen Che) reveals in the disparaging tone of the essay quoted in the last section, how the left despised Americanization and mass culture. From Saigon to Paris to Chicago, the sixties of the barricades was an egalitarian protest from below against the sickness of consumer capitalism as well as its masters.

In complete contrast, the left in the Soviet Union, that now seeks to introduce sixties-style change, is not only doing so from above, but aims to encourage anti-egalitarian, consumer-oriented values. This contrast, between the Soviet reformers' desire for modernization and sixties-style scepticism about economic growth, is only partial. On ecological issues the Gorbachev programme – to judge from his speeches – is quite close to the doubts about giganticism and nuclear power expressed in the western peace movements that the Stalinists once tried but failed to capture. Nonetheless, the differences are more important than the similarity. 1968, while opening the way for Americanization, was also a protest against it. Twenty years later, the Kremlin's espousal of the spirit of the sixties seeks to embrace many of the values the sixties protesters found repugnant.

What is happening in the USSR is not therefore a repeat of the Western experience twenty years ago, even if a period of Soviet riots and rebellion may lie ahead. Should its changes lead to a socialist version of consumer and cultural pluralism, then the new left in the Kremlin is likely to prove more successful than the New Left in the West. The result may well be a divergence from, not a convergence towards, the trajectory of capitalism.

THE DEVIL

In the short term the most immediate difference between the two systems is that their nuclear forces point in opposite directions: towards each other. The paradox is well known. Never has so much been spent on weaponry, and never before has military force been so destructive. But because the earth will become uninhabitable except for insect life, after the first strategic exchange, the more money that is spent on it, the more difficult it becomes to translate military into political power.

Star Wars seems the key issue here in military terms. President Reagan claims that his Strategic Defence Initiative is just that: defensive. Which, of course, is what the Soviets say about their tanks in Eastern Europe. But any weapon that can be deployed in defence may also be deployed in an offensive operation. In terms of military science the Red Army is correct to see the US policy of combining a huge space shield with cuts in strategic rockets as a potential means to give America the power to smash the Soviet Union while remaining safe from counter-attack. In their recent talks in Moscow, Gorbachev is said to have asked Secretary of State Schultz why his administration wants to spend billions and billions of dollars to protect the USA from a reduced number of Soviet ICBMs, when it could have a verifiable agreement that would dismantle every single rocket presently aimed at his homeland, that would not cost a cent.

There is no specific record of the reply to this question.

Although it makes sense, it is hard to believe in the possibility of real strategic disarmament as opposed to limitations on deployment. There is no precedent and it seems to challenge human nature, especially the nature of human power. Furthermore, the socialist record is a warning rather than a positive example.

The socialist ambition aspires to a society which is consciously determined by all its citizens, a world in which all choose how they live, so that one person's advantage is not furthered at the expense of another. Yet the actual experience of socialism has been marked by dictatorship and the annihilation of choice. In Pol Pot's Cambodia even the family meal was abolished and private eating forbidden, as the slightest zone of free choice was considered a danger to the 'great leap forward' of the country's construction.

Thus socialism is doubly cursed by choice. First, an impossible ambition – the attempt to choose the future itself. Second, some of the most oppressive negations of choice ever witnessed.

Its enemies argue that the promise of socialism inevitably turns into a nightmare. They have done their best to ensure that this is so, as Nicaragua testifies today. Socialists led the overthrow of the dictatorship of the Samoza family, who had been kept in power with US support for two generations. The Sandanistas began to increase the degree of choice in their country, politically and economically. The US regarded the possible loss of a sphere of influence as a threat to its interests. It embargoed, quarantined and assaulted Nicaragua, creating and funding the Contras against it.

What does this do? It leaves the country with less and less choice. It has no choice but to survive, its national ideology becomes dedicated to sacrifice, as a militarization takes place which will be internalized over time to become second nature. Meanwhile, blockade means rationing, hence uniformity and shortages – Nicaraguan socialism comes to mean 'no choice'.

If choice is the curse of socialism, it may also be the curse of life itself. God offers us heaven, provided we behave. The devil offers us a choice!

And capitalism is the devil's brew. Wicked greed, the desire to profit at the expense of others, will bring benefit to all, it claims, at least in a perfect market situation. It presumes that human motive is nasty, and tries to turn this to advantage. Whereas socialism presumes that human motive is virtuous and has no theory about what to do when it isn't.

Nuclear weapons, however, seem to reverse this profound difference in philosophies. Those who, like Mrs Thatcher, praise the bomb, claim that it has kept the peace, and presume it will always do so. They assume a lasting rationality in the conduct of those who run the world's military affairs. These days, it is the Right that insists we have perfected government to such a degree that the destiny of the human species is secure, and the power of armageddon is safe, behind the locked doors of the National Security State. While it is the Left that insists such a belief is utopian and emphasizes the imperfect nature of human administration.

The revolutionary conundrum, from both points of view, is that antagonistic systems must cohabit, this side of kingdom come. At present, the Soviet one lags behind the western one in productivity and democratic rights. But there are also structural flaws and inhumanity in the capitalist system. Nor is it impossible that within the stunted and disfigured growth of the socialist bloc are inscribed the genetic codes of a preferable social order. So we have to ask, towards our conclusion, whether there might be a positive legacy locked within the Soviet experience.

There are lots of ways to ask about this. I'm going to address what I call the politics of sincerity. Because issues of meaning and motives play a large part in perestroika.

GENERATION GAPS

The generation gap in the USSR envelops a much deeper contrast of human experience than in the West. The seniors knew not only Stalin and the war but also the shift from peasant to urban life that began with collectivization and lasted until the 1960s. Now that colour television is everywhere and rock is irreversible, the confrontation embedded in the difference between the millions of active Communists over sixty, and the millions of youngsters who sing to the Time Machine, will eventually be won by biology.

Rock music – or if you will, its noise – is an expression of a new style of life, a life that demands individual style. Its content finds its form in films. Far more than books, movies influence the young. The response to two of them clarified for me another generation gap, between those inspired by the thaw of the Khruschev period, and the modern young.

Liberals of around forty and over regarded the mass screening of Tengiz Abuladze's *Repentance* as a turning point. It is a very effective, surreal yet alarmingly believable film, made in Georgia under Shevardnadze's protection, before he became Foreign Minister. It filled the Moscow cinemas and shattered the taboo on talking about the Gulag and what it was like for the victims of Stalin. It also has a strong Christian theme.

But the under-thirties were electrified by Juris Podnieks's *Is*

It Easy To Be Young? Its title is a riposte to the oft-heard refrain of the war-time generation – that, unlike for us, these days it is easy to be young. A stunning documentary, the film starts with a rock concert outside Riga, shows a trial for vandalism, interviews youngsters about their beliefs and prospects, discusses the drug problem, follows punks, shows young ecologists cleaning up the old city, and ends with a dramatic sequence on the Afghan war that forced Nella to interrupt her translation as she wept in a Moscow cinema.

It presents no answers to those who watch it. Instead, it films young people who are looking for values they can live by. Few in the Soviet Union have found any that are satisfactory, but to judge by the movie, they are searching. Thus *Is It Easy To Be Young?* is a disturbing inquiry into belief. It has been attacked for its 'cynical indifference'. Petrova found it 'permissive', and disapproved, although not of its being shown. For her, the film of the year was *Repentance*, which she had seen three times. Talking to some eighteen-year-olds, I asked if they had seen *Repentance*. They nodded. Did they know what it was about? 'The regime, Beria.' They didn't make much of it. Then I asked about Podnieks's film. Their faces lit up, 'Yes, that really was an event!'

This contrast illuminates a difference between the anti-Stalinist intelligentsia and post-Stalinist youth. At present there is a wave of publication of major books and collections of poems that have been forced underground, or locked in drawers, for twenty or even thirty years. The arts have been the first major beneficiaries of glasnost. A generation bore witness but was silenced. Now its testimony has given legitimacy to perestroika, has enlarged its support and, with time, it will help people to believe in themselves. The *Times Literary*

Supplement headlined a survey of seven recently published, historic Soviet novels: 'At last an exorcism'.[121]

It seemed to me, however, that this middle generation felt ill at ease with the Party-inspired reforms. After Stalin they came to life in the thaw and then, when the thaw chilled over, they were frozen – preserved, but powerless. Like mammals found under the ice in Siberia, whose flesh is still fit to be eaten, many from this generation have not found their resting place in the past, but nor are they at home in the present.

I put this to Nella in a letter and she disagreed. The argument is central to any assessment of glasnost. The prime cause of the reform programme is the flip side of Soviet achievement – the vast social and economic catastrophe that faces the USSR if nothing is done. But there is no law of history which says that what needs to be done shall be done. On the contrary, if the political and economic system that demands change also resists it, then how *can* it transform its own character? Societies that are confronted by the necessity of deep structural transformation usually collapse – the necessary revolution coming from an overthrow of the State by war or insurgency.

If the Soviet leadership – or at least part of it – does wish to oversee changes that will transform the system, we must ask not 'why?', because that is obvious. Those with foresight realize that neither domestically nor internationally can they hope to retain their positions over the next twenty years without radical measures. What we must ask is *how*, in their closed system, can they argue for such change? What experience can they appeal to, to persuade the multifarious and resentful opposition to support their revolution without the shots?

My answers looked to the outside: to the influence of America and the new culture of modern life, not to speak of science. Nella insists that an indigenous, rooted pre-Soviet tradition also makes a vital contribution. Her terse response follows in the next section. It led me to reflect on the relationship between the Party's Leninist tradition and the Russian literary one.

NELLA'S RESPONSE

If we take the Russian word for dissidents, *inakomysliatchiye*, its literal meaning is 'those who think otherwise'; if we now enlarge the term to include any kind of resistance to central State power in thought and act since the October Revolution, we find ourselves before a specifically Russian body of public opinion, which persisted even through the worst years of the terror. The arts, literature and above all poetry, played a very special role in forming and keeping alive a public conscience concerned with both individual liberties and social events. The power of the written word was all the greater because democratic rights, in the western sense, were being trodden underfoot. This was true for the Russia of the Tsars as for the Russia of Stalin and Brezhnev. The experience is reflected in the Russian proverb:

What is written with the pen
No axe can cut down.

Consequently the arts and literature became the main oppositional stronghold – hence also the attacks against a Pasternak or a Sinyavsky.

The fact that today the poems and writings of Pasternak, Mandelstam, Akhmatova and others are beginning to be published cannot be considered a mere literary event: it is itself an opening of and towards the public opinion I'm talking about.

Equally, the fact that films like *Repentance* and *Is It Easy To Be Young?* have been made and widely shown since the period of glasnost is far more than an artistic breakthrough. Such films are already an expression, if in a new form, of the 'école civique' whose civilizing tradition has been reproduced in Russia before and after the Tsars, by the written word.

This is to say that the period of glasnost has not come out of nothing, but is the result of a long distillation of social conscience. To a large degree writers and poets helped to form this conscience. But above all, it was formed by the millions who passed through the Gulag and whose experience spread out, soaked into and touched the whole of society. And here one must emphasize that those men and women who claim publicly to be dissidents are but a tiny fraction of the millions, direct and indirect victims of the camps, who think otherwise. One of the paradoxes of my country is perhaps this: Gorbachev and his associates and followers are also among those who to some extent think otherwise.

The bringing to light of the past, and the debate about Stalin and his reponsibility for what befell the Soviet Union, are questions which particularly concern the generation who are now the parents and grandparents of those whom we see in *Is It Easy To Be Young?*. In the film we feel a constant if subdued reproach against parents who have failed to give an example to follow, or ideals by which to live. Yet there is something more important here. The film testifies to the spiritual deprivation of youth today. It was made by a young man for the young. What is hopeful is that it has provoked a truly passionate response. It has been seen by millions and debated and argued over in the press, on television and in people's homes. Such a phenomenon is unthinkable in the West, where an austere documentary about the values by which people live could never light up the imagination of the young as if it were Madonna singing in Central Park.

LENIN'S FROWN

When tourists talk about Lenin they comment usually on two things: the mainly out-of-town Soviet citizens, who line up in the morning to see his preserved corpse in the Red Square mausoleum, and the ubiquity of his icon-like presence in streets and shops. His gaze is unavoidable in public and has a quasi-religious function, incarnating supposedly shared values. But I was struck by his frown.

It is not a realistic portrayal. Lenin had a well-known and much recorded habit of screwing up one eye very tight as he scrutinized strangers or tried to calculate developments. Photographs and film footage of him did not record this, but make him seem either businesslike or, when posed, avuncular. The paintings, social-realist and made after his death, project a classic paterfamilias image of tough but tender. Familiar with these, I expected to see them in Moscow. Instead, I was taken aback by the graphic image of Lenin often inscribed on statues – for example, the one in the military museum – and posters. Two powerful knitted brows concentrate fiercely, as if pushing the intelligence towards a goal still just out of reach. Quite unlike the classic image of Mao as an inscrutable arbiter of power, Lenin's image transmits the example of a terrific mental exertion – a symbol of effort and will.

But also frustration. Don't feel bad about Lenin, feel sorry for Soviet people. You go into a bookshop to get a book. It isn't there, but in the window is Lenin's frown. You look in the army museum for a display about Afghanistan. It isn't there, but at the top of the stairs there is Lenin, frowning.

One of the most remarkable new buildings in Moscow is the *Mezhdunarodnaya* or International Hotel. A forbidding brown complex from outside, it encloses a piazza with trees, water and glass walled lifts, as if it was in Manhattan. It connects, via an air-conditioned mall, to the international trade centre. The whole complex is well guarded. Inside, it is a hard currency zone only. I was reminded of the Galata Tower in Istanbul, built by the Genoese in the fourteenth century at the apex of the fortified Christian settlement. Later, feudal Moscow also had its foreign enclaves. Nella and I had a coffee and ice-cream there and strolled around. The supermarket that is supposed to sell western goods for western money was shut. Resident foreigners complain that it is always shut because of incidents of corruption or robbery of stock. This proves how feckless and incapable the Soviets are, is the usual conclusion. I felt, although one doesn't dare say so in Moscow, that it proved a rebellious if not revolutionary spirit was still alive among the Muscovites, and that they resist slavish behaviour in circumstances of such gross inequality and privilege.

After the ice-cream we wandered into a bookshop selling art-books and expensively bound tomes. There was also a pile of bright red pamphlets. They were by Vladimir Ilyich Lenin himself, on *How to Organise Competition*. Irresistible. But I had to pay with hard currency. So there was only one way for me to buy Lenin on competition at the International: with my American Express card.

Far from extinguishing competition, socialism, on the contrary, for the first time creates the opportunity for employing it on a really *wide* and on a really *mass* scale, for actually drawing the majority of working people into a field of labour where they can display their abilities, develop their capacities, and reveal those talents, so abundant among the people whom capitalism crushed, suppressed and strangled in thousands and millions.

Workers should compete therefore, writes Lenin, to find the best forms of the practical organization of labour. The Paris Commune of 1871

gave a great example of how to combine initiative, independence, freedom of action and vigour from below with voluntary centralism free from stereotyped forms.

But what about 'the rich and the rogues', he asks, the 'two principle categories of parasites'?

Thousands of practical forms and methods of accounting and controlling the rich, the rogues and the idlers must be devised . . . Variety is a guarantee of effectiveness here, a pledge of success in achieving the single common aim – to *clean* the land of Russia of all vermin . . . In one place half a score of rich . . . will be put in prison. In another place they will be put to cleaning latrines. In a third place they will be provided with 'yellow tickets' after they have served their time, so that everyone shall keep their eye on them as *harmful* persons, until they reform. In a fourth place, one of every ten idlers will be shot on the spot.

Oh dear . . .

In a fifth place mixed methods may be adopted, and by probational release . . .

and so on. But how can it be done? Only through 'talented organizers':

> There is a great deal of talent among the people. It is merely suppressed. It must be given an opportunity to display itself. It *and it alone*, with the support of the people, can save Russia and save the cause of socialism.

And thus the pamphlet ends. It was published in January 1918.

Desperate stuff for desperate times. As we know from his own words, only a few years later Lenin could not think – it's a wonderful list – of anybody who would be more tolerant, loyal, polite, considerate and less capricious than comrade Stalin, to replace him as General Secretary, although he regarded such a replacement as of 'decisive importance'. Yet the same Lenin calls for the talent among the people to save Russia, not just the Bolshevik leadership. The talent! Locked away in part, because, Lenin argues:

> The workers and peasants are still 'timid', they have not yet become accustomed to the idea that *they* are now the *ruling* class; they are not yet resolute enough . . . The workers and peasants are still 'timid' (he repeats); they must get rid of this timidity and they *certainly* will get rid of it.

You've got to hand it to Lenin, he really tried. Today, the Soviet people try too. Perhaps they inscribe the fierce furrows upon his brow as a signal of their effort. Or is it their failure, or even disapproval of their timidity, that is encoded in Lenin's frown?

'Bolshevism,' I said, 'is the unity of word and deed. Lenin's entire merit consists in his will to carry out his programme . . . Land to the peasants, factories to the working class, power to those who toil. These words have often been spoken, but no one has ever thought seriously of passing from theory to practice. Lenin seems to be on the way.'

'You mean,' said Sergei, bantering and incredulous, 'that socialists are going to apply their programme? Such a thing has never been seen . . .'

I explained that just this was going to happen in Russia.

Thus argued Victor Serge in Barcelona in 1917, as he tried to explain the singularity of the Russian situation to his comrades. It's worth an emphasis: 'Bolshevism is the unity of word and deed. Lenin's *entire merit* consists in his will to carry out his programme.'[122]

In February 1986 Gorbachev told the 27th Party Congress: 'It is by the unity of words and deeds that the Soviet people will judge our work.' This implies action against Party members who resist the new policies. Nor is it such good news for the average Soviet, who likes to disparage glasnost and perestroika, and say that they are just another campaign, for many people prefer slogans they can easily dismiss to ones which oblige them to change their lives.

Such resistance has ensured that the leaders of the new, self-proclaimed revolution in Moscow are literally obsessed with the need to bring about a unity of words and deeds; to make the words honest and deeds themselves speak of the conviction that motivates them. The issue sounds philosophical. Its objective is material. They mean to introduce a new discipline – internally motivated, to be sure, whether by positive incentives or the negative threat of bankruptcy – to replace the failed discipline of the command economy.

Gorbachev is also attempting to administer to a Soviet sickness summed up by the word *pokazucha*, a colloquialism for 'show' or false appearance. Sometimes it is as if he and his colleagues fear the Party can only have a Potomkin programme.

Lenin and Stalin, not to speak of Khruschev, shared a Party attitude about the need to cut through bureaucracy – an attempt to match word and deed, however, that functions to preserve bureaucracy. Just as those who run filling stations perpetuate the lines of those who wait, so as to sell their petrol on the black market, so the utility of Party connections becomes redundant if the state bureaucracy does its job. Now the papers and the Party speak out against the flatulent, deceptive language of stagnation, but can they get the Soviet Union to work?

Take, for example, one issue of *Moscow News*, of 4 October 1987. Page two carries an article on science which complains that today's science managers in the USSR give – and the emphasis is the paper's – only the '*appearance* of efficiency', lead only a '*semblance* of discussion' while they 'substitute ersatz science for the real thing'. On page three, writing about film and theatre, Konstantin Shcherbakov attacks propaganda performances, 'We must secure by deeds the traditions and the spiritual values of our Revolution'. On the centre spread an article about Mikhail Shatrov's play about 1917, concludes with Shatrov on Rosa Luxemburg:

> She also says another topical thing: Bolsheviks are the people of deeds, not of words.

On page 13 the paper's editor reports from the big car works at Togliatti about the changes there:

> The usual gap between word and deed is still alive within each and every one of us . . . As long as I can remember there have always been more loud words about good deeds than there were actual deeds . . .

In its supplement, the same issue carries Foreign Minister Eduard Shevardnadze's UN speech, which opens:

> The Soviet Union and the United States have, together, finally authored the first word in a nuclear-free lexicon. When this word becomes deed . . .

A cynical explanation for this chorus is that if Gorbachev emphasizes the need to match words with deeds, *Moscow News* must echo his tune.

Yet the paper's writers are no longer parrots. To be sure, there are times when the formula is a mere slogan. At other times it is evident that the authors are striving to be truthful and to help achieve a public life – and labour – that avoids deceit.

There are at least three strands converging on this aspect of glasnost. First, revulsion from Brezhnevism, and the chasm between official 'good news', which corrupted the vocabulary of public life and turned it into a rotten farce. Second, an attempt to return to Lenin as a source for a practical vocabulary that will help to legitimize the regime. Third, a wider cultural passion about truth and language.

Because we can now read in its own press hard-hitting accounts of events in the Soviet Union, it is difficult to estimate how far the old presentation still holds sway. But Mary Dejevsky went to Gorbachev's home town of Stavropol, down in the warm south, at harvest time, in 1987.

For the centre of one of the richest farming regions in the country, Stavropol town is poor. Beyond, a transitional region of single-storey wooden houses with luxuriant gardens and fruit trees gradually gives way to the golden grain and maize fields on which Stavropol's farming reputation rests. But the harvesting has been patchy. The combines have produced loose, untidy sheaves. Rusting machinery stands idle in the sunshine. Monday afternoon in harvest time and fields have been left with grain only half-gathered and no sign that work is to be resumed.

The following day the announcement was made with fanfares, on national television news: Stavropol region has delivered its millionth ton of grain to the state. It must have been another district.

This seems to be another example of the appearance of success projected ever since the first five-year plans. Under Brezhnev, as results diminished their proclaimed success increased. And as Brezhnev, who was only a political officer in a relatively insignificant sector of the front during the War, became the most decorated war hero in the Union, disbelief became chronic.

Vaclav Havel, the Czech writer and signatory of Charter 77, begins some reflections on the 'The Power of the Powerless' with the example of a manager of a fruit and vegetable shop who, 'places in his window, among the onions and the carrots, the slogan: "Workers of the World Unite!"' Why does he do it? Havel asks. Not because he thinks it will increase trade, or because he believes that it will persuade anyone. The sign really says, 'I am a greengrocer, and I know what I must do.' Apart from that, he, like everyone else, ignores it. For Havel, the ubiquity of such senselessness means people are obliged to 'live within a lie'. This creates a society inscribed with a moral crisis, but also a resistance that can be put at its most simple as the attempt to 'live within the truth'.[123]

Today the Soviet Party has begun to turn against the hacks and hired academicians of its old prose, textbooks and slogans. It demands glasnost not because the new leaders love truth as an abstract concept, but because they realize that the USSR can only overcome its moral and economic crisis by turning its back on official deceit, if not sloganizing.

For many in the West the fact that Lenin's authority is cited in support of glasnost seems proof that it is more of the same old soup. But Lenin did stand for truthful policies (and, incidently, the founder of the USSR has not been reported as having uttered such an outrageous falsehood as 'Father, I cannot tell a lie'). He dedicated his life, at some risk, to the overthrow of autocracy, he wanted to win emancipation for the toiling masses and to drag Russia out of its servitude. Lenin was practical, experimental and capable of energetic thought: he said what he meant and he meant what he said.

Too much so. For while it is doubtless these qualities that led Gorbachev to say, 'I read and re-read Lenin', when we look at the nature of the relationship between word and deed in Lenin, we touch the double-helix of Soviet political culture.

Perhaps there is no better place to start than *What Is To Be Done?* Written in 1902 as a critique of reformism – of the belief that socialism could replace capitalism gradually by electioneering – it is the founding text of revolutionary strategy within the Russian working-class movement. To understand its significance one fact needs emphasis. Today, two sources in the West conspire to project Lenin and his associates as a small group of conspirators. First, those on the Right who want us to see the 1917 revolution as a coup, as if the Bolsheviks were just a left-wing version of Pinochet's Chilean junta, rather than the leaders of a Party with around 300,000 members at the head of a much larger mass movement.[124] Second, contemporary, self-proclaimed Leninists in the West are limited to small groups, consumed by the passionate enchantment of their own role as a historic vanguard. By contrast, Lenin debated as an equal with the leaders of the social-democratic movement; Bolsheviks and Mensheviks (in 1902 they had yet to separate by name) were two opposed strands within it. And if their formal numbers were reduced by Tsarist proscription, nonetheless the Russian working class had no other political representation. Thus, from the beginning Lenin and his colleagues were national leaders equivalent to those heading the Labour Party in Britain, or trying to win a majority for the Social Democrats in Germany.

What Is To Be Done? is an argument for an 'All-Russian political newspaper'. Lenin insists:

> Far from representing the fruits of the labour of armchair workers, infected with dogmatism and bookishness . . . it is the most practical plan for immediate and all-round preparation of the uprising.

There is an important formula here: a dismissal of bookishness ('the academic stratum' is also regarded with contempt), goes along with insistence on the need for more information and knowledge. In the pamphlet's first section Lenin made his famous argument:

> Without revolutionary theory there can be no revolutionary movement. This idea cannot be insisted upon too strongly . . .

Furthermore, it has to be 'the most advanced theory', which has to be brought to the workers 'from without', as 'the working class, exclusively by its own effort, is able to develop only trade-union consciousness'. What is needed is to *train* workers in the breadth of revolutionary activity:

> Working-class consciousness cannot be genuine political consciousness unless the workers are trained to respond to *all* cases of tyranny, oppression, violence and abuse, no matter *what class* is affected . . . to observe *every* other social class in *all* the manifestations of its intellectual, ethical and political life . . .
>
> Why do Russian workers still manifest little revolutionary activity in response to the brutal treatment of the people by the police, the persecution of religious sects, the flogging of peasants, the outrageous censorship, the torture of soldiers, the persecution of the most innocent cultural undertakings, etc? . . . We must blame ourselves . . .

Lenin faced a twofold problem: to organize a qualitative increase in the intellectual and cultural level of the Russian worker, yet defeat the bookish blather and reformist wordmongering of both exiled and domestic progressive intellectuals.[125]

This tension in his perspective intensified a traditional Marxist contempt for 'talking shops', 'pieces of paper', mere political chatter, as ephemera compared to 'real' material interests. Just prior to the revolution in 1917, Lenin codified a vision of the construction of socialism in *State and Revolution*. His view of bourgeois assemblies and legal systems was that they were no more than a machinery for hoodwinking. That is, an apparatus of deception. In essence:

> Under capitalism, we have the state in the proper sense of the word, that is, a special machine for the suppression of one class by another.

During the transition away from capitalism, a special apparatus will still be necessary:

> But *the people* can suppress the exploiters even with a very simple 'machine', almost without a 'machine', without a special apparatus, by the simple *organization of the armed people*.

As if that was simple! Only a few months later when in power he was lamenting the dearth of talent and excessive timidity. Even so, he was willing to discuss the experimental shooting of one rascal in ten, without any consideration of the mechanisms through which the one should be selected from the ten.

As for the economy: 'Accounting and control – that is *mainly* what is needed for the "smooth working", for the proper functioning, of the *first phase* of communist society':

> From the moment all members of society, or at least the

vast majority, have learned to administer the state *themselves* ... from this moment the need for government of any kind begins to disappear altogether. The more complete the democracy, the nearer the moment when it becomes unnecessary.

For the first time there will be a democracy of the poor. Then a withering away of the state, so that there will be no further need for any apparatus of coercion whatsoever and, he quotes Marx, 'it becomes possible to speak of freedom'.[126]

It is the other way around. Should the time come when all coercive forces have been abolished, there will be no need to talk of freedom. It is long before then, and above all here and now, when there is so much coercion, that we must make it possible to speak of freedom.

The utopianism of *State and Revolution* has often been criticized: by some, by way of apology for Lenin's visionary prelude to the actual experience of revolution, while others have been more severe. Alec Nove, the historian of Soviet economic history, argues that for Lenin while problems of technique and of accountancy certainly exist: 'Economics as such disappears'. In a more wide-ranging critique, *Lenin and the End of Politics*, Tony Polan goes further, suggesting as his title implies, that Lenin's arguments

abolish any possible distance between the gross economic position of an individual and his motivations ... abolish space for "values" and, consequently, for disagreement over values; (hence) there can be no genuine differences of *opinion* within political life.[127]

As a final judgement on Lenin, this is unjust; it stems from excessive concentration on the text of *State and Revolution*. But there is a compelling aspect to Polan's thesis. Under feudalism politics was not a separate sphere; legal, military, religious and economic power were fused (though not centralized). With capitalism there is a unique separation of economic from political power. The crude Marxist interpretation says that nonetheless, despite appearances, politics is decoration, and that in reality the state is just a machine for the suppression of one class by another. Taken to extremes, such an argument denies the reality of politics altogether, which is seen exclusively as a means of masking class rule. Bourgeois politics and constitutions are thus seen as forms of mere misrepresentation.

In a curious way, this view is paralleled by the tradition of political philosophy in the West. In her essay on 'Truth and Politics', Hannah Arendt observes that the two have usually been on bad terms:

> Lies have always been regarded as necessary and justifiable tools not only of the politician's or of the demagogue's but also of the statesman's trade.

Truth, she argues, is not only non-political; it may be 'anti-political':

> To look upon politics from the perspective of truth . . . means to take one's stand outside the political realm.[128]

Contemptuous of the egoism and lies of the statesman's trade, Lenin looked forward to a society 'cleansed' of such vermin. In effect, Lenin sought to abolish, if not politics, then at least politicians. And who can blame him for loathing the complacency demonstrated by the other world leaders of his time, who together drew up at Versailles the peace treaty that paved the way for the next war?

Understandable and inspiring, Lenin's capacity to unite word and deed was also dangerous. Not just for his opponents but for his supporters. To get rid of politicians, of the profession of knaves and fools that proliferates in the drink-sodden confusion and double-dealing of the space between speeches, votes and policies, also meant to close the door on the development of civil society. Because social organization becomes more complex, not more simple, Lenin's simplification of the state machine did not liberate, it threatened the citizen. Stalin was to exploit this potential.

Lenin sought unmeditated popular power along the lines of the Paris Commune. He underestimated the influence that constitutional processes may have despite the effort and interests of those who hold office within them. He thus found it difficult to establish a structure of government when he himself took power. There is a vivid description of his 'white, concentrated expression' as he concerned himself with the fate of small pelts in a full session of the Council of People's Commissars (while at the same time dealing with an important telegram of state). He was criticized for his absorption with such 'vermicelli' by Preobrazhensky, who said it was ruining his health.[129]

An absolutely tragic example, in the sense that it signalled a seemingly inevitable destiny, came a few months after the revolution. Already, disputes among the Bolshevik leaders over peace with Germany had become so vehement that many began to fear their revolution would drown them in their own blood. Bukharin drafted *An Anti-Thermidorian Catechism*, so called because its purpose was to prevent a 'Thermidor', or a counter-revolution from within (as happened in the French Revolution in the month they called Thermidor). The *Catechism* – which the dictionary defines as an oral instruction of first principles – 'consisted of rules and regulations designed to restrain inner-Party controversy and to prevent it from degenerating into a fratricidal struggle'. Bukharin wanted it circulated widely among Party members. The politburo members read it, and waited for Lenin to speak.

> Comrades, I see no need to circulate this among Party members. I do not see what purpose any such catechism may serve. I trust we shall never seek to settle our inner-party differences in a Jacobin manner. But if events were ever to drive us that way, if any of us were ever to be tempted to settle our differences by means of the guillotine, then God have mercy on us, for no anti-Thermidorian catechism will help us then. It is a childish idea, Nikolai Ivanovich, that we could stop or forestall so fatal a development with the help of a sheet of paper like this.[130]

Far from being childish, Bukharin had sensed his own fate. Twenty years later he was shot. Lenin had been wrong. It would certainly have helped to lessen, even prevent, the purges if Stalin had been obliged to contravene flagrantly fundamental Party regulations. The publication and circulation of Bukharin's *Catechism* would also have legitimized the co-existence of differences within the Party, even as it forbad their resolution by extreme measures against the person.

Lenin's disbelief in the autonomous role of constitutional regulation is accompanied by that fatalism which often seems the twin of voluntarism in the chemistry of revolutionary self-sacrifice; a fatalism which ultimately contributed to the acceptance of the purges and show trials by the old Bolsheviks.

And it is chilling to think that Stalin, with his excellent

memory, was probably present when Lenin turned down Buk-harin's *Catechism*. For while Stalin personally was the opposite of Lenin as a principled socialist, he inherited and then used Lenin's contempt for sheets of paper. This is a very sensitive issue in Soviet history – to what extent was it Lenin's legacy that led to the bloodbath first in the countryside and then throughout the Party?

Lenin genuinely sought to subject the deed to the word; this was, if not his entire merit, a signal part of it. Stalin inherited a political machine built to sustain this extraordinary fusion. And discovered that it had the power to make words mean anything he wished. He used it to turn Lenin's unity on its head. He bent words to his deeds and crushed language of its content, so as to meet his own purpose. Lenin was perhaps the most truthful man of power this century. Stalin was the least.

Despite the great difference between Lenin and Stalin, we can see that the radicalism of Lenin's unity prefigured Stalin's, even while its intention was so fatally reversed. By refusing the mediations, safeguards, restrictions, rights of appeal, and other aspects of constitutional life, there was little to prevent Stalin from exploiting Lenin's awesome achievement, first by retaining the unity of word and deed and second by pulling it through the looking glass.

The way that his rule embodied both a continuity and the antithesis of Lenin's legacy is crucial to comprehending why Stalin was both detested and adored. Earlier I quoted Pasternak's description of collectivization. He concluded that 'every means of intimidation had to be used to make people forget how to think and judge for themselves, to force them to see what wasn't there and maintain the contrary of what their eyes told them'. For Victor Serge also, the transition from

Lenin to Stalin meant everything changed – the aims, the political system, the Party ('from the organization free in its life and thought and freely submitting to discipline . . . to the passive obedience of careerists') and morality:

> from the austere, sometimes implacable honesty of heroic Bolshevism, we gradually advance to unspeakable deviousness and deceit.

Serge wrote this in 1936, having escaped from the Gulag, thanks to the fame of his writing, just before the final extermination of most of his colleagues. For those who knew literature and worked with words, including almost the whole Bolshevik elite, it was Stalin who ruptured the bond between word and deed of which they were so proud.

But at the same time young men and women in Russia *were* freely submitting to discipline, to use Serge's terms. They saw in the transformation and construction of Soviet power not deceit but candour. Stalin said Russia would never again be beaten; they would make sure he was right. He was right. Between the 1920s and the 1950s, many Soviet citizens experienced Stalin quite differently from Pasternak and Serge and other far-sighted members of the political and literary intelligentsia. For those to whom Stalin meant the first fruits of modern life, he personified the same quality which attracted many to Lenin: he meant what he said.

When Stalin said 'execute' at a person's name, you could virtually hear the cartridges being loaded. It was less a word than the deed itself: the closure of the gap between the spoken and the achieved was absolute. There would be no trial with its pieces of paper, no appeal with lawyers and all their clever talk. There would be no process of argument and consideration.

The job was done. Equally, if a factory was to be constructed, a mighty river dammed, the enemy stopped at Moscow (even though he should never have got there), Stalin's will – the ruthless fusion of judgement and action that never spared the men – forged the deed. That is why millions loved Stalin as Victor Serge loved Lenin.

Their commitment established a tradition we can call 'honest Stalinism' which survives to this day and honours the unity of word and deed in the form of military command transcribed into the civilian context. Uncorrupt but orthodox, it regards public argument as the disunity of words, the disabling of deeds, and the gift of an unnecessary advantage to the enemy. It regards democracy with the contempt Lenin had for politicians. Democratization in the Soviet Union will need to meet this inheritance head on if it is to succeed.

We can see Soviet reform as an attempt to do this, and to bring 'truth and reality' into a credible balance. A balance that at one and the same time abolishes Stalinist command politics and Leninist simplification, while refusing to surrender the possibility of an administratively honest, politician-free society.

This latter ideal links up with a wider relationship to language, about which Russians care with a rare passion. They worship words as if they are icons. We in the West have an instrumental relation to words: we see them as a means – what else? – to transmit narrative and information. In the Soviet Union such instrumentality is often regarded as philistine – after all they have had the example of Stalin. The difference may also be rooted in the millennial contrast over the role of images. In the West these were defended against the iconoclasts as a narrative device, yet were refused the status of religious objects to be venerated in themselves. In Byzantium, however, images could become icons, venerated as direct intercessors between man and God.[131] Today, many in the USSR worship language as the incarnation of truth. Pasternak suggests:

> Language, the home and dwelling of beauty and meaning, itself begins to think and speak for man and turns wholly into music . . . by its very movement, the flow of speech creates in passing, by the force of its own laws, forms . . . until now undiscovered, unconsidered and unnamed.[132]

The same impression of the God-like power of language possesses a later Russian Nobel Prize winner, Joseph Brodsky:

> Time worships language, it means that language is greater, or older, than time, which is, in its turn, older and greater than space. That is how I was taught, and indeed I felt that way . . . isn't a song, or a poem, or indeed a speech itself . . . a game language plays to restructure time?[133]

To attest that language itself is the home of meaning, or is greater than time, is a religious claim. Yet it is also a rejection of religion in its traditional form of received truth codified by doctrine and authority. The arguments of Pasternak and Brodsky (who have very different attitudes towards Soviet history), can be seen, in part, as a refusal of all organized belief. To claim for language a superiority over history is to assert that language is ultimately untouchable by deeds: that it can always escape the reach of the Cheka, Stalin or any future Stalin.

The new General Secretary's call to unite word and deed draws upon a Party tradition of honesty of purpose that goes back to Lenin. In another form it finds an ominous predecessor in Stalin. Finally, it appeals to the moral authority of language itself, which the country's writers have helped preserve since the 1920s.

Gorbachev has one advantage. The Soviets have so far avoided the corruption of public language now found in the West. Rupert Murdoch, for example, who is among the world's most powerful newspaper and television magnates, instructed *The Times* and *Sunday Times* to publish extracts from 'Hitler's Diary'. They did so. It turned out to be a forgery. Murdoch showed little concern. 'After all,' he said, 'we are in the entertainment business.'[134] Such contempt for truth and history is enough to make anyone prefer Lenin.

THE WOMANLY MISSION

Rupert Murdoch is also one of the world's major soft pornographers. Every day, his topless page three girls fill millions of copies of his papers. The absence of such western style sexual titillation from the streets of Moscow is one of its attractive characteristics for a visitor from the West, and gives the city a charm that has been swept away in our own capitals of commodity fetishism.

Are the Soviets more civilized than ourselves in their policies and attitudes towards women, or is this another expression of their backwardness? It is probably a bit of both, a mixture that is also a living example of the gap between word and deed. In public and at home – in the street, market or across the kitchen table in a discussion with foreigners – women play a strong role and are treated with equality in Moscow. In this respect, certainly, it is not the capital of a Third World country.

But what people say about relations between the sexes makes it seem so. Sexual relations before marriage are difficult, which doesn't help. In part this is due to crowded living conditions which in turn make marriage with children especially claustrophobic. Divorce is relatively high. Among women the joke goes, 'One child is enough'; in other words, men have yet to grow up. Men work, which under the developed socialism of Brezhnev means non-work. As non-work means non-pay, women also have to work, usually at harder jobs and they oversee the child (more rarely children), and do the cooking and housework, not least the washing. Meanwhile men, as they say, stick to:

THE THREE Ts:

Tapochka	Slippers
Tachta	Sofa
Televisor	We all know what that means!

Contraception and sanitary towels are scarce and poorly made, so rather than being a necessary yet awesome right for women, abortion has become a means of birth-control – in effect, another instrument in the familiar story of a male society punishing females for their fertility.

In occupational terms, it is well known that the Soviet Union trains and employs great numbers of professional women, notably in medicine and education. At the same time, their presence even in the top echelons of those professions, let alone government and Party, is scanty. There is a double mechanism operating: on the one hand it draws women into skilled employment, where their care, reliability and restraint with respect to alcohol make them especially valuable. On the other, it positively blocks them from senior positions, where recruitment in no way reflects the high proportion of women in the qualified workforce. Female emancipation has thus been exploited by a system that remains thoroughly – almost totally – male dominated.

Or rather, to use the phrase of the English sociologist Maxine Molyneux, under existing socialism women have been mobilized without being emancipated.

Just as the development of civil society has been frustrated in the USSR, so also has sexual freedom been repressed in the public domain. And these two heavy influences are linked by the style of Party direction. The competitive atmosphere of an intense, all-male, self-selecting elite, in which even the secretaries are men, must play a large part in perpetuating the Party's 'boss-like' nature – a state of affairs that has yet to find its novelist.

A significant loss of talent and initiative is not the only price the system pays for its discrimination. The tone of the Yeltsin affair, for example, the way he was denounced and admitted himself guilty towards the Party, the exaggerated and personal venom of the exchanges, is characteristic of a single-sex institution. It is not that women can't be as hysterical as men, or as swayed by the herd instinct, although educated women tend to be the more balanced of the sexes. Rather, all institutions that shut out the other sex from any significant intervention in their affairs, are prone to collective infatuations, and an excessive rigidity that follows from the exclusion of the other half of humanity. If democracy includes differences of view – 'arguing honourably, listening to another's opinions' – then it is much more likely to happen in circumstances where both women and men exercise authority.

In his speech to the Central Committee in January 1987, Gorbachev pointed out that women hold many junior Party and State positions and called for them to be actively involved in more senior, all-Union tasks. 'We have such possibilities. All we have to do is trust and support women.' Such a feeble conclusion may only encourage those who wish to ignore it altogether. And it is most unlikely that the men (and they are all men) responsible for top appointments, men who have probably spent an average of thirty-five years in a predominantly male environment, will trust, let alone support women as their equals and possible seniors. For such promotions are bound to change the familiar chemistry of command.

Article 35 of the Soviet Constitution, however, states that women have equal rights. It continues:

> Exercise of these rights is ensured by according women equal access with men to education and vocational and professional training, equal opportunities in employment, remuneration and promotion . . .

The same clause of Article 35 then adds explicitly that this includes 'political activity'. Furthermore, women also have the constitutional right to additional support and child care to ensure they can make full use of their equal right to promotion. There can be no excuse in law. So it is hard not to conclude that the Party is in flagrant violation of the Constitution. Perhaps it should be taken to court for rectification . . .

Putting legalism aside, while Communist ideology proclaims a superior (because truly equal) treatment of women compared to the West, the Soviet reality of socialism belies this. The combination of large numbers of trained, articulate and relatively experienced women and their almost zero presence in principle positions, means that there is no better place for speedy gains through affirmative action than the Kremlin.

The remarkable constitutional assertion of real equality and its lamentable actuality may be another case of the gap between word and deed, yet the fact that intention is well ahead of reality need not provoke scorn. Provided, that is, there is tangible momentum towards improvement. But this, there doesn't seem to be. On the contrary, many women now resent the way that in the *name* of equality they in fact have had to suffer a triple inequality: in the home, in the Party and, above all, in the economy. For in the name of equal rights their sex has been cast as the front line managers of the system – especially the battle-axes of the retail system – where they bear the brunt of public resentment and respond by becoming over-weight harridans. In other words, men screw up the system and women take not only the burden but also the blame.

Although Mikhail Sergeyevich usually avoids the stereotype reactions of his more traditionally minded compatriots, on this topic he seems to have slipped rather badly. On page 117 of *Perestroika* he says, and the passage needs to be quoted in full:

We have discovered that many of our problems – in child-ren's and young people's behaviour, in our morals, culture and in production – are partially caused by the weakening of family ties and slack attitude to family responsibilities. This is a paradoxical result of our sincere and politically justified desire to make women equal with men in every-thing. Now, in the course of perestroika, we have begun to overcome this shortcoming. That is why we are now holding heated debates in the press, in public organiza-tions, at work and at home, about the question of what we should do to make it possible for women to return to their purely womanly mission.

The misunderstanding here seems blindingly obvious. Equality between men and women does not mean 'to make women equal with men in everything', i.e. to make women like men. The prospect would be utterly repugnant. On the contrary, the equality of men and women involves a greater change in the psychic and behaviour patterns of men rather than women. First, men should share in domestic labour, from laundry to child rearing – a way in which a fruitful, stable and enjoyable family atmosphere can be reproduced in an urban environment. Second, men need to accept women in positions of equal and superior authority at work, while they do the grind.

Instead, it seems that women are now being asked to pick up the tab for perestroika. They must make it their womanly mission to take primary responsibility for renovating the USSR's morals, culture and production, no less, while – it goes without saying – leaving the boys to their manly mission, haranguing each other in the Central Committee.

But when I asked an outstanding Muscovite about her attitude to Western feminists – it was before Gorbachev had sat down to write his book – she prefigured his argument: 'We are not interested in feminism, these days we want to become more feminine.' For her, the actual experience of existing, Soviet socialist equality has terminated any interest she may have had in the political improvement of the role of women.

It is the same for the younger generation. Even if Soviet rock seems shocking to war veterans for its apparent licentiousness, Artemy Troitsky regards it as 'blatantly de-feminized', with very few female bands, players or singers.[135] Yet the desire for freer sexual expression is another of the urban tides the old guard can delay but will resist in vain. The younger generation is determined to be more sexy, as well as stylish. Young Soviets are keen on fashion, and Liliya Orlova, the Editor-in-Chief of *Fashion Magazine*, takes it very seriously indeed:

Taste, culture, an understanding and knowledge of the laws of building up an outfit, moreover the creation of the

311

very image of a person, in keeping with the times, that is
what is most important.[136]

In these circumstances, 'feminization' – looking and being
more sexy and encouraging a more open and frank enjoyment
of sex – is seen as an essential emancipation for the mental as
well as physical health of Soviet society. It may be improbable
to hope for this in the Islamic Republics of the USSR,
apparently the only part of the country that has yet to produce
a good rock group. On the other hand, Vadim Sidour, a
Ukrainian-born artist who worked in Moscow, and died in
1986, created very lively and impressive sculpture, sometimes
dramatic, often humorous, and with a forthright sexuality that
is perhaps unique. It is neither pornographic in the Rodin
tradition, nor romantic, nor does its explicitness do violence to
the person, as so often happens in Western art.

Sidour's work bears witness to the human body in war, love
and the city. Typically, he was neither driven out of town nor
allowed to exhibit. His first Moscow show came after his
death. But the fact that Soviet culture could produce such an
artist means that it is capable of lifting its taboos.

How far should it do so? Soviets can hardly be blamed if they
are unimpressed by the capitalist model of relations between
the sexes. Just after I returned from Moscow I went by the
London underground to an appointment. While sitting waiting
for the train, I was reading the newspaper intently, to try to
follow events in the USSR. I put aside the paper and suddenly
found myself looking straight down the flimsy negligee of a
girl with black hair, as if I was flying a few feet over her head. I
could see the outlines of her breasts, and her long, young and
naked legs stretched up and curved slightly towards me, for

they were plastered against the wall of the tunnel opposite. Because she was so much more than life-size, the distance diminished her optically to perfect human proportions, and being short-sighted and having hardly ceased to focus on the latest story from Moscow, I felt momentarily that I could put my hand out to touch her. Nor did the way she lay offer any resistance to this. In my momentary embarrassment I turned my attention to the words. These assured me in suitable detail that a newly developed cream was now the best means of removing female body hair. 'Ah, my country', I said to myself, and thought of Nella looking out of the aircraft window as we banked before landing in Moscow.

SEVEN REFLECTIONS

I

Even if Gorbachev's 'revolution without the shots' is less revolutionary than he and his close colleagues would wish, or even if, despite his wish, it leads to some shooting, the Communist Party of the Soviet Union is evidently trying to grow up. This is not a very scientific description. But sociological and Marxist terminology for development, modernization and so forth are often gobbledegook for elementary human perception.

Within the Soviet Party-Establishment, a generational change is underway, from those fashioned by the militant defence of socialism in one country, to those formed by the international experience of an uneven but partial parity with America and independent socialist neighbours (in the East).

The change in experience and perception is profound. Gorbachev belongs to a generation unculled by the mass slaughter of war. The transformations of modern urban living, new technology, mass communications and education, must find expression in the USSR. In the process both culture and personal life are becoming political, as people feel that the crisis of values cannot be resolved by the traditional appeal to received authority – which includes old-fashioned Communism.

For thirty years the multinationals have pumped out their

values as they sought to profit from the West's version of this transformation. The Soviet Party, deeply hostile to innovation, and rooted in a country traumatized by the physical and military cost of 'catching up', held itself at bay. This handed the West an easy victory. For the Soviet inability to respond meant that progress and capitalism become synonymous.

Beneath the ice they were learning. Today, the Party-Establishment feels itself to be not only intellectually and culturally ahead of its own people, but just as far-sighted and intelligent as its equivalents in the West. Perhaps more so, as symbolized in the contrast of Gorbachev and Reagan. The tension generated by falling further behind while seeing further ahead, is not hard to imagine. What is difficult for Western officials to accept is that the Soviets might indeed see further and better than themselves.

True, their dedication to language and public values, and their refusal of pornography and the gross debasement of popular culture, have been preserved through long years of massive dishonesty, oppression and repression. Blocking out the development of a civil society has been a serious business. But that very seriousness could mean – could, not will – that a Soviet civil society, socialist yet free from state control, might become an example of interest to many on my side of the Iron Curtain.

The key requirement for this to happen is economic and political democracy in the Soviet Union.

II

Democracy may now develop in the USSR. The qualitative difference between East and West will remain for many years. The West is more free because people and groups of people, including those who can publish, or make videos, have the right to say things, give opinions and judgements, argue and expose facts and figures, while the state does not have the legal right to stop them – at least not within limits supposedly established in law.

Right-wing opponents of the Soviet Union have exploited this qualitative superiority of the West to argue a case of black and white. By saying, 'There, over there, there is totalitarianism', they have been able to suggest that, 'Here, over here, there is freedom'. Through the use of this sharp contrast they have been able to project the West as being in a state of almost perfect, and certainly healthy liberty, with a political and economic system that needs no fundamental modification or improvement, even though it naturally throws up the odd difficulty.

The problem for such ideologists of the Right is that if glasnost and then some freedoms are established in the USSR, this will rebound upon their interpretation of capitalism. A Soviet Union that becomes relatively democratic will begin to undermine the absolute superiority of the West projected by its most outspoken representatives. That the qualitative difference remains today is clear, as I've described. But already its quantitative extent has narrowed. Should democracy begin to grow in the USSR – if its provincial press (and not just a few papers in Moscow) and the local language television stations of the Republics become regularly more explicit and hard-hitting; if a new legal code for people's rights and autonomous organization is enacted; if family firms and farms are able to produce and sell; if workers really elect their managers, and elections to the Soviets are not just multi-candidate but have candidates who stand for different policies – then the difference of the two worlds will narrow still further.

To say, 'We are the more democratic' is quite different from saying 'We have democracy and they do not'. The former concedes the relative nature of this complex term. Then the whole argument changes. We may have more freedom, per- haps even much more, but do we have enough? They have some democracy, we have a lot – but is ours sufficient? Do the people really rule in the West? Are we our own masters, even to our own satisfaction? The glib response in the past was: 'If you don't like it here, go to Russia.' That meant: choose between *our* freedom or *their* unfreedom. It meant: any attempt to improve our way of life through collective action can only make it worse. Either be ruled by politicians and the profit motive, or by bureaucracy and the KGB. There is no alterna- tive . . .

III

We must judge the Soviet Union by its deeds, and only by its deeds. Yet today, with profit, we can also listen to its words. For now interesting and thoughtful arguments can be heard in the Kremlin. In his speech to the gathering of international representatives, mainly from the Communist movement, at the 70th anniversary of the Russian revolution in Moscow in November 1987, Gorbachev argued that 'modern living' demanded an end to 'stereotypes':

No one has any ready-to-use prescriptions. It is hardly likely that anyone holds Ariadne's thread, which would help find the way out of the labyrinth of the present-day's contradictory world. As we set forth our concepts of the

new way of thinking, we do not in the least claim a
monopoly on the truth: we are engaged in search ourselves, and invite others to look jointly for the ways along
which humanity can cross the minefield of our times and
emerge in the twenty-first century, in a nuclear-free and
non-violent world.

He went on to attack 'the arrogance of omniscience', and called
for 'a more sophisticated culture of mutual relations among
progressive forces'.

In the late 1950s a New Left emerged in Western Europe and
America, as confused as it was creative. It defined itself nega-
tively. It was against escalation of the nuclear arms race. It was
energetically anti-Stalinist and deeply hostile to control from
Moscow or by pro-Moscow parties. At the same time it was
against colonialism and imperialism; hence it was swept into
the anti-war movement in the 1960s, during the American
intervention in Vietnam. Of course, it was also against traditional Social Democracy – the idea that one could gradually
incorporate the representatives of the working class into existing parliaments and change the system thereby. One of the
foremost (and least stuffy) of England's social democratic intellectuals and reformers was sure that the Western Europe of the
1950s could no longer even be described as capitalist.[137] The
New Left argued that, on the contrary, it was becoming more
so. It was correct. Anti-consumerist but for individual choice,
sensitive to culture and hostile to officialdom, the thinkers, and
often non-thinkers, of the New Left helped lay the ground for
feminism – which then, with good cause, made the New Left
its own first object for the feminist critique. The New Left also
became the victim of less benign intellectual and organizational

dogmatism and terrorism. It has survived and thrived most obviously among the Greens and in the renewal of the peace movements. Now many of its themes find expression in the one place I would have predicted was absolutely the least likely of all: the Kremlin.

Democracy, an end to dogmatism, some real pluralism, genuine individual initiative, ecological responsibility, a determined effort to get rid of nuclear weapons, glasnost . . . together these present a very different socialism from that we have been led to expect from socialist countries. If it succeeds, it is bound to change the Left, old and new, in the West.

IV

It can't happen!

Perestroika and glasnost are certain to be attacked. Hatred for the freedom of others is widespread in the USSR. The personal, sexual, financial, moral and therefore, finally, political costs of years of crowding, shortages, queues, speeches and militia; of fixing, of connections, of the price of failure, of the price of success, of jealousy and boasting . . .

> I and the public know
> What all schoolchildren learn
> Those to whom evil is done
> Do evil in return.[138]

Schoolchildren are not always taught the truth. The real evil is usually done by those who have already been wicked and nasty. When people are full of hate it is because of what they have done to others rather than what has been done to them. It

319

is not the victims but the victors, whom we have to watch out for.

In their hearts a majority in the nineteen million Communist Party members (particularly those who joined during and after the War) can hardly desire change. But they have been trained to accept discipline. Furthermore, it may not be what they want, but what alternative do they have? How are they to raise morale and productivity if they shut down glasnost and replace Gorbachev with a leader who likes medals? While it is easy to guess how they can slow down, it is hard to see how the old Communists can turn back reform, without cutting themselves off from the world, even handing over the flag of socialist modernization to China.

As part of my research I went to see an acquaintance who is a merchant banker in the City of London. He speaks fluent Russian and handles much of his bank's financial dealings with the Soviet bloc. We talked late after work, in a City wine bar, that became progressively more crowded. It was at the height of the financial boom. I asked him about the prospects for change in the USSR.

'It will take them at least ten years. First, many do not trust that the reforms will not be reversed. More important, they need a complete change in their mentality. That's going to take a long time.'

The conversation got around to what had been happening in the City. 'Only a few years ago, except for the Japanese, you would not have seen anyone around here after six o'clock. In my bank people used to come in at ten in the morning; now the canteen serves breakfast for executives.'

'If you can change your mentality so quickly,' I asked him, 'why can't the Soviets change theirs?'

'Here, innovation is built into the system. There, it is built out of the system – it's excluded from it.'

This is an intriguing way to look at reform in Moscow. Gorbachev and his allies seek to implant innovation into their system. Naturally it recoils because the new is necessarily the unpredictable, the unplanned, the unorthodox.

Is there an alternative? In writing this book I have found it difficult to estimate the likely chances of success for Soviet democratization over the next decade. What the reformers are trying to do is magnificent. They are outnumbered, but they are smarter and should have youth on their side. Indeed, the support of the young is essential. But they have been so depoliticized by their education under Brezhnev, that their support may not be forthcoming. All this makes me think Gorbachev will lose; when good and evil are balanced, the latter usually triumphs.

On the other hand, the conservatives in the Soviet Union, and they are by no means evil just because they loath democracy, do not have a coherent programme. Take the key issue of prices. There are likely to be disturbances, as the system of massive subsidies is ended by the reforms. But is it credible just to carry on with subsidy indefinitely? No. In this, as in so many other respects, the old system is over. The reformers may win simply because the conservatives have to go along with them *faute de mieux* – for want of anything better.

It can happen.

V

If it does, it will be because the Party is socialist, a source of strength not understood by many in the Western press corps.

Speaking the language, with a real feeling for the people, close to intellectuals who are non-Party members, even the best of Western journalists tend to see the country through Russian, rather than Soviet, eyes. They argue, as for example the *Washington Post*'s Dusko Doder wrote in the conclusion to his recent book, that Gorbachev should be perceived as a benevolent despot.[139] Benevolent and enlightened, to be sure, but unthinkable without despotism. In other words a good Tsar. In short, no historic change.

Yet it was Brezhnev who was like, let's say, a quite good Tsar who sought to modernize the autocracy: his detente and imported Western technology went along with resistance to Western ideas. In this sense he was very much a child of Stalin – who, while a Soviet patriot, called on Russian traditions. Gorbachev's break with this heritage signals something that comes from outside that tradition of rule, but which finds a legitimacy in Lenin.

It is very difficult for Americans to comprehend this. Hedrick Smith ends his often absorbing bestseller, significantly called *The Russians*, with a story about how he drew up at a petrol station outside Moscow and found 'a mildly comic scene . . . of great disorder . . . it struck me as a great scene for pictures.' So he took four or five photographs until the burly manager of the service station demanded to know who he was, what he was doing and told him to stop. Hedrick Smith attempted to reassure him by claiming that Brezhnev and Nixon had agreed that each others' satellites could photograph their respective rocket emplacements. This did not assuage the manager who said he would call the police. Smith and his wife drove off, shaking their heads at Russian peasant-like suspicion: 'It was the same under the Tsars. They're the same people', they concluded – the final words of the book.[140]

I would not envy the Soviet visitor who drew up at a clapped-out service station west of Kansas in a Soviet-made car and began to take pictures of the mess without permission or offering to pay. As for what would happen if he tried to justify his action by pointing out that the Kremlin had satellites overhead, that were authorized to photograph . . . he'd be fortunate not to look down the wrong end of a shotgun.

A similarly bizarre incomprehension can be found in the essay *Time* magazine published on the eve of the 70th anniversary of the Revolution. It was, I should stress, a genuinely sympathetic attempt at understanding, with some fine and funny observations of the ambiguous relationship between the Soviet people and their State. But when Roger Rosenblatt visited the museum of Stalin at his birthplace in Georgia, where there were photos of Stalin with Lenin, Churchill and Roosevelt, he asked:

'Where are the photographs of Stalin with Hitler?' – a needling question to the decorous museum guide, who did not skip a beat. 'Oh those,' she says. 'They must be in the archives.'

A doubly amusing exchange, for unlike British Prime Minister Chamberlain, Stalin never actually met Hitler! Then Rosenblatt writes:

It is unsettling for Americans to realize that to Soviet citizens, it is *they* who defeated Nazi Germany, and history gives them a point.

A point! Who *do* Americans think defeated Hitler? But for me the strangest moment in the *Time* essay comes when

Rosenblatt describes a conversation with a young woman teacher who suggests that he cannot understand 'How it is we can love and fear our country at the same time.' It is because, she tells him, it is 'home'.[141]

He agrees it is 'hard for an American to comprehend how Soviet citizens can love the country that makes war against them'.

I have yet to meet Americans, perhaps it is just the kind I meet, who do not both love and fear their country. The quality of that fear is different, certainly. It may concern what the USA will do to Central America, to the Gulf, or with military over-spending; that is, its capacity for making war on other people, while at home it concerns less what the US government does than does not do: as it allows the sale of millions of guns that shoot hundreds weekly, refuses medical care to the needy, makes it hard to walk through a city centre unmolested, and builds up budget and trade deficits with barely a care. I know why people love America, but those who do not also fear it do not love the world.

VI

Observers say that the majority of the occupants of the high-rise flats and the ill-served provincial towns would much prefer another strong boss, who will make the chips fly: that far from the Soviet people wanting democracy, they'd like even more rule from above. If this is true, why have the Party leaders opted for perestroika and glasnost?

The old guard in the Central Committee would prefer a

relatively efficient and reliable orthodox socialism. But even this would still demand a cultural revolution. After the years of stagnation, the Politburo has therefore only two alternatives apart from complete immobility. Either it falls back on the, supposedly popular, tsarist model as modernized by Stalin, to clean up the country and force it to work, or it breaks from tsarist and autocratic traditions altogether. The Brezhnev years can be seen as an attempt to put off this choice, which was understandable as either option threatens to set in motion an irrevocable momentum.

Under Gorbachev the Soviet Party has made its choice. It has set its course for democratization, not only because of the American example, or the need to catch up with capitalism, or because the young desire freedom, if not small aeroplanes, but also because its socialist ideology allows democracy to be perceived as preferable. The revolution was made to overthrow Tsarism. That it was poisoned by the imperial legacy is evident. But that recovery, however slow, may now be possible is thanks to the founding inspiration behind the events of October 1917: that the people of the country should be their own rulers.

An American leftist shook his head in disbelief when I told him that I was convinced that Gorbachev and his allies want democracy in the USSR. 'No ruling class ever gives away its power,' was his response. There are two aspects to such scepticism, it seems to me. One is a leftist refusal to place any hope in Moscow, or indeed in any State; a good reaction to the long history of fellow travelling. But scepticism too can be a kneejerk reaction. And this one fails to comprehend the circumstances of the Soviet reforms, for it assumes that things can go on as they are.

In fact the Party is being forced to change. And in part by a major protest from below. True, this has been social rather than political, but the society-wide go-slow and biological strike, that I tried to describe at the beginning of this book, is evidence of massive discontent with the system of privileges in the Soviet Union. At once atomized and everywhere, this protest has had profound economic consequences.

Today, the economies of Western Europe, if combined, are decisively greater than the Soviet Union's. In the east, Japan on its own could now outstrip the USSR in the production of nuclear armed submarines, if it so decided. It was advanced Toshiba equipment sold to the USSR for the engineering of its submarine propulsion systems that led to a recent confrontation between Washington and Tokyo. The Soviets either transform the productivity and growth rate of their economy or their global position will collapse. To put it in the terms of my American interlocutor, the Party leadership must trade off a loss of power at home if it is to retain its power abroad.

The real question, therefore, is not whether the new leaders want democracy, but why, given the overwhelming rationality and national self-interest of the course they have chosen, there should be any doubt as to their success.

There must be such doubt. History has many examples of social systems that were unable to transform themselves despite the obvious. The loss of authority and privileges inherited from Stalin will be acute and will be resisted. A catastrophic regime of repression and decline remains a real likelihood in the Soviet sphere. It is the new leaders' attempt to avoid this which motivates their reforms.

VII

In the judgement of some, for example the now exiled dissident Vladimir Bukovsky, democratization is impossible. His long stay in America has led him to conclude that the myth of the obedient Russian character is wrong. If anything Russians are more individualistic than dutiful Germans and Americans, and would be 'no worse' as citizens of a democracy. But:

> It is my deep conviction, and that of many of my friends, that the Soviet *system* cannot exist as an open society. You can open it up a bit to let off steam and assist you in installing a new leadership – but then you have to close it down again or face the consequences.[142]

Against this there is the view of Zdenek Mlynar, an exiled Czechoslovak, who was one of the leaders of the Prague Spring, and who as a student in Moscow once shared a room with Mikhail Gorbachev:

> I am convinced that the Soviet political system is capable of reform, that it can continue to develop, and can finally attain a qualitative transformation which will not mean dislocation of the socialist regime, but its genuine development. This is actually a much harder task than changing the economic system.[143]

Mlynar suggests that Soviet success might lead to something different from Western society, because here, in the West, the struggle for democracy is, he argues, one for control over a technocratic society and its corporations. Here, democracy is posed against the science-driven intensification of capitalism.

In the Soviet Union it is the other way around. Democracy is an anti-bureaucratic programme that seeks to release and promote efficiency and innovation, now desperately needed above all by scientists. In the post-war West scientists were among the most servile and least critical segment of the intelligentsia, either because they knelt directly before the State, or because they have preferred the calm of ideological neutrality to the arguments about our destiny that rage outside the laboratories. By contrast, in the USSR, many chose science to preserve their political integrity and strongly held beliefs from distortion. Andrei Sakharov and Zhores Medvedev are outstanding examples of scientific democrats, well known in the West because they have clashed with the regime in the past. Behind them there are thousands of the finest researchers in the USSR for whom glasnost, democracy, freedom to travel, is professionally a matter of life or death. Their hands also, and not just the Party's, shape the Soviet future and may fashion Soviet freedom.

When I went to Moscow, one of my questions concerned the sincerity of Gorbachev and his colleagues. Do they mean what they say when they talk about democracy? They do, I concluded, but this is not really the point. For sure, they would like to have democracy if this does not upset their own authority too much – what they might lose by way of direct power they can gain in popularity and prestige. The question that matters is whether they and, more importantly, the system of rule from the Kremlin, can tolerate such a massive transformation.

In a sense, it must. Everything, from the development of Soviet science to the country's role in world trade, demands an end to direction from the centre. Modernization entails both destruction and construction; as we know in the West its freedom may also enslave. But without it, the Soviet Union will fall fatally behind, and then may collapse with awesome consequences for the world.

Glasnot should be seen in this context. If it is merely an attempt to graft some journalistic and artistic liberty on to the trunk of the old order, the graft will not take and its limited freedom will wither and fall away. The economic reforms legislated to come into effect from the beginning of 1988 will decide the future. The self-financing of enterprises is designed to end the Stalin-style command economy: it is Moscow's version of the Big Bang. Will the Soviet system, its bureaucrats and workers, its privileged elite and its broken families, be able to live with the intense rationalization, the massive redeployment, the price rises and the insecurity that must accompany such reconstruction? If it can, then the Soviet Union can change politically.

LEAVING

There was no problem leaving Moscow. My typewriter, my papers, a large painted rocking horse, were all waved through, as they should be. I was on a flight with a party of British students on their way back home. For the last three months they had been learning Russian at a well-known language school in Voronezh. It is a city of about 850,000 that was utterly destroyed in the war. Today it makes aircraft, although foreigners are not supposed to know this. One of the students described the city as 'an architectural disaster, with only one nice building not in grotty condition – the puppet theatre'. There are, 'only two restaurants; one has a poor menu, the food at the other is execrable, but it sells drink'. In the last weeks vodka had disappeared completely, a woman student told me. Six months before the supply of cigarettes had run out. She thought the cause was just bureaucratic bungling but said it created intense spasms of black-market profiteering.

They were full of praise for the quality of the teaching. But the sanitary conditions in the hostel were not wonderful. Some of their party got dysentery, and once there was no running water for two days. The girls said that while they fancied some of the men from other countries, they wouldn't touch Soviet youths because they were convinced that venereal disease was rife among them. More important, the diet was very poor.

One guy, who admittedly seemed to be a vegetarian, said that he had eaten only four apples in three months (apples weren't in season). They felt starved of vitamin C. Oranges were 6 to 8 roubles a kilo on the free market, brought in by traders from Azerbaydzhan. They said that the basic diet was bread and cheese. They did not know how the Soviet students survived on their allowance of only forty roubles a month – foreign students got 170 – supposedly worth £170 a month or $300. They found that the men lost weight while the women students gained, because they ate more sugar to compensate.

As many consumer goods are distributed in the USSR through administered allocation, the workers in the aircraft factories will not necessarily be short of cigarettes or fruit, which are probably available for employees at the enterprise supermarket. This is one of the aspects of the Soviet economy which makes it so difficult to estimate the realities of life from outside. But the students' experience made me realize how privileged I'd been, with dozens of satisfying meals in Moscow under my belt.

The students thought that glasnost sounded great but that it was still cosmetic, and they said that the younger Soviets in Voronezh felt that the anti-vodka edicts had diminished even further what little freedom they had. The same applied to my young compatriots. They could hardly wait to climb on the British Airways jet for the alcohol. The boy across the aisle from me immediately ordered five small bottles of gin – each one a double – chased by three large cans of lager. One of each went to a friend, the rest he consumed non-stop. The singing was unbearable. A thin, serious and thankfully quieter student next to me said, 'You'd forgive our unruly behaviour if you knew the way we have been treated by the Soviet people and the way they treat their own socialist people.' We talked some more, and he said he wanted very much to return to the USSR, as did many of the others, although as individuals rather than in a group. There was a tangible attachment for the country they were so excited to leave.

The pilot announced that the plane was out of Soviet airspace and there was a great cheer. A young woman shouted in a piercing voice, 'For the West! For freedom! For capitalism!' at which the man with the gin inside him shouted even more loudly, 'Bollocks!'

There was a sudden silence at this ideological exchange. After a second or two everyone started to chatter extra noisily. The disagreement was soon forgotten and they went back to their drunken singing. It gave me a headache, and made me hope that the economic reforms being promulgated by the June plenum would be very far reaching indeed.

But this was not the last of my trip to Moscow. It marked the beginning of my thinking about what I had seen, heard and learnt; reflections that I now had to gather up and turn into prose.

Four and a half months later, a young Soviet who had talked to me in Moscow arrived in London. It was his first visit to the West. I wanted to hear his impressions, and above all to learn of his reaction to the draft manuscript of this book.

He read it rapidly. 'The form', he told me sternly, 'is impressionistic. Sometimes there is no logic.' After many months he is still searching Moscow – one of the largest cities in the world – for an apartment. And he wants logic!

As for the content, he made some very constructive points, and emphasized how different things are in the Republics from the capital. Then he complained that there were too many quotes about whether glasnost went far enough and perestroika could succeed.

'For me these are boring questions. People here in the West all ask about whether the changes are irreversible. I say that anyone can speculate and no one can predict, it is a total gamble. It is best to do something. Only this will help guarantees to emerge and make sure that the changes are real.'

'But you', I replied with some emphasis, perhaps because I was wounded by his aspersion against the subtle logic of my pages, '*you* were one of the people who told me that glasnost didn't go very far. Even though you supported reform, you emphasized to me how it was still very limited.'

He looked surprised. Then, admitting as much with his wry smile, he replied, 'My opinion must have matured since then'.

ONLY THE START OF
THE BEGINNING

'For us,' he spoke quietly, 'for our generation, it is a last chance. One I did not expect. We laughed at Brezhnev when he was old, and at Chernenko. We knew something had to change. But we could do nothing. Today, we admire Gorbachev as a man, but still what can we do?

'People are much more tired than in 1956. They are fed up with politics and especially with slogans and declarations about how wonderful we are. Twenty years under Brezhnev have sent the people into a deep sleep. It will not be easy to wake them to political life, and why should they be when it is so dangerous?

'They can wake up, and the best waking up was the war. This showed that the people are patriotic and active and brave. But it is a sad fact that under Brezhnev a new people have arisen, bred to be passive, cynical and cunning but without skilful work. They expect everything from above, economically as well as politically, and give back as little as possible while stealing as much as possible. And all was stolen. No one came back from the factory without something that could be removed from the factory. It is hard to work for eight hours when there is little to do, and so you turn to stealing. You have an expression for this in English I think, about idle hands . . .

'Now perhaps we will start, but it is the start of the beginning only. There will have to be consistency in Central Committee policy. Without this, no one will believe in anything. Everyone will just wait for the campaigns about glasnost and perestroika to come to an end, like previous slogans.'

A couple of days later, in the south of Moscow, a hoarding proclaims:

> THE 9,000 WORKING PEOPLE OF THIS AREA OF MOSCOW
> WILL FULFILL THE ASSIGNMENT OF THE FIRST TWO YEARS
> OF THE 5 YEAR PLAN BY THE ANNIVERSARY OF THE
> GREAT OCTOBER REVOLUTION

And to the side, on a smaller space:

> PERESTROIKA IS EVERYONE'S CONCERN IN EVERY WAY

CHRONOLOGY

1812 Napoleon invades Russia. Enters Moscow, city burnt, he retreats through winter.

1853–6 Crimean War, British and French invade.

1861 Edict abolishing serfdom by Tsar Alexander II after wide-ranging discussion in the press.

1887 Lenin's brother, Alexander, executed after failed attempt to assassinate Alexander III.

1902 Lenin (b. 1870) writes *What is to be Done?*

1905 Uprising establishes the first Soviets (councils). A Duma (parliament) formed, later abolished.

1914 First World War begins; Russia invades Germany, defeated at battle of Tannenberg.

1917 February revolution, Tzar forced to abdicate, civilian government continues war; October revolution, Lenin leads the Bolsheviks to power with slogan 'Bread, Land and Peace'.

1917 War Communism, the Reds defeat White intervention.

1921 New Economic Policy (NEP) allows peasant and commercial trade.

1924 Lenin dies after long illness; struggle for power.

1927 Stalin (b. 1881) supreme, Trotsky (b. 1879) later expelled.

1928 Start of crash industrialization; first five-year plan.

1930 Forced collectivization, accompanied by famine.

1933 Hitler (b. 1889) to power in Germany.

1934 Kirov (b. 1886) assassinated, political purges and trials.

1936 Stalin's new Constitution adopted.

1937 First 'elections' to the Supreme Soviet.

1938 Munich agreement between Chamberlain (b. 1869) and Hitler dismembers Czechoslovakia.

1939 August: Molotov-Ribbentrop pact, between USSR and Germany; September: Germany and USSR partition Poland, UK declares war on Germany.

1940 Hitler's forces overrun France.

1941 German army of 3.5 million invades Soviet Union, reaches outskirts of Moscow and Leningrad.

1942–3 Battle of Stalingrad turns the war.

1945 Allies divide Europe.

1947 The Cold War.

1949 New purges.

1953 Stalin dies.

1954 Khruschev (b. 1894) consolidates power.

1956 February: Khruschev speech denounces Stalin for his crimes; November: Soviets crush Hungarian rising.

1961 Cuban missile crisis.

1964 Khruschev overthrown; Brezhnev (b. 1906) made General Secretary with help of Suslov (b. 1902).

1967 Andropov (b. 1914) made head of the KGB.

1971 Grishin (b. 1914) enters Politburo; SALT I treaty signed in Moscow by Nixon (b. 1913) and Brezhnev.

1977 Brezhnev becomes President as well as General Secretary; new Soviet Constitution promulgated.

1979 Gorbachev (b. 1932) made youngest Politburo member.

1982 Brezhnev dies, Andropov succeeds him.

1984 Andropov dies, Chernenko (b. 1911) made General Secretary.

1985 Chernenko dies, Gorbachev defeats Grishin to become General Secretary.

ENDNOTES

[1]*Moscow News*, No. 19, 3 May 1987.

[2]The meeting with the writers took place on 19 June 1986. At one point Gorbachev said, 'restructuring progresses with great difficulty. We have no opposition party. How then can we control ourselves? Only through criticism and self-criticism. Most important, through *glasnost*. Democratization without *glasnost* does not exist. At the same time, democracy without limits is anarchy.'

[3]*The Autobiography of Lincoln Steffens*, the life story of America's greatest reporter, New York 1958, p. 799.

[4]Bertrand Russell, *The Practice and Theory of Bolshevism*, London 1920, pp. 15-23.

[5]Ronald Clark, *The Life of Bertrand Russell*, London 1975, p. 380.

[6]Hans Magnus Enzensberger, *The Consciousness Industry*, New York 1974, pp. 129-157.

[7]Laurens van der Post, *Journey into Russia*, London 1986, pp. 143-5.

[8]The *Economist*, 15 August 1987.

[9]Speech in Bucharest, 26 May 1987.

[10]Margaret Gardiner, 'Moscow Winter, 1934', *New Left Review*, No 98, July-August 1976.

[11]Laurens van der Post, as above, p. 18.

[12]Mikhail Bulgakov, *The Master and Margarita*, trans. Michael Glenny, London 1985, p. 137.

[13]Walter Benjamin, *Moscow Diary* trans. Richard Sieburth, London 1986, p. 47.

[14]*Financial Times*, 25 August 1987.

[15]Martin Walker, *Guardian*, 14 April 1987.

[16]Michael Ryan, 'Funding for the Soviet Health Service', *British Medical Journal*, 12 September 1987.

[17]*Moscow News*, No 34, 23 August 1987.

[18]Marshall Goldman, *Gorbachev's Challenge*, New York 1987, p. 262.

[19]In 1970–1972 Zhores Medvedev worked in Borovsk, 60 miles from Moscow, where D. S. Polyansky was given a 300 acre forest as his private hunting ground, a right 'Brezhnev gave every high official', *Andropov*, Oxford, 1983, p. 138.

[20]*Moscow News*, No. 39 (supplement), 27 September 1987.

[21]Mikhail Gorbachev, *Perestroika*, London 1987, pp. 25, 47, 57, 84, 85.

[22]As above, pp. 62–63.

[23]*International Herald Tribune*, (from the *New York Times*), 19 November 1987.

[24]Alexander Yakovlev, *Modern Socialism Must First and Foremost Know Itself*, Novosti Press Agency pamphlet, 1987, pp. 8–9.

[25]*Moscow News*, 9 August 1987.

[26]Vladimir Gubaryev, *Sarcophagus*, trans. Michael Glenny, London 1987, p. 67.

[27]*Moscow News*, as above.

[28]From the March *Literaturnaya Ukraina*, quoted in Martin Walker, *The Waking Giant*, London 1986, p. 225.

[29]Richard Nixon, *Memoirs*, London 1979, p. 611.

[30]Roy Medvedev, *All Stalin's Men*, Chapter 3: 'Suslov: Ideologist-in-Chief', New York, 1983.

[31]M. Heller and A Nekrich, *Utopia in Power*, London 1987, p. 624.

[32]Roy Medvedev, *On Stalin and Stalinism*, Oxford, 1979, p. 181.

[33]Abbreviated from, 'Appeal for a Gradual Democratization', trans. Marilyn Vogt, in *Samizdat*, ed. George Saunders, New York, 1974.

[34]Richard Nixon, *Memoirs*, London 1979, p. 619-20.

[35]Mark Frankland, *The Sixth Continent*, London 1987, p. 151.

[36]Zhores Medvedev, *Gorbachev*, Oxford 1987, p. 207.

[37]Nadezhda Krupskaya, *Memories of Lenin (1893-1917)*, London, 1942, p. 3.

[38]Julian Semyonov, *Tass is Authorized to Announce*, London 1987, p.15.

[39]Xan Smiley, *Sunday Telegraph*, 19 July 1987.

[40]The exchange is reproduced in *Soviet Weekly*, 11 July 1987.

[41]*The Spectator*, 19 September 1987.

[42]Teodor Shanin, *Russia as a 'Developing Society'*, Vol. 1, London 1985, pp.85-85.

[43]V.I. Lenin, *Collected Works*, Vol. 36, pp. 594-596.

[44]*Pravda* (monthly English language edition), August 1987.

[45]Leonid Ilyich Brezhnev, *Memoirs*, trans. Penny Dole, Oxford, 1982, pp. 26-27.

[46]Moshe Lewin, *The Making of the Soviet System*, London 1985, p.230.

[47]The phrase is Alec Nove's, from *An Economic History of the USSR*, London 1982, p. 169.

[48]L. Kochan and R. Abraham, *The Making of Modern Russia*, London 1983, p. 378.

[49]Quoted in Roy Medvedev, *On Stalin and Stalinism*, as cited p. 76.

[50]Boris Pasternak, *Dr Zhivago*, trans. Max Hayward and Manya Harari, London 1958, p. 453.

[51]John Erickson, *The Road to Berlin*, London 1983, p. x.

[52]Petro Grigorenko, *Memoirs*, trans. Thomas Whitney, London 1983, pp. 211-212.

[53]Semyon Lipkin, 'The Story of Vasily Grossman's Novel', *Moscow News*, 18 October 1987.

[54]*Sunday Telegraph*, magazine section, 'My Country Right or Wrong', September 1987.

[55]Basil Liddell Hart, *History of the Second World War*, London 1970, p. 141.

[56]Paolo Spriano, *Stalin and the European Communists*, trans. Jon Rothschild, London 1985, p. 79.

[57]Mark Frankland, *The Sixth Continent*, London 1987, p. 156.

[58]Martin Walker, the *Guardian*, 16 October 1987.

[59]CPSU: Documents and Analysis, Novosti Press Agency, 9 July 1987, p. 18.

[60]*Moscow News*, 3 May 1987.

[61]*Moscow News*, 5 July 1987.

[62]Zhores Medvedev, *Gorbachev*, as above, p. 6.

[63]Dusko Doder, *Shadows and Whispers*, London 1987, p. 246.

[64]Bohdan Nahaylo, *The Spectator*, 19 September 1987.

[65]Mikhail Gorbachev, *Selected Speeches and Articles*, 2nd edition, Moscow 1987, p. 437.

[66]Rudolf Bahro, *From Red to Green*, trans. Gus Fagan and Richard Hurst, London 1984, p. 39.

[67]Jorge Semprun, *The Autobiography of Federico Sanchez*, trans. Helen Lane, Brighton 1979 (with the daft title: *Communism in Spain in the Franco Era*), p. 105.

[68]As above, pp. 110 and 215.

[69]*Marxism Today*, February 1987, p. 15.

[70]*New Socialist*, December 1985

[71]*END Journal*, Summer 1987, pp. 11-12.

[72]Antonio Gramsci, *Selections from the Prison Notebooks*, trans. Quintin Hoare and Geoffrey Nowell-Smith, London 1971, p. 238. There is a useful discussion of Gramsci's complicated argument in Perry Anderson, 'The Antinomies of Antonio Gramsci', *New Left Review*, 100, November 1976.

[73]Archie Brown, 'Soviet Political Culture through Soviet Eyes', who need not be held responsible for my interpretation of his data, in Archie Brown (ed), *Political Culture and Communist Studies*, London 1984, pp. 100–110.

[74]*New Socialist*, May 1985, p. 23.

[75]*Encounter*, September–October 1987, pp. 62-4.

[76]*Newsweek*, 7 September 1987.

[77]Zhores Medvedev, *Gorbachev*, as cited, p. 169.

[78]Yegor Ligachev, *Activating the Human factor – the Main Source of Acceleration*, Novosti Press Agency, Moscow 1987, p. 29.

[79]Alexander Yakovlev, *Modern Socialism Must First and Foremost Know Itself*, Novosti Press Agency, Moscow 1987, pp. 30-31.

[80]Yegor Ligachev, as above, p. 12.

[81]Quoted in *Newsweek*, 25 May 1987.

[82]*Literaturnaya Gazeta*, 6 March 1958, quoted by Roy Medvedev, *On Socialist Democracy*, trans. Ellen de Kadt, New York 1975, p. 166.

[83]Martin Walker, *Guardian*, 14 July 1987.

[84]From the translated version in *Soviet Weekly*, 17 October 1987.

[85]'The Russian Complex – the Eidelmann-Astafiev Correspondence', *Detente*, No. 8, Winter 1987, pp. 5-7.

[86] Alexander Yanov, *The Russian Challenge*, Oxford 1987.

[87] Dusko Doder, as cited, pp. 126, 134.

[88] Julian Semyonov, as cited, p. 218.

[89] Private communication.

[90] Jonathan Steele, *Guardian*, 12 September 1987.

[91] *Moscow News* No. 37, 13 September 1987.

[92] Alexander Yakovlev, *Modern Socialism Must First and Foremost Know Itself*, as cited, p. 23.

[93] *The Times*, 2 November 1987.

[94] Central Intelligence Agency, Statement to the Subcommittee of National Security Economics, Joint Economic Committee of the United States Congress, Washington D.C., 14 September 1987, p. 21.

[95] Alexander Yakovlev, *On the Edge of an Abyss*, no trans., Moscow 1985, pp. 46, 75, 97, 318.

[96] Fraser Harbutt, *The Iron Curtain; Churchill, America and the Origins of the Cold War*, New York 1986, p. 283.

[97] Artemy Troitsky, *Back in the USSR*, London 1987, p. 4.

[98] p. 14.

[99] p. 56.

[100] Dmitri Likhachev, *The 21st century Must Be an Age of Humanism*, Novosti Press pamphlet, 1987, p. 24.

[101] Charlie Gillett, *The Sound of the City*, London 1971, p. 291.

[102] David Widgery, *Beating Time*, London 1986, p. 116.

[103] *New Times*, 28 September 1987.

[104] As cited, p. 53.

[105] The *Independent*, 16 September 1987.

[106] From 'The War and Russian Social Democracy' (1914), Collected Works, Vol. 21, pp. 28–29.

[107] As above p. 28, and *Imperialism, the Highest Stage of Capitalism*, New Introduction (1920), Collected Works, Vol. 22, p. 194.

[108]'The War and Russian Social Democracy', as above, p. 33.

[109]Paul Kennedy, *The Realities Behind Diplomacy*, London 1981, p. 145.

[110]'Socialism and War', *Collected Works*, Vol. 21, p. 301.

[111]William Langer, *An Encyclopedia of World History*, London 1972, p. 976.

[112]Ronald Clark, *The Life of Bertrand Russell*, London 1975, p. 246.

[113]Alexander Solzhenitsyn, *August 1914*, trans. Michael Glenny, London 1971, p. 375.

[114]Isaac Deutscher, *Stalin*, Oxford 1949, p. 129.

[115]Short Course, Moscow, 1945, p. 314.

[116]See 'Churchillism', Chapter 2 of Anthony Barnett *Iron Britannia*, London 1982.

[117]'A Modest Contribution to the Rites and Ceremonies of the Tenth Anniversary', *New Left Review*, May–June 1979.

[118]The contrast comes from Lawrence and Jeanne Stone, *An Open Elite? England 1540-1880*, Oxford, 1984, p. 32

[119]Jonathan Steele, *Guardian*, 12 September 1987.

[120]I wrote a brief article about this for the *Guardian*, 'How Mrs Thatcher hijacked the thrusting class of '68', 14 April 1987.

[121]Geoffrey Hosking, 9 October 1987.

[122]Victor Serge, *From Lenin to Stalin*, trans. Ralph Manneheim, New York, 1973, p. 9.

[123]Vaclav Havel and others, *The Power of the Powerless*, London 1985, pp. 23-96.

[124]Alexander Rabinowitch, *The Bolsheviks Come to Power*, London, 1979.

[125]From *What Is To Be Done?*, V.I.Lenin, *Collected Works*, Vol. 5, Moscow 1961, pp. 369, 412-3, 514.

[126]From *State and Revolution*, V.I.Lenin, *Collected Works*, Vol. 25, Moscow 1964, pp. 462, 463, 473, 474, 476.

[127] Alec Nove, *Political Economy and Soviet Socialism*, London 1979, p. 77; and Tony Polan, Lenin and the End of Politics, London 1984, p. 175.

[128] Hannah Arendt, 'Truth and Politics', in her *Between Past and Future*, New York 1968, pp. 227, 258, 260.

[129] T.H. Rigby, *Lenin's Government*, Cambridge 1979, pp. 75, 227.

[130] Isaac Deutscher (and David King), *The Great Purges*, Oxford 1984, p. 30.

[131] Judith Herrin, *The Formation of Christendom*, Princeton 1987, Chapter 8 especially – she has also helped to form my thinking on many other matters.

[132] Boris Pasternak, *Dr Zhivago*, as cited, pp. 391-2.

[133] Joseph Brodsky, *Less than One*, London 1987, p. 363.

[134] Harold Evans, *Good Times, Bad Times*, London 1983, p. 404.

[135] Artemy Troitsky, as cited, p. 97.

[136] *Pravda*, English monthly digest, July 1987, p. 26.

[137] About the Britain of 1956, Tony Crosland wrote, 'To the question, "Is this still Capitalism?", I would answer "No"', *The Future of Socialism*, London 1956, p.76.

[138] W.H. Auden, *September 1, 1939*.

[139] *Shadows and Whispers*, as cited.

[140] Hedrick Smith, *The Russians*, New York 1976, pp. 508-9.

[141] All quotes from *Time*, 26 October 1987.

[142] Interviewed by George Urban, *Encounter*, November 1987, p. 15; my emphasis.

[143] Zdenek Mlynar, 'Political Reform at the Crossroads', *END Papers*, No. 15, Spring 1987, pp. 51-53.

John Pilger
Heroes £4.95

'A tough, responsible book . . . Pilger's strength is his gift for finding the image, the instant, that reveals all: he is a photographer using words instead of a camera' SALMAN RUSHDIE, OBSERVER

'Pilger's *magnum opus*: a passionate and utterly absorbing collection of reports from the firing lines, both abroad (Vietnam, Cambodia, South Africa) and home (the East End, the miners' strike, Fleet Street) by one of the dwindling bunch of journalists in this country with heart as well as a hard nose' TIME OUT

'Pilger is the closest we now have to the great correspondents of the 1930s . . . The truth in his hands is a weapon, to be picked up and brandished – and used in the struggle against evil and injustice' GUARDIAN

'Some remarkable reporting is reprinted here . . . It contains some memorable snapshots of a harsh world' TIMES LITERARY SUPPLEMENT

'He is a true model for his peers and followers. Let them study for instance the awesome opening pages of the long chapter, 'Year Zero', which unforgettably describes the hideous and desolate remains of murdered Phnom Penh . . . mark, shudder, reflect and profit. There are other passages just as fine' SPECTATOR

'If I were a modern history teacher, I'd start the year's course by slinging copies of it across the desk and telling them to get on with it' DUNCAN CAMPBELL, CITY LIMITS

'What makes Pilger such a compelling writer is his sharp use of irony – his sense of the ridiculous makes the tragedies of his heroes seem all the more vivid' TODAY

'A number of these pieces are humdingers' CLANCY SIGAL, NEW SOCIETY

'Powerful . . . scathing . . . impressive' CHRISTOPHER HUDSON, LONDON STANDARD

Charles Humana
World Human Rights Guide £4.95

This unique survey – the very first of its kind – of 120 major countries throughout the world records human rights performance and responses to the Universal Declaration of Human Rights and United Nations treaties. The information on which it is based has been drawn from world human rights organisations, official and unofficial sources, international institutions, as well as individuals.

The survey is in the form of forty questions and answers, covering both traditional human rights, such as freedom of expression, association and movement, and the wider area of state power-censorship of the media, telephone tapping, extrajudicial killings, independence of courts, the right to practise any religion, to use contraceptive devices, to practise homosexuality between consenting adults. The results are calculated and summarized by an overall rating.

Basic data about each country is also provided, together with a short commentary on factors affecting human rights and a list of compulsory documents required by citizens.

'Useful and telling . . . shows, in the clearest possible way, how the world is divided at present between the free and the unfree' SUNDAY TIMES

'A valuable resource book . . . it offers a considerably wider perspective than can usually be gleaned from AI's own publications . . . sure to prove indispensable' AMNESTY!

'Its value lies in the extent to which he has achieved what would have seemed impossible until he did it, and indeed has never previously, as far as I am aware, been done' BERNARD LEVIN, OBSERVER

Christian Schmidt-Häuer
Gorbachev: The Path to Power £3.50

Mikhail Gorbachev's rapid rise to supreme power caught the West completely unawares, for few knew much about this 54-year-old technocrat whose charm and wit and ability to communicate, not to mention his relative youth, suddenly gave the Soviet Union a human face.

Christian Schmidt-Häuer, one of the West's most distinguished Soviet experts, was among the first to spot Gorbachev's potential when the provincial party leader arrived in Moscow in 1978. In this comprehensive personal and political portrait he examines Gorbachev's career from his youth in the Caucasus, his student days and his rise to high office under the patronage of Yuri Andropov and Mikhail Suslov – two of the Soviet Union's most powerful figures. By bringing together previously unknown material from Gorbachev's past, Schmidt-Häuer identifies the patterns which portend the future.

Far more than just a study of the man, this book paints a fascinating picture of the factions and personalities in the Kremlin, of the tense power struggle that led to Gorbachev's rise, of the new men of power around him, and most dramatically, of the influence and role in Soviet policy making of his wife Raisa, an unorthodox and innovatory political thinker in her own right.

'Excellent . . . the author certainly knows what he is talking about and he has used his evidence well. This book will last'
PROFESSOR JOHN ERICKSON, DIRECTOR, CENTRE FOR DEFENCE STUDIES, EDINBURGH UNIVERSITY

'Excellent, well observed and well informed . . . the author's analysis is the most penetrating I have seen and is thoroughly readable . . . in the same league as Hedrick Smith's *The Russians*'
PROFESSOR HARRY SHUKMAN, MODERN RUSSIAN STUDIES, ST ANTHONY'S COLLEGE, OXFORD

Ryszard Kapuściński
Another Day of Life £3.50

'Angola . . . the last months of Portuguese rule and the dramatic days of the transfer of power. Factions fight for power, the South Africans invade to install their proteges, the Cubans land to prop up theirs. Guerillas, refugees, spies, and the lonely reporter who had run out of money for food weeks before, connected to the outside world by one vulnerable telex line. Kapuściński is in the thick of it. He goes to the front line, flies to isolated garrisons, makes it in a truck across hundreds of miles of hostile bush . . . he has a good eye for the specific, the gesture, the phrase, the universal expressed through the particular'
SUNDAY TIMES

'The book seems informed by the novelist's eye rather than the journalist's. It might be a product of a Graham Greene or a V. S. Naipaul . . . fragmentary, anecdotal and impressionistic. This idiosyncratic eye, and the laconic, candid way its observations are recorded are what make *Another Day of Life* so memorable. More important, the author pins down the nature of war in modern Africa, its particular terrors, lunacies and disasters. Mr Kapuściński has captured this quite brilliantly. Throughout the book in the decaying surreal city or the tense journeys through the bush, one senses just how fragile is our sense of order, our idea of a comprehensible world'
NEW YORK TIMES BOOK REVIEW

'A fine reporter . . . Kapuściński infiltrates each inferno with the weary knowledge that revolution is a dialogue between the bad and the worse. There are no solutions, only reports from the midnight of high noon'
DAVID CAUTE, OBSERVER

'One Kapuściński is worth a thousand grizzled journofantasists; and through his astonishing blend of reportage and artistry we get as close to what he calls the incommunicable image of war as we're ever likely to by reading. Ours is the most cryptic of centuries, its true nature a dark secret. Ryszard Kapuściński is the kind of codebreaker we need'
SALMAN RUSHDIE, GUARDIAN

Humphrey Jennings
Pandaemonium £3.95
The Coming of the Machine as seen by contemporary observers

'Jennings sought to use the writings of others to create something
entirely new. What he was after was a continuous narrative on the
Industrial Revolution, woven from contemporary observations and
opinions, and with a minimum of editorial or authorial interference . . .
Like all great ideas, it is breathtakingly simple. And it has produced a
book which is at once a treasure-chest of quirky, unusual pieces and a
memorable account of the most devastating and exciting sea-change
which has yet engulfed mankind' OBSERVER

'An extraordinary and wonderful book . . . Letters, poems, novels,
reports and diaries – almost 400 of them altogether – create a picture of
such vividness that you can almost smell the sulphur, hear the
monotonous thud of the steam hammer, and see poor Huskison run
down by Stephenson's rocket' SUNDAY TIMES

'The first thing that strikes you is the high quality and enormous variety
of the 'images' that he assembled. Much of his material comes from
little-known sources, while familiar names tend to be represented by
unfamiliar excerpts. Almost all the excerpts have powerful points to
make, and most of them are examples, at the very least, of good,
vigorous English prose. Some of them are superb . . . It is what Ezra
Pound called an 'active anthology,' a book that sets ideas in motion and
establishes a complex network of internal cross-references'
NEW YORK TIMES

'A very fine book . . . the extracts are brilliantly chosen and suggest a
history more complex and interesting than that implied in several recent
polemics against 'Cartesian reductionism'. We are spared none of the
horrors of child labour and mining, but the book also conveys with great
subtlety the ambivalent and constantly changing attitudes to the
railways and London, the peculiar and exciting new worlds opened up
by geology, palaentology and ballooning, and the farcical lengths to
which theology was driven to adapt to the spirit of the age'
TIMES EDUCATIONAL SUPPLEMENT

All Pan books are available at your local bookshop or newsagent, or can be ordered direct from the publisher. Indicate the number of copies required and fill in the form below.

Send to: **CS Department, Pan Books Ltd., P.O. Box 40,
Basingstoke, Hants.   RG21 2YT.**

or phone: 0256 469551 (Ansaphone), quoting title, author
and Credit Card number.

Please enclose a remittance* to the value of the cover price plus: 60p for the first book plus 30p per copy for each additional book ordered to a maximum charge of £2.40 to cover postage and packing.

*Payment may be made in sterling by UK personal cheque, postal order, sterling draft or international money order, made payable to Pan Books Ltd.

Alternatively by Barclaycard/Access:

Card No.   ☐☐☐☐☐☐☐☐☐☐☐☐☐☐☐☐

                        Signature:

Applicable only in the UK and Republic of Ireland.

While every effort is made to keep prices low, it is sometimes necessary to increase prices at short notice. Pan Books reserve the right to show on covers and charge new retail prices which may differ from those advertised in the text or elsewhere.

NAME AND ADDRESS IN BLOCK LETTERS PLEASE:

....

Name ——————————————————————————————

Address ——————————————————————————————

——————————————————————————————————

——————————————————————————————————

——————————————————————————————————

                                                                        3/87